James Albert Harrison

Spain in Profile

A summer among the olives and aloes

James Albert Harrison

Spain in Profile
A summer among the olives and aloes

ISBN/EAN: 9783337240134

Printed in Europe, USA, Canada, Australia, Japan

Cover: Foto ©Andreas Hilbeck / pixelio.de

More available books at **www.hansebooks.com**

SPAIN IN PROFILE:

A SUMMER AMONG THE OLIVES AND ALOES.

BY

JAMES ALBERT HARRISON,
AUTHOR OF "GREEK VIGNETTES," ETC.

Neque flere neque ridere, sed intellegere.
SPINOZA.

Un peu de chasque chose et rien du tout, à la françoise.
MONTAIGNE.

BOSTON:
HOUGHTON, OSGOOD AND COMPANY.
The Riverside Press, Cambridge.
1879.

RIVERSIDE, CAMBRIDGE:
STEREOTYPED AND PRINTED BY
H. O. HOUGHTON AND COMPANY.

To

BAYARD TAYLOR.

> J'ai un voyage à faire
> Aux pays étrangers ;
> Il faut que je m'en aille :
> Dieu me l'a commandé.
> Tenez, voici ma bague,
> Ma ceinture à deux tours,
> Marque de mon amour.
> *Cantique Pop. sur St. Alexis.*

NOTE.

THERE is a class of readers whom the unscientific traveler would gladly reach and interest, — the light skimmers of summer books between whom and distant countries lie, — not one, but many seas, and whose only hope, in all probability, of seeing them is through the more favored eyes of others. For these — not for those who have personally 'undertaken the adventure of Spain' — this volume is specially written, — a series of profiles projected more or less vaguely by a Spanish sun. The author feels his errors of omission and of commission quite as keenly as the most hostile critic could desire, and would hesitate to publish his sketches at all — for more they do not profess to be — if the general impression pervading them were unfavorable to the Spaniards. Much has doubtless been overlooked, much inadequately seen; but the book is in no sense a guide-book, and wherever it has been possible, details such as are found in guide-books are left to those compilations. The realities of landscape, the mode of life and of travel, the aspect of the old Spanish cities, the habits of the people, the vicissitudes of a summer journey set down just as they appeared, form the staple of these pages. Personal impressions may, peradventure, have a sort of value ; and if this slight record, which pretends to nothing beyond being a faithful transcription of personal impressions, should awaken the interest of a single reader and persuade him to study a most interesting country for himself, its aim will be more than accomplished.

LEXINGTON, VA., 1879.

CONTENTS.

		PAGE
I.	OVER THE PYRENEES	1
II.	GLIMPSES OF ARAGON AND NAVARRE	24
III.	AN OLD ROMAN CAPITAL	37
IV.	JULY BULLS IN VALENCIA	44
V.	PALMS	73
VI.	BETWEEN THE CONTINENTS	82
VII.	THE CITY OF THE KHALIFS	92
VIII.	THE ALHAMBRA IN SUMMER	105
IX.	ON THE GUADALQUIVIR	147
X.	A CORDOVA SCRAP-BAG	191
XI.	A SPANISH FONTAINEBLEAU AND CANTERBURY	222
XII.	MADRID	247
XIII.	STATISTICS À VOL D'OISEAU	288
XIV.	A SENTIMENTAL JOURNEY	314
XV.	PHILIP'S FOLLY	331
XVI.	CINTRA IN AUGUST	340
XVII.	THE CITY OF INEZ	355
XVIII.	A GLASS OF PORT	364
XIX.	CLOUDLAND IN SPAIN	375
XX.	IN OLD CASTILE	387
XXI.	BURGOS AND A SPANISH SPA	406

SPAIN IN PROFILE.

I.

> The king of Aragon look'd down
>   From Campo Veijo, where he stood,
> And he beheld the sea of Spain,
>   Both the ebb-tide and the flood.
>   FRERE, *Romance del Rey de Aragon.*

THE blonde light of yellow Spain! At sunrise this morning we arrived in the capital of the Basque provinces, Bayonne, the bishop's see, the home of the Jews exiled under Philip, the spot that has for some inscrutable reason given its name to the bayonet, — for it was not invented here, — the paradise of ham, chocolate, and patois! All night we had been climbing towards it from Bordeaux, the vast wine metropolis, which loomed over the river at us through innumerable lights and gathering mist. The moon followed through the night, and we were enabled to isolate and individualize the groups and successions of landscape that detached themselves from the silvery dusk and left a vivid impression on our no[t] too wide-open eyes. The country seemed t[o] grow poor as we approached Bordeaux, and noth[ing] seemed to indicate the existence of, or ap[-]proach to, a great city. From Bordeaux to Ba[-]yonne the journey is monotonous. The yellow light of morning illuminated extensive stretche[s] of pine, quaint Basque stations embowered i[n] vines and trees, just awakened peasants saunter[-]ing to work with the leisurely pace of the South and a long train full of weary travelers. Th[e] air meanwhile had grown delightfully fresh an[d] keen, an overcoat was welcome, and the fres[h] fragrant presence of the sea — the blue Bay o[f] Biscay — was felt. Then suddenly the train ra[n] in under huge fortifications built by Vauban him[-]self, and we were at Bayonne.

In this remote corner of France, locked in b[y] the French and Spanish Pyrenees, one woul[d] expect many survivals of antiquity in costume[.] But such is not the case. Costume survives i[n] Bayonne only in the peculiar blue turban-lik[e] caps and broad-brimmed straw sombreros of th[e] men and women. A bright red sash — a rem[-]nant of the Far East — is found now and then[;] brown faces, brilliant eyes and black hair, smal[l] figures and feet, great animation of manner an[d] profuse gesticulation, announce the vicinity o[f] Spain.

Two picturesque little rivers, the Nive and the Adour, run together here and produce a charming variety in the landscape. Bayonne is a great starting-place for the tour of the Pyrenees baths and water-cures, little French-Spanish Alpine nests perched among the cliffs and valleys of the outlying Pyrenees and combining many pleasant peculiarities of the two countries. The Pyrenees are nowhere much beyond ten thousand feet high; but there is a peculiar cordiality and politeness in the manners of the people that compensates for Alpine altitudes and makes you feel at home. Several trains leave the place every day for Pau, and the boat penetrates the idyllic scenery of the river, while south runs daily the great current of travel to Madrid and the peninsula: so the Bayonnais do not lack for the usual excitements of frontier towns.

The profusion of gold lace and scarlet breeches also announces the existence of a near frontier; little fierce-whiskered, tight-laced, sworded and emphatic gentlemen, who take their *café noir* under the arcades of the Place d'Armes, promenade up and down, and ogle the pretty milliner girls, indulge frequently in absinthe and cognac and are willing to fight for any government in office at the present moment. No blame to them; one must live. Life is sufficiently agreeable whether Henri Cinq or MacMahon Premier be on the throne; and the grisettes take their evening promenade all the same. A handful of red-legs comes to dress-parade of an evening, accompanied by a multitude of the loudest drums and shrillest fifes in Christendom; immense aplomb and bravura; vivid reminiscences of La Belle France; wonderfully straight, proud figures wonderfully dressed and self-conscious; tremendous sensation; marchez! So it goes in France. The French shops are all façades; the French people have only front teeth and front hair; there is brilliance and wit and culture and the best foot foremost; then the Germans come. Alas for light hearts, singing chambermaids, *table d'hôte*, and *grand confortable*. They all vanish down the back stairs and hunt up their stockings full of hoarded gold to pay the milliards with. Is this all such fascinating civilization is fit for? France gives us our wine and our perfumes and our manners; has she no great example of self-restraint and self-abnegation to give? Looking on this little bit of hid-away, happy French life at Bayonne, haunted by the lovely light of the blue sea and the shining river and the morning-glory-tinted Spanish mountains, — a life shut in by the tall Basque houses, the dim arcaded streets, the shadow of the beautiful twelfth century cathedral lying in benediction on it, — the question recurs with tenfold intensity: What will the French come to? The country is under exquisite culture; every foot of it is painfully, even pitifully nursed and coddled and pampered, like a spoiled child; the ripe wheat and mellowing grapes and multitudinous vegetables followed us in superfluity about thirty miles an hour, as fast as we could travel, from Paris to Bayonne; the fields were shot with poppies of magenta, and purple of corn-flowers, and white trumpets of tangled convolvulus, interspersed with brilliant green meadows, mill-wheels with their lazy abundance of falling water, ancient villages and cities like Orléans, Angoulême, Blois, and Poitiers; vineyards, sugar beet, poplars; white turnpikes, new-mown grass-fields, spiritually present in the perfumed air; harvest people asleep beside the slain gold of the harvest; song of birds and effulgent presence of flickering and chanting streams; but what is coiled at the heart of this dazzling picture, Heaven only knows. The sad heart says the French cannot be trusted; their fields can, their pockets can, their honor and honesty can, their great bank can, and their great artistic and imitative instinct can; but what is a-top and at bottom of all this, the mainspring and working principle of it, viz: the French themselves, cannot.

From Bayonne to Biarritz, the summer sojourn of Eugénie and the emperor, it is but a few miles.

Think of the poor widow in exile, doomed to German baths when she will go any whither, with her own pleasant Villa Eugénie nestling in the rocky glens of Gascoigne far from her and all her race. The place has an interest more tragic than that of Miramar. Flowers, music, light, loveliness, and — exile. The place seems to languish for the far-away empress. It will not be itself again without her; and the magnificent hotels look out over the sea as if ever expecting somebody, — the blue delusive sea, with its perpetual smile, its fickleness, and its summer beauty. Rocks of singular formation lie at the feet of the bay and form islets where confluent lines of sea gather into what seem like vast foam-flowers, and break in delightful waves when the wind is still. Set in this blue mirror, with the foam foliations and foam fringes surrounding them, these masses of rock look like huge sea-anemones ruched and serrated. To-day it was strangely calm; the sky was a warm gray; the sea serene as any lotus-eater, save when these rocks vocalized it and fascinated it into efflorescence. A light-house stands opposite on a promontory approached by a drive penetrated with musky pine odors. This is the famous drive from Bayonne by the Barre and Phare. The pines are everywhere slashed and cut, with earthenware pots attached to catch the resin. Everywhere one sees bleeding trees;

everything is wounded and *hors de combat*, and there is a disagreeable sense of mutilation in gazing on these splendid trunks treated in such a way. The white road meanders through the green pines all the same, and the world is none the wiser.

Biarritz is the Brighton of the Basses-Pyrenees; it is very hilly and contains many handsome villas. The drive back on the imperial of the omnibus — does not Victor Hugo ride on the imperial of an omnibus? — through spacious grounds and along elegant summer residences, is very pleasant. Particularly elegant is the Villa Sofia, with its sward, its grouped and glorious geraniums, its white figures of pedestalled and dancing marble, and the graciousness and spaciousness of its verdant park. Then the omnibus traverses arcades of green interwoven sycamores and poplars and elms, past men winding hemp into cord, past the two-towered façade of the Gothic cathedral, past the fortifications dotted here and there with diminutive French soldiers, past the ever-present *octroi* and its recollections of mediævalism, in under a resounding arched gateway, dashing round it and the Place d'Armes with its cafés and balconied hotels, up to the stopping-place in the Rue du Gouvernement, — altogether a charming drive for eight cents. I see a forerunner of Spain in the numerous fleas which have jumped to meet me on the frontier; in the very miscellaneous dinner and coiffured waiting-girls of the Hotel St. Martin, and in the unsavorinesses which accompany the hostelry dedicated to that long-suffering saint. The wine is sour; gravy over everything is already in the ascendant; the bread looks as if it were aged; and the ham is intensely salty. The celebrated Gascoigne and Galician porkers have already suffered in my estimation. Bayonne prides herself on ham, on little feet, on sparkling eyes and dusky hair, and on her mariners. She is the z, not the zero of the French provinces; two nations go to make up her nationality; linguistically she is unique, since neither Prince Bonaparte nor Mr. Vinson has been able definitively to settle the relationship of her patois. French life has here run down into an intense drop of highly concentrated individuality; and painter, poet, and historian have all enough, and more than enough, to detain them pleasantly for weeks.

Leaving Bayonne at half-past five or so, — for you never know precisely when you do leave, being in the land of inexactness, lazy watches, and comfortable time-tables, — the train arrived at Saragossa at eleven in the evening, with more or less of punctuality. Indeed, the perfect indifference with which advertised arrivals and departures are ignored as works of supererogation, the accommodating spirit of the trains, which stop everywhere and take in everybody, the easy *insouciance* of conductors, railway clerks, and porters who smoke the *cigarrito* and dangle the Spanish leg from every conceivable support, box, bench, or fence-rail, remind one of North Carolina in the olden time, when engineer, fireman, and passengers all had to get out and drive the pigs off the track. It will not do to fuss and fume up and down Spanish railway stations in the usual way.. Everybody 'takes it easy;' the traveler from England and the Continent soon abandons the acute distress he may suffer for fear of being left, and falls into the take-your-time-and-enjoy-yourself fashion of lazy Spain. Nobody is ever left in this obliging country, be he even the tortoise of the fable; '*cinco minutos!*' (five minutes), cries the man when the train arrives at some mud-colored Basque village. You are delighted at the prospect of so soon departing; but delight changes into woe, as ten, fifteen, even twenty minutes pass away without leaving and without assignable reason for remaining. There is nothing in the place but a yellow-skinned Basque woman in colored bandanna and voluminous skirts, who walks around crying *Agua! agua!* (water! water!) which she serves out of an earthen-ware caraffe used for cooling by evaporation; a gendarme paces up and down in red breeches, blue coat, yellow straps, and cocked hat, with a loaded rifle; two or three dirty peasants in the national *boina* hang indolently over the fence and gaze listlessly on the thinly populated train; the conductor parleys with half a dozen different people, quells a row in the third-class carriage, drops in and talks with the passengers; people get in and out with no dread of being taken off, run to the *fonda* (buffet) for wine and water; wash their faces at the pumps; eat, drink, and are merry; in short, *mañana, mañana* (to-morrow, to-morrow), the national Spanish word, is in full play and keeps the peevish northerner in continual annoyance with its ceaseless suggestion of procrastination. A lady traveling in the same carriage with me asked a gentleman passing by when we should get to Valencia, a town lying at no great distance from where we then were; '*Mañana! mañana!*' answered he, with decision; whereupon the poor lady had an attack of ejaculation beheld in its perfection only in this country of superlatives: '*Madre mia,*' exclaimed she; 'it is impossible!' On being assured firmly and positively from the same source that to-morrow it was, and to-morrow it would be, she lapsed into the depths of the *guia oficial*, or official guide for the railways, and appeared determined to work out her salvation with fear and trembling out of that. She was willing to arrive at nine the same evening — but to-morrow! There is a mysterious charm for the Spaniard in to-morrow, there are so many possibilities and probabilities; so much may happen 'twixt now and then; you may be here, and I there; my ship may come in and your château be built. The poesy of yesterday is as nothing to the events and eventualities of the time to come. Poor Spain! In the same way Philip II. had looked forward, and Isabel II. had worked, and Cervantes had died a hooded monk. In thinking of the great to-morrow, the beautiful daughter of Lope immured herself and her genius in a cloister; and the king of Navarre burnt ten thousand Jews in the market-place of Pampeluna. With eyes fixed on the supreme future, all Spanish victories and losses, Inquisitions and expulsions, are more or less mixed up with delay, procrastination, — the element of futurity; and Spain has put off being civilized till she will never be.

After leaving Bayonne the road ascends gradually through some wonderful engineering work, tunnels, bridges, steep grades, and sharp culverts, into a region of Alpine loveliness and charm. The northern part of the peninsula — the six hundred and fifty miles from Cape Cruz on the Mediterranean to Cape Finisterre on the Atlantic coast — is luxuriantly clad with vegetation. Pine, spruce, oak, birch, chestnut, heather, ferns, and gorse, Alp flowers and moss, fragrant lichens, sparkling waterfalls and rivulets, glens full of Swiss scents and scenes, and valleys vividly draped in the most living emerald, meet the eye everywhere. Not the least charm of the Basque region are the quaint watering-places and baths perched in among the almost inaccessible mountains; the sulphur, saline, and chalybeate springs that gush out of the towering Pyrenees, and form nuclei for adventurous travelers, mountain châlets, and picturesque, semi-civilized summer life. The peaks of the Pyrenees are frequently over ten thousand feet in height, on the French side tropically rich and forest-clad, on the Spanish side far less so from the almost vertical character of the precipices. Four or five roads put the two countries in communication, — little enough for a stretch of over two hundred leagues. Great wealth of game, fish, primeval forest, and unexplored flora, exists in this wild border-land; and the inhabitants, especially on the south side, are a fine, stalwart, manly, and independent race; prone to the savage virtues of war, love, and hospitality, a stronghold of conservatism and the contraband; of hunters, fishers, smugglers, Carlists; splendid Basque, — whom Voltaire described as 'a lively little people that dance on top of the Pyrenees,' — Navarrese, Aragonese, and Catalonian fellows, as far removed as possible from the languor and listlessness of the lower provinces. The passes even excel the Swiss passes in height and magnificence. The French, true to their nature, have utilized their side to the utmost: it abounds in fairy retreats and mountain hermitages, tiny baths with graceful casinos, straight rows of poplars, meandering boulevards, nooks, and cafés, bands of music, light hearts, bright flowers, and green turf. Railroads penetrate the valleys and plain. Bayonne, Toulouse, Agen, and Perpignan are centres from which tours may be made to them ; and, in a word, there is Swiss comfort added to French alertness, intelligence, and taste.

On the other side, *tras-los-montes* — how different! The wild, almost uninhabited plains of Navarre and Aragon, a solitary railroad from Bayonne to Barcelona, faces and forms and costumes as if just flashed on you from Velazquez' portraits, a sixteenth century look in the eyes of the people, conventual and monkish life with its deep impress on the land, roads, country villages, wide sombreros, priests, peasants in knee-breeches, women in veils and mantillas, savage looking boys and beggars, splendid cathedrals and wretched family-life, donkeys and muleteers, diligences, intolerable dust and pitiless sunshine.

San Juan de Luz is the first village reached

after leaving Bayonne, and a picture of poetic landscape it was as it nestled in the silvery, dewy morning light, just enough concealed and just enough revealed by the mist to make it a magnet for the eye. The crown jewel in its necklace of memories, say the chronicles, is the marriage of the great Louis XIV. here in 1660 to Maria Theresa, daughter of Philip IV. of Spain. The little place seems never to have recovered from the shock, and looks out to sea from its strange Basque houses as if still dreaming of the august event. The whole country through which we passed is redolent of Wellington and the wars of 1813. Battles, stormings, slaughters, victories, retreats, glory, triumph, and death are inextricably intermingled with its fields of butter-cups, its purple heather, and its changeable hued tufts of blue-green pines. Théophile Gautier contemptuously called the famous isle where Louis XIV. met Maria Theresa, near Hendaya, a 'fried sole of middling size.' Other famous memories cluster about this locality; the great Velazquez contracted a cold here and died, while fitting up the salon for the conference between the Spanish and French kings; Francis I. was exchanged at San Juan in 1526, leaving his sons behind as hostages: and wherever you go, everything is salted and peppered with souvenirs; here this, yonder that, took place; here an assassination, there a wedding; history, like a loom, crosses its innumerable threads till the whole is woven into a glittering fabric.

Next comes Irun, where everything and everybody coming from France is emptied out and examined for the delectation of the Spanish custom-house people. I will do them the justice to say, however, that they were courteous and passed us without difficulty. Custom-house officers have an infallible instinct for their victims; they seldom trouble the right-minded and innocent stranger; it is the nervous, fidgety, conscious, conscience-smitten wretches into whose shrinking eyes and abnormal wallets they look, drawing their conclusions. Irun is a fisher-village, but it too has great things to say of itself. La Fayette sailed hence for America; a battle or two took place between the English and French in the vicinity in 1813, etc. All through Spain one is pursued by this abominable date until it becomes a positive nightmare. The town is not of sufficient interest to demand more than a few words. From Irun the train brings us to San Sebastian, a town of very striking situation on the Bay of Biscay, and quite recently celebrated for its bombardment. It lies on an isthmus and is surrounded by water on three sides, — water curiously enlivened by the Bayonne and Basque boats (called *trincadours*). It is the Madrid Long Branch;

there are delightful bathing, a fine promenade, military music, a bull-ring, handsome women, brilliant verdure of summer on the hills, pure air, and purer water.

From the railway window the town is a real picture; we happened to pass on Sunday and saw the Basque women in their Sunday gear, with bright bandanna kerchiefs and long tresses of blue-black hair hanging down behind after the fashion of a Chinese pigtail. The foot-gear of the men — as all through Aragon and Navarre — is truly antique; a sandal, made of felt, with straps coming over the toes, crossing the instep and tied around the ankle, and worn with or without stockings. More pretentious people have white cloth or white canvas shoes, now and then variegated with strips of leather. It seems to be an easy, delightful, and open sort of foundation, such as to make one's feet, rendered feverish by confinement and heat, envy their lucky wearer. This sandal seems quite what we read of in ancient story before the torture of box toes, shoe-buckles, and high heels had been instituted. How we complicate the simplicities of ancient civilization; compare the plain tunic of a Greek woman with a costume of Worth's; Socrates' *obolus* with the Bank of England!

The scenery as we ascend toward the Pyrenees, — for we really seem to be ascending thither, becomes wilder and lonesomer. A keen brush of Alpine air smites the cheek and titillates the lungs now and then, the ferns with their wonderful ribbons of foliated lace become heavier and heavier, there is a delicious sheen on the green fields, sounds of falling water touch the ear of July like liquid heaven. The fire and faintness of the low, painted, and panting plains melt into the dewy freshness of sharper altitudes; the eyes are bathed in the suffusing moisture of these upper regions; summer is forgot and spring has come again. We wandered on and on up the charming valley of the Urumea, fields on the right and fields on the left, blue perspectives aeriform, the mountains in the distance snowless and sunshine smitten. Stoppages at strange little towns where women with veils and marketbaskets got out and peasants with tresses and kerchiefs got in; stoppages for water, stoppages for no earthly reason except the fun of the thing, to breathe the bright Sunday air, and look down on the yellowing harvest marching carnival-like through this idyllic landscape. Happy Spaniards! *Muy leal y muy hermosa España!*

We were not in a hurry that summer morning: it was all so beautiful; the light of the fresh dawn was over us; we were passing great fortresses and turreted battlements, and the sea looked in and smiled and sang to us, and men drank *chacali* and gazed and laughed and talked broken Spanish and listened to the harmonious inflections of the Basque, and nobody seemed to think it was Sunday. Presently Tolosa, a town of some ten thousand inhabitants, was reached, shut in between the Loaza and Ernio hills, — not, however, before we had passed Hernani, famous to lovers of Victor Hugo, who just missed being a Spaniard. Everybody seemed to be at the stations; chatter, chatter, chatter all the time with an animation and an eagerness unknown in less impressionable countries. The third-class is always crowded in Spain, — and such a scrap-bag of nationalities and costumes, patois, odds and ends of eccentric and impoverished humanity as it is! Whenever we stopped the noise of some adjacent third-class carriage was deafening, everybody talking at once, everybody gesticulating, everybody declaiming and haranguing, from the market-women to the abbé in black skull-cap. It was like a nest of blackbirds. You meet people who can read and people who cannot; you see Spanish life and get your pockets picked. I felt as if I was in one of Caravaggio's pictures. Doubting Thomases explored one's empty-looking pockets; sneering Pharisees picked up cuartos, and asked one the superscription and image; valiant Peters swore eternal friendship, and long-tressed Magdalens sat at one's feet. And here, too, were all the sons and daughters of Eve that sat under the pencils of Murillo, Ribera, and Zurbaran, whether hung to crosses, suffering agonies in the garden, or enjoying our common existence under the golden radiance shed over Murillo's beggars; the same eyes of coal, skins of tan, hair of purple, and features in perpetual curves; the rags and ruin, the gayety, the passion, and the pathos; Spanish life in marvelous encyclopædic merriment and synthesis and sympathy; all traveling cheap, all large-eyed and happy! All over the peninsula the same jumble is found, the same *canaille*, the same eating, singing, and carousing manhood and womanhood, trying to get the best of everything for the least possible price; trying to outwit you and everybody else in a bargain; trying to drive you farther than you engage for to make more money; trying to show you castles and abbeys and churches and palaces, whether you will or not, for a few cuartos, bidding you 'go with God,' when they are done; begging in every imaginable crevice and corner; throwing coins out of their poor poverty-stricken pockets over the silver railings as an offering at the shrine of some sumptuous Virgin; eating and dancing in the street with delightful naïveté; going to bed to wrestle with *pulgas* and *chinches*. An American's idea of Spain and the Spaniard is apt to be clearer than his idea of other countries, owing to the much that has been written and painted on the subject, the geniality and romance of the national character, the soft beauty of the Mediterranean landscape, the intimate relations between Spain and America, and the presence of so many of our distinguished men in Spanish diplomatic offices. The novelty of a tour to Spain has its edge greatly taken off by many of these circumstances and the books they have produced,—an enduring and charming literature now extensive enough to form a library in itself.

At Alsasua in Navarre the carriages are changed for Pampeluna and Saragossa, unless you desire to go direct to Madrid, a long and tedious journey over the arid plains of Castile, past wretched little towns, with but a collection of beasts and unhappy-looking people by way of evidences of civilization. Immediately on entering the train for Pampeluna you feel that the management has changed hands. The road belongs to the Rothschilds. The speed is not great, but the carriages are comparatively clean and broad. In France the roads are narrow-gauge, in Spain broad-gauge, and this accounts for the much greater width of the Spanish cars. Traveling rates are very cheap; every ticket has the price stamped upon it in reals and cuartos; the conductor walks along the side of the train in the old-fashioned way and collects the fares; everything is easy-going and good-natured. The ticket offices so far are true abominations, a sort of stye out of which a pig-faced individual peers and talks Catalonian Spanish at you, no matter what your nationality.

All along until we came to Pampeluna ruined stations met us, relics of the Carlist war; soldiers paced up and down with loaded guns, and a general air of uncertainty and uneasiness seemed to prevail. The country is now, I believe, quiet, — quiet as this caldron of Spain can ever be. The plains, wheat-fields, and mountains of Navarre lay before us, yellow, yellow, yellow. The day was fortunately gray, or the ocean of yellow light might have swallowed us up. Imagine yellow roads, yellow fields, yellow rocks, yellow people, yellow houses, yellow dust, yellow earth, yellow sky, with just the green neck of the bottle through which you have come from Bayonne expanding into the immeasurable yellow plains of Castile, Navarre, and Aragon; and the yellow sea sweeping down from the Pyrenees and covering everything with its saffron waves; yellow daffodils, yellow sun-flowers, yellow sunsets, fruits yellow, and grain yellow, and yellow ague in the eyes of the people; imagine the Mediterranean turned to yellow pigment and flowing over the land; imagine all the rays of the spectrum yellow and all of those rays throwing their jaundiced light over Spain, and every chemical substance and re-agent doing the same till the soul faints with glut of yellow light, and its sole, fervent prayer is for the greenness and sweetness and freshness and purity it has just left behind on the benignant slopes of the Urumea, and you have a pale conception of the blonde light of yellow Spain. It is well the people have black hair, for that might be yellow and increase the trouble.

Tudela and Calaborra are passed, both bustling Navarrese towns, with the whole population, as it seemed, hanging agape over the station fence gazing at us. A very good *mesa redonda* (*table d'hôte*) is got for three pesetas (francs) at Calaborra, and one wonders where the Spanish get so many savory morsels from in the general sterility of this part of the country. They dine twice and do not breakfast at all. The *almuerzo*, or eleven o'clock breakfast, is a dinner in every respect except soup and sweetmeats: wine, course after course of meats, eggs, fish, stews, fowl, salad, cheese, and fruits. *Comida*, or six o'clock dinner, is the same, with greater elaboration. Coffee may be got — at least at the hotels, in the restaurant. The wine is too much like cordial to be pleasant in the long run, — fiery, sweet, fruity, garnet-colored, and rich.

At four we arrived at Pampeluna, the capital of

Navarre, a town of about thirty thousand inhabitants, full of the Carlist spirit, — Carlist and old Navarrese grandees, and antiquity of aspect. It is of little interest to the tourist, — a dreary, yellow, ancient, dilapidated town, which has corrupted the former *Pompejopolis* into the modern *Pampeluna*, — stands about a mile off the railroad, and looks infinitely sad and still on its yellow river. An hour — the official twenty-three minutes — was spent at the station, apparently waiting for the *sala de espera* or waiting-room to fill with passengers before we started, and then the train crept on into fertile, treeless Aragon, over the winding Ebro, into the city of Saragossa (Cæsarea-Augusta). The transition from Navarre to Aragon and Catalonia is like that from Mississippi to New England.

II.

> In a somer sesun, when softe was the sonne,
> I shaped me into a schroud, a scheep as I were;
> In habite of an hermite unholy of werkes,
> Wende I wydene in this world wondres to here.
> *Piers Plowman, prologue.*

EVERYBODY knows a little about the story of Saragossa — its foundation by Noah's nephew (!), its fortification by Cæsar and his legions, the Moorish corruption of its name into Saracosta, its capture by the Suevi in 452, by the Goths in 466, by the Berbers and Charlemagne, and its subjection to the kings of Aragon; its rise into the capital of Aragon before Ferdinand married Isabella and united the two kingdoms of Castile and Aragon, its celebrity in the Peninsular War of our days, and the famous sieges of 1808, when the town held out so marvelously against Lefèvre, Junot, and Lannes. One is surprised on walking through its dusty thoroughfares to find so much history lingering amid their quaint ugliness. The town lies, or rather sprawls, along the Ebro, — a great, shallow, turbid, tortuous stream that fertilizes this thirsty province, and is everlastingly turning itself in the way of the railroad, being jumped by bridges, and administering refreshment to the wayside pilgrim with the sight of its crawling water. It is the incarnation of mud and misery, with long lines of dyspeptic looking poplars throwing their haggard shadows on the banks, — vineyards of fierce Aragonese grapes ripening their garnet fire in the sun, and now and then a cluster of miserable hovels, with *Posada* (resting-place, inn) written on the side in letters almost as big as the huts themselves. It was welcome and delicious night when we arrived, — night, that pearl of seasons in this dazzling peninsula, — and the quaker gray-green of the olive plantations, in which Saragossa is embowered, could not be seen. We dashed along through the rattling street (oh! the unspeakable comfort of having no trunks to detain us at the stations!), and drew up at the *Hotel of the Universe* (does not that sound Spanish?).

A good night's rest prepared the way for enjoyment on the morrow, aided by the softest murmurs of the fountain splashing in the *patio*, on which the chamber looked. These patios are one of the characteristic charms of Spain: courtyards, often edged exquisitely with flowers and urns, a jet of sparkling water in the centre, canvas awnings oscillating gently in the wind above, and mysterious chambers, before which hang the floating and twilight-cherishing persianas of straw, opening out on these spots of perfumed tranquillity. The Moors left the *patio* behind as a legacy to Spanish señoritas, who sit behind the curtains, reading or embroidering, a prey to the imaginative reverie of the South. You generally enter these enchanted abodes through a great arched doorway, sometimes a cluster of fluted pillars or the filigree of a Moorish screen flinging their intervening grace between you and them. Now and then there is a deep vista, a delicate colonnade, a series of monumental vases that have caught fire with flowers; a pavilion all gilt and airiness and honeysuckle, sunny lines of shelled or pebbled walk, a glory of far-away oleander and orange, and a glimmer of winged and light-poised statuary. There is everything to put out the world and keep in the indefinable sweetness of perfect stillness and peace. Our dining-room at the hotel looked out on the court-yard and its fountains, and as we tasted or toyed with the curiosities of Spanish culinary art before us, we could catch the freshness of the dropping water and enjoy the sensation of coolness it always produces.

I sallied forth on a walk before breakfast and found the streets almost thronged. It was my first experience of a genuine Spanish town.

Saragossa is so far from the ordinary lines of travel that it is neglected more than it deserves. If you want to see the sixteenth, seventeenth, and eighteenth centuries in their Spanish architectural peculiarities, their walls, their fortress houses, their twisted streets, tiny *boutiques*, and infinite nonchalance and dilapidation; if you want to go to bed and wake up two hundred years ago; if you want to compare the insane elaboration of the modern *table d'hôte* with the simplicities, the unchanging habits, the domestic conservatism, the town life, the household economies of a hundred years gone by, Saragossa is the place to transport yourself to. Not that there is anything the least wonderful about the place, for there is not; a brown, provincial, sleepy, satisfied Spanish town, gazing into its sluggish river until it has become stupefied and comatose; it has nothing of the vividly picturesque to detain a sensation hunter, still less to tickle the luxurious few who travel *en grande toilette* and are particular about kid gloves. But to the artist, the antiquary, the thoughtful and curious student of epochs and manners, there is much to see, and much to carry away. Every window has the invariable balcony, with the green woven persianas hanging out over the balustrade; the high houses all have the projecting *para* at the top; on the ground floor the shops are entered through flowing curtains like the Italian churches; over many there are massy coats of arms, scrolls, quarterings, devices, and blazons molded in plaster;

before every two or three there is a beggar stationed, with some astonishing deformity, invoking all the saints in heaven to smile on you whether you give him a cuarto or not. (How one would like to do to these people as old Chaucer once did to a Franciscan monk who had insulted him,—give them all a sound thrashing around!) Dark-eyed señoras, with lace mantillas flowing over heads and shoulders, hurry by, going to mass; groups of funny little Spanish street waifs play at the never-ending national *pelota*, or turn and ask your *worship* to give them a penny for the love of God; an *arriero* saunters by, driving his hay-laden mules and donkeys; not a carriage is to be seen, and the yellow omnibuses with their quaint berlina in front come along at a truly antediluvian pace; there is no haste, no eagerness, only great flakes of golden sunshine everywhere, great clouds of lazy, whirling dust, fruit hanging over the garden walls, and scents of gathering summer wafting from the new-mown fields. You walk in the middle of the narrow street, stroll into the choired and cloistered coolness of parish churches, seek the shadow of providential walls and gaze out on the glittering atmosphere through half-shut eyes; you wonder that this white and yellow light does not burn the eyes of these people out of their sockets. How could the Spaniards endure it if they were a reading people? As it is, the book-shops are mean, dark, and full of Paul de Kock ; the newspapers are printed in Lilliput, and people who get in and out of trains have to have their tickets spelled out for them. IGNORANCE is written in characters as big as the wedges of Babylon all over these mendicant faces ; you instinctively feel that they have never looked into a book. And those who do read sometimes make a singular choice : viz., two young ladies poring over Boccaccio in the carriage coming to Barcelona, then drinking wine out of various bottles end foremost, powdering and making their toilettes before a whole carful of passengers in entire unconsciousness, and, as a crowning horror, washing their faces with a quantity of pomade-like stuff which they finger-nailed out of a pot ! They were evidently very decent, but very naïve people, who seemed habituated to this sort of thing, — Boccaccio and all, — offered luncheon to their neighbors, laughed and talked and joked merrily as we crawled along, and finally were met and welcomed by very nice-looking people at the Barcelona station. They had a whole carpet-bag full of towels, bottles, hand-mirrors, cold-chicken, rice-powder, combs and brushes, peaches, slippers, bread and butter, fans and cake, — all in delightful confusion. The day was insupportably hot, but they would get out wherever practicable, promenade up and down in the sun, buy a plate of soup here and there, cry '*O Dios! Maria! Maria!*' when anything out of the common run happened, and were as natural as so many kittens on a first holiday excursion. They may hardly, however, be regarded as specimens of the Spanish ladies, who are the prettiest women and have the prettiest manners in the world.

Saragossa has two cathedrals, the Metropolitan La Sea, and the Del Pilar. La Sea is more like a wide, magnificent Gothic cloister, mysteriously dark and vast as you enter, and becoming more and more beautiful as the slender columns unfasten themselves from the encrusting twilight and shoot up their sheaved pilasters to the ribbed and rosetted roof in almost too ethereal lightness. Golden wheels and roses hang from the vaulted roof, where each column spreads out like a spider-limbed palm and the worshiper stands as in some sacred wood. The light percolates through white wheel-shaped windows very high up, which gives admirable illumination to the piers, buttresses, sculptured cherubs, and pilaster capitals of the upper portion. The spectator is himself almost in the dark as he gazes up at this vaguely illumined groined grotto, with its dome-covered side-chapels, thrilling abysses and recesses, and silent beauty. It realizes most perfectly Dr. Johnson's 'horrible feeling of immense height.' What a contrast was this serenity with the garish day

I had just left! You felt it was a holy place, with its sanctity of eight hundred years, its far flickering tapers, the noiseless worshipers kneeling around in the dusk of the mighty pillars, and the sweet spell of its over-arching presence strange and tender on the silent heart. The choir is in the middle and shut in by a carved screen on which a whole population of interlacing arms and legs, *en monogramme*, saints and sinners, legends and Bible stories, disport themselves in marble and gilt. How little has all this dancing *canaille* to do with the majestic pillars about which they cling, and the starry heights of the ogive arches! As I sat gazing up at them with delight, the verger approached and made me uncross my legs. It was irreverent!

The other cathedral, Del Pilar, is a modern, seventeenth century structure, reminding one of a section of St. Paul's in London. It is overloaded with gilt, paintings, lamps, shrines, chapels, and sculpture. The Virgin used to come down and visit this favored place in the good old times, whence the church, and the stone is still shown — now transferred and set in the wall for the devout to kiss — on which she alighted! A lady knelt and kissed it while the guide was telling me this. It is just as well: why not?

The La Sea cathedral stands in a quaint square, with the archbishop's palace on one side and the ancient lonja or exchange opposite.

All imaginable styles run riot over the façade of this cathedral: Corinthian pillars surmounted by prophets and apostles, bits of antique Mauresque brick-work, Romanesque and Byzantine buttresses and apsis, light and elegant allegorical statues on the eight-sided tower; in short, it is not exactly a mass of 'fricasseed marble,' but something strangely like the national *puchero* or Spanish hash. It is with strange surprise that one enters the dingy little door stuck in a corner of the church, and suddenly finds oneself breathed and blown upon by the delightful atmosphere of the shaded interior, with its distances and altitudes, its severe and sombre antiquity, its grand air of breadth, the boldness of the arches, and its splendid recollections of by-gone times. The kings of Aragon were crowned here. An alabaster retablo stands behind the choir with its effigied multitude, devout relievos and elaborately wrought seats, organ and lectern. The grandeur of the cathedral is greatly diminished when one has done looking up into the pillared sky of the roof, and turns to the side chapels to be met by tawdry pictures, greasy candelabra, and dingy gilt.

The legend goes that the Del Pilar cathedral was founded by Santiago after the crucifixion, who came to Spain and preached the gospel in the first century. The Virgin appeared to him mounted on a pillar of jasper, surrounded by angels. A conversation ensued, in which she expressed a desire for a chapel on this spot, which Santiago courteously erected, — small and unpretentious at first, then more and more costly, till in 1686 it grew into the present Del Pilar Cathedral. Nothing can be uglier than the domes on the roof with their white, green, and yellow tiles, suggestions of a series of soap-boilers. The great heart of Don Juan of Austria lies buried here, and there is a very fine alabaster retablo by Fument. The Holy Image worshiped in this cathedral has a wardrobe worthy of Elizabeth, — pearls, diamonds, necklaces, mantas, silks, and satins; and the devout gaze at her blazing shrine through a *reja* or balustrade of massy silver. As I stood and looked at the curious scene a troop of Catalonian peasants in velvet knee-breeches open at the knee, long white stockings, sandals, gorgeous sash, with the long Santa Claus-like Catalan cap, came by and bent the knee. One of them unwound his sash, took out a copper cuarto and threw it over the silver railing at the feet of — what? the Santa Imágen. She did not bow as the wooden doll of Montserrat did to the Infanta of Spain; but one could not help being touched by the simple piety of the poor fellow. He made the offering out of a full heart and (doubtless) a by no means plenteous pocket: Peter's pence require Job's patience.

The streets swarm with the vermin evoked by the most catholic injunction to be charitable. One longs for a cleansing law disfranchising beggary! Spain would be half redeemed from her worst enemy — herself. You can hardly step out of your hotel without treading on some supplicant. The ingenious devices resorted to by the blind, the lame, and the halt to collect alms, — the bags, boxes, plates, and nets suspended round every limb of their unimaginable bodies, held out, rattled imperiously, or attached to some point of support, — are a never-ending study. Hundreds of years of such doings have produced great skill in this privileged class; half the same spent in good honest work would have developed the country and fed the people who now every twenty steps elevate their deformities as if they were a host, and instead of the charity they expect, get simply — horror and detestation. The streets should be cleaned of such things and the hospitals filled with them, where the wretched nuclei of perambulating disease could be cured and attended to. As it is, crooked feet, ophthalmia, limbs distorted in every conceivable manner, masquerade on the street like a carnival of death, and are regarded by their happy possessors as a true fortune. A cure would no doubt in many cases be stoutly resisted, for then the blind would *have* to see, the lame to walk, and the halt to work. A Spanish plaza where the liberal light throws broad shadows through the arcaded walk is the favorite resort of teeming mendicancy; there is a beggar for every streak of light across the pavement and a beggar for every shadow, and apart from these a squadron of imps is employed by those who are too lazy to move, to adjure the promenader by everything on the face of the earth to stop and look at that object of charity yonder, to give the *pobrecito* a glance out of his blessed eyes and a *limosna* out of his most illustrious pocket, etc. You are tapped on the shoulder, addressed through the *reja* of the house-window, assailed at the entrances to shops, and beleaguered at church doors. I had heard and read of Spanish beggars, but I had never, as the ministers say, 'realized' them before. Nor is there that excuse for this class which was urged in the sixteenth century by one of their great writers: '*La hermosura tiene fuerza de despertar la caridad dormida:* Beauty hath power to awaken sleeping charity.' But then one may add with the same writer: '*De todo hay en el mundo:* There's something of everything in the world.'

Apropos of a famous mystery acted in the La Sea Cathedral before Ferdinand and Isabella during the Christmas of 1487, occurs an item in the archives of the cathedral, which curiously illustrates the spirit of the age. The mystery represented the Nativity of Christ and the archive reads as follows: 'Seven *sueldos* (*sous*) for making up the heads of the bullock and donkey, in the stable at Bethlehem; six *sueldos* for wigs for those who are to represent the prophets; ten *sueldos* for six pairs of gloves to be worn by the angels.'

III.

> But lordes and knyghtes and othere noble and worthi men, that conne not Latyn but litylle, and han ben beyonde the see, knowen and understonden if I seye trouthe or no, and if I erre in devisynge, for forgetynge, or elles; that they may redress it and amende it. — SIR JOHN MAUNDEVILLE, *Prologue*.

WHAT a lovely old place is Tarragona! I dropped in here last night in the dark and woke up to find myself transported to Carthaginian, Roman, and imperial times. I cannot understand Hare's volubility of abuse lavished on the town, for in just such seldom visited places lie the traveler's most frequent surprises. This is the Carthaginian Tarchon, the winter residence of Augustus in one of his rambles, the old town that clung to Pompey — 'ein Mädchen, das an meiner Brust mit Aeugeln schon dem Nachbar sich verbindet'[1] — and then kissed Cæsar,[2] the residence of Roman proprætors, the capital of Roman Spain, the scene of once great prosperity, a hill of palaces, theatres, aqueducts, and temples, now no more. The town runs all over a hill some eight hundred feet high, commanding the most lovely views of the vast and pallid Mediterranean

---

[1] *Faust*.   [2] Hare, *Wanderings in Spain*.

at its foot, and the garden-like Campo de Tarragona towards Valencia. It is surrounded by high walls, with gates, bastions, battlements, and forts, relics of one and another time, left here to become infinitely picturesque and mellow in this balmy light.

The street in which the hotel lies, called, like so many other Spanish High streets, the *Rambla*, from the rivulet that once flowed through it, — like the *Fleet* in London, — runs in a straight line to two of these gates, through whose spacious arches delightful views may be had, at the one end of the blue-fired sea, at the other of the wonderfully fertile plain and mountains of Tarragona; opposite are the quarters for the infantry, and all the morning most charming music has been floating through the hotel windows, as battalion after battalion of red-legged fellows marched into the adjacent church to attend military mass. As soon as mass was over the band broke out into tuneful dance music, and I looked down into the street and saw two tiny damsels chassée-ing up to each other on the brilliant, sunlit pavement. The immensely broad window of my room has a balcony with iron railing, over which is let down from above — as usual in these Spanish towns of fluttering curtains and mysterious half-lights — a broad green persiana, giving ample ventilation, light, and protection from inquisitive eyes. You can look up the street and see hundreds of the same sort, of every hue and color and material. Nothing can be more interesting than the perspective of one of these streets with the innumerable rain-spouts reaching out over the sidewalk, the twinkling and swaying curtains sweeping down from windows high and low, the bits of ancient sculptured wall, with here and there a splendid grape-vine growing out of them, rooted twenty feet above your head; a garden, over whose wall hangs a peaceful and mighty palm, a bastion planted with rows of light-leaved china-trees, a palace looking on the sea out of a labyrinth of mimosa, aloe, cactus, orange, and myrtle; a portal with the lions and lilies of Spain graven in marble over it, a long plaza which was once the great Roman Circus, but is now given up to soldiers, civilians, and fountains; a strange church steeple in glazed green and yellow tiles, with its peal of bells hanging out through grouped windows; a palace of the archbishop or the captain general, with severe and solemn stillness reigning about it; a flight of marble steps surmounted at the top by the glorious cathedral; an oriel window high up on the side of a house, through which there is a glimpse of square, grated openings, as of a prison; a gallery running across the street and connecting two odd Tarragonese houses by its umbilical cord, — in short, a series of very pleasant and very striking illustrations of Spanish street architecture, life, and custom. The whole livelong day, nearly, bells have been ringing, bands playing, congregations hearing mass, and the streets filling with people. A neighboring fife has been continually cutting its musical zigzag on the air as if the fifer were writing arabesques and monogrammed initials in sound on the crystalline atmosphere; then wild clashing of silvery bells from the groaning *tartanas*, — a vehicle of Arab origin; then murmurous and multitudinous talk welling up from the street below, from the people sitting before the inns and shops. Early morning and late evening are the noisiest times in Spain; the middle of the day is consecrated to in-doors.

Apart from the antiquity of the place, the tomb of the Scipios, and the noble Roman bridge in the vicinity, the special object of a sojourn here is the grand Norman Gothic Cathedral and cloisters of the thirteenth century, truly a

'Santo templo del immortal Amor'

of that sweetest of the old Spanish poets, Fra Luis de Leon. I do not know of a lovelier bit of color than is the outside of this noble mass; the golden under-ground stain softened into pink and brown and mellow ochre by the hallowing touch of time. It has an unfinished look, indeed is, externally, quite unfinished. It is approached by a flight of marble steps flanked by two very old fountains, and encrusted all about by venerable houses. Could the envelope of close-clinging habitations with which it is built about be removed, the cathedral, cloisters, and adjacent churches might almost rival Pisa. The entrance is by a deep-recessed door divided in the middle by a column which supports a canopied Virgin, above whom sits Christ, looking rather superciliously, it must be confessed, down on the Holy Mother. A score of life-sized saints and apostles, some with books, some with scrolls and swords, stand under canopies round the upper part of the door, and receive the visitor with all manner of smirk and salutation. Long black curtains wave before the entrance, and when these are drawn aside and you enter, the effect is very striking. This cathedral is nothing like those of Barcelona and Saragossa: it is plain, three-aisled, majestic in its gray and grave simplicity, illumined by stained glass three hundred years old, and three superb rose windows; and there are massive buttresses out of which shoot pillars with elaborate capitals which in succession give birth to the ribbed and groined vault. The church is cross-shaped, and high up the jeweled windows distill their painted dew till, at sunset, the upper domes are a fountain of color.

There is not the mystery and gloom of the Saragossa Cathedral nor the reverential stillness; all is large-limbed, massy, and revealed. There is beautiful carving around several of the chapels, and high altar, choir-stalls, and pulpits, all deserve regard. Attracted towards a candle burning in one of the side chapels, you are half terrified to find yourself gazing on the undecomposed corpse of San Olaguer in a glass case, lying before you surrounded by gigantic figures in stone, so life-like that they look as if about to speak. A box with ' *Limosna para la Tierra Santa* ' written on it lies at the saint's feet.

After you have done wandering under the heavy Norman arches, a door to the left is glimpsed, which leads to the glory of Tarragona and the rival of the Campo Santo and Westminster — the cloisters. What a delightful retreat for monkish feet in those olden days of yore! For one hundred and eighty-six feet on four sides the cloisters extend, embracing in their caressing arms one of the most old-fashioned of cathedral gardens. It is all a tangle of box and ivy hedges, cypress, orange, and sweet scented herbs and flowers, — a perfume box for the poetic old monks, and a fragment of thirteenth century sweetness for us. The gem of this cloister is the series of arches supported by sheaves of delicate marble pillars, which runs around it, and has given birth to a world of charming imaginings in the curiously carved capitals. The Gothic imagination has gone mad in these traceries: fighting cocks, mice burying the cat, cooing doves, eagles standing on hares, geese plucking owls, serpents interwined, masques, fruits, flowers, the star and story of Bethlehem, fighting gladiators, satirical scenes from monkish legends. All these have gathered into tiny tableaux on these remarkable capitals, and lend grace to the buttresses on which the six large ogive arches rest, together with the groined roof. Small Norman windows, Moorish basket-work, Roman capitals, vestiges here and there of the palace of Augustus and a mosque, are scattered up and down the cloisters; while along the framework on the garden side run arabesques, dentellated work of various patterns, and gracious Moorish ornamentation. It was full of people this cloudless Sunday morning, and through the open Byzantine door leading from it into the cathedral pealed the sweet-toned organ, like the stained glass, more than three hundred years old. I visited it again this evening and found the floor studded with kneeling señoras and señoritas, nearly all with the national fan and lace headdress. The evening sun streamed in gloriously through the windows and left its iridescent blaze along the cloister wall.

IV.

The surviving shadow of the Bull-God is as the shadow of death on past and passing ages. — SWINBURNE, *Essays*.

NEVER dream you have seen Spain till your eyes have rested on Valencia. Here you are fortunately rid of cathedrals, and your eye dwells solely on the inexhaustible beauty of landscape, *huerta*, and sea. The approach from Barcelona is unrivaled, and should never be made by night, however hot it is. The railroad winds with all manner of languishing and serpentining along the labyrinthine coast, and involves in its folds most enjoyable glimpses of the great lazy Mediterranean, the lamb-fleece sky, the scarred and castellated sea-shore, and the teeming wealth of the unexhausted soil. After the desert between Saragossa and Lerida such a bath and brilliance of verdure is beyond description. It looks as if the whole wealth of Spain had unlocked itself upon this land of fruit and flowers, and had suddenly broken out in vast plantations reaching as far as the eye can see, — thanks to the heirloom of thorough irrigation bequeathed by the Moors to their most Christian descendants. The land is a network of canals, water-wheels, ditches, and rivulets furnished by the various rivers that take their way through this jewel of Spain; distribution of water is under government control; and though the highways in summer whiten and glisten with insufferable dust, — cast a glance across them and see to what greenness and gloriousness water can bring things, — the ablutionary apple of the Moor's eye, and the principle which he so generously applied to assist the good gift of Allah.

The train moves (not too fast!) through a most picture-like country — the scenery and spacious envelope of Barcelona, with the Llobregat zigzagging across it and touching its roots with beneficent moisture. On the right hand dances the exquisite apparition of Montserrat etherealized and poetized by distance, perhaps unique in the history of mountain-groups; a cluster of mountains faintly resembling the thousand-pinnacled Milan Cathedral, though incomparably finer, staining the sky with its sharp and sudden blues, its evening towers and ambient heights, its transformations into unimaginable shapes as you gaze on it from the ever-changing track, its shrine and fortress-like convent, the hermitages and grottoes; you know not what to call it or say of it, for it suggests everything fantastic as it looms hazy-clear across the trail of this divine atmosphere, an element of poetry and devotion in a landscape so given up to worldly needs. Silius Italicus's '*Divisque propinquas rupes*' come to mind in looking at it. Then ancient towns are approached, such as Martorell, with its fine Roman bridge called *Puente del Diablo*, through whose arch of one hundred and thirty-three feet (a work of the Moors) the winged dragon of Montserrat is caught sight of soaring into the sky; then Villafranca and the ruins of Saguntum, Tarragona, Tortosa (where the *reino* or kingdom of Valencia begins); then rich-wined Benicarlo, whose famous juice connoisseurs tell us goes to build up the bloodless Macon of Burgundy; then Alcala, where Hannibal swore vengeance against the Romans, Castellon, and other stations. To describe this journey would be to write the words rice, citron, almond, pomegranate, vine, fig, orange, olive, and mulberry a hundred times over. The country is undulating till the province of Valencia is reached, when it levels out into an emerald floor of two hundred and forty square leagues; rich in silk, fruit, grain, and wine, where you see quaint little straw-thatched huts as in Normandy ('*Parva, sed apta mihi*' stood written over Ariosto's door), each surmounted by a cross or a palm-leaf, to keep the lightning off; churches and towers embowered in green, groups of magnificent palms shooting heavenward from the surrounding flatness, fields of flax, carob, alfalfa (mowed five or six times annually), melons, maize, avenues of mulberries and forests of oranges, a world of vegetable wealth compensating for the rarity of minerals. The railroad breaks its way with difficulty through the thicket of opposing growth, every foot of which is sending up something to blossom and ripen in the powerful sun, or scent the summer air. I had imagined the 'Valencianets' lazy and careless; they are anything else.

The climate is a balm which seems to stimulate rather than enervate; and in spite of the culinary solecisms, such as chicken stewed with rice, the greasy ham with greasier eggs and tomatoes, the fish in the middle of the dinner, the soup made of floating reminiscences of yesterday, the enormous peppers devoured as if they were bread, the *habas*, the *chorizo*, and the *gazpacho* (made of onions, vinegar, oil, bread, salt, and red pepper mixed together in water), etc., etc., the people seem healthy; chills and fevers are frequent on account of the great humidity arising from the constant irrigation of many districts, and no doubt other sicknesses springing from the excessive use of fruit are prevalent; but who without positively looking over the mortality tables or going into the hospitals would suspect this voluptuous atmosphere of harm? It is the softest, sunniest, sweetest air in the world; the sea distills its honeyed coolness into it, and fills it with pleasant salt scents,— there is a saffron mist of white pervasive light dwelling over it, hamlets nestled in cypress and palm lie around the mother city like so many hovering chicks; bright costumed and mantillaed señoras move about with oriental lightness; there is perpetual peal of church-bells, mass-going, picturesque chaffering in the strangest old markets and market-places in the world; market-places sometimes surrounded by a *lonja* with a mighty clock bedded in plateresque carving looking out strangely still across the bustling plaza, and a series of fluted and twisted pillars running up into a groined ceiling which canopies many a scene worthy of Sir David Wilkie; then the streets wind like the thread on a spool of cotton, round and round until they meet in the same place, or expand like pebble-struck water into wider and wider rings until the towered and battlemented wall is reached, where the *octroi* stand in the sculptured gates and pierce the contents of every peasant's cart with a long thin blade, to keep out the contraband; then the boddiced women with their classic jugs held slantwise under the arm wait their turn around the fountains or lay their jugs in long rows on the side till their turn comes, or your wandering feet bring you to the *alameda* (lit., alley of poplar-trees) along the river where the fashionables promenade from sundown to midnight, and where you see every style from Jouvin kids to the many-colored *manta* and *alpargatas* (hempen sandals) of the sashed and waistcoated peasant, head in gay silk handkerchief, and legs orientally loose in huge trousers. There is no lack of artistic bits! Try to gather up one of the dissolving views as they appeared the other night on the occasion of the great July Fair in the wondrously illuminated alameda of Valencia; catch the multitudinous booth scenes, the fanning and flowing mistresses of an Albacete knife establishment dealing out wares to astonished and simple-faced *paisanos*, or a dim table full of roulette-players staking the last cuarto in the light of a wind-blown lamp, fascinated by the hope of gain; or a brilliant pavilion where there is a *rifa* (raffle) going on amid a glittering heap of treasures at two reals a chance, the numbers being little rolled cigarette-like papers which you draw out of a large glass jar; all which is to buy Nuestra Señora de los Desamparados (Our Lady of the Forsaken, the national saint) a new gown or a splendid manta, while Valencia streets (mark you) are swarming with beggars. Pictures and pictures might be made out of all this, not to speak of the châlets and *pabellones* all ablaze with chandeliers and crimson curtains, where the fair Valenciennes dance to titillating music during this great festival; the gay little *horchateria* gardens where ices of all sorts are dispensed, and the *estoque* booths, where an unceasing stream of men and boys are purchasing ivory-headed bamboo canes or heavy hooked shillalahs for the *corrida de toros* (bull-fight) to-morrow. *Agua fresquita!* (here's your cold water!) rends the air from *jarro*-bearing women; *Fosforos! fosforos!* (matches! matches!) from boys in blouses gleaming phosphorically about along the dusky walks. It is a ten or eleven days' carnival in July for the kind-hearted Valencian people, whose affability, gayety, quick temper, and ready poniards are so well-known. It is not much to say they are imaginative, for that one sees everywhere in their highly-colored phraseology, dress, jewels, proverbs, and churches; nor nervous, for they are fidgetty as tarantulas; nor excitable, for their broad Limousin-like dialect, — so like the old Provençal of Bartsch's Chrestomathie Provençale — resounds on the streets in high key all day and all night long. I never saw gracefuller, tinier women, brighter eyes, or more beautiful hair, — like silk; and among the peasant women the long plaits at the back are held together by a silver pin, to which a very gorgeous silver comb of quaint design gives greater accent.

At the *plaza de toros*, or bull-ring, in Valencia,

I saw a big burly countryman with shirt buttons of clustered pearls in front, — a confirmation of what I had read, that many of the peasants wear jewels and stones of classic form and great value handed down as heir-looms from a considerable antiquity. The tinkling guitar and clashing castanets are heard everywhere, from the poor blind men leaning pathetically over the fence which separates the railway from the road, where they stand and play in the hope of beguiling a copper out of the traveler when the train stops, to the wanderers that make the music in the streets under the balconies and hotel windows, even before one is up in the morning. Take it in good humor, for it is better than begging, and there is so much beggary in this blessed land.

I saw my first *corrida de toros* in Valencia — and my last? I think so, for the present. To think of such verdure, and *verdura es carne*, says a Valencian proverb, being watered by such blood! Perhaps the passionate wealth of vegetation springs from such fertilization? But then the tawny blaze and barrenness of the rest of Spain, — sterilized and saffronized Castile, sandy Navarre, and the yellow mourning of glowing Cordova. It is a land of contrasts; now the green magic of England, now the glooms and eternal fatigues of Siberia, now enormous and luscious fruit, now leagues on leagues of hopeless railway travel past station after station and town after town, without even a drop of water or a grain of mustard-seed to be had for love or money. And you gaze out over the endless illuminated mountains, ribbed and fluted like a Gothic cathedral, and lighted from morning till evening with the most exquisite effects of painted distance and pallid purple air, parched in throat and panting for breath, willing to give your poor little kingdom of a purse for just one peach! But it is Spain always and ever, remember that. Carry water-jugs and fruit-baskets and alleviating comforts with you, or suffering the martyrdom of San Sebastian will be luxury to it. One looks on grilled San Lorenzos and blazing Smithfields with utter indifference in comparison with summer traveling in this sun-struck peninsula.

The first *corrida de toros* in Valencia! It was an experience. Walking one evening down the busy Rambla of Barcelona, I saw posted up beside one of the railway ticket offices a large variegated advertisement, telling with the true Iberian pomp of adjectives of the great *feria* (fair) at Valencia during the last eleven days of July, during which wonders were to take place. First, and foremost, the great fair of Santo Somebody, patron of Spain, then immense display of fireworks, dancing *al fresco*, opening of museums and botanic gardens, gala nights at the theatres, concerts, competitions of various kinds, and last and best, three days' bull-fighting 'initiated' by the celebrated *espadas*, Lagartijo and Frascuelo, assisted by the *banderilleros* Calderon and Templao, the *picadores* Mariano, Agutejas, etc. Considering that the most solemn funeral mass for the repose of the soul of Doña Mercedes, Queen of Spain, had just been performed in Barcelona Cathedral, this advertisement struck a foreigner as rather curious. The sweet young queen, so beloved, so ill-fated, hardly cold in the mausoleum of the Escorial, and the good Valencianets a-thirst for Santiago and his bulls! I confess I did not feel the regret which I should have felt. To depart without seeing a bull-fight was to have the mere shell of the almond. I thirsted with true Spanish ferocity to gaze on the triumphant scene and go away with its noble enthusiasms, its rigid excitements, its hair-breadth and hair-splitting escapes indelibly branded on my memory, — and so they have been.

Thousands — without exaggeration — flew to Valencia from all parts of Spain; half-fare tickets brought in throngs of Carthaginian and Berber-looking peasants from the populous Mediterranean lands; Barcelona, Tarragona, Alicante, and Albacete emptied themselves into the first, second, and third-class cars to be disgorged in the great *plaza de toros* in Valencia. The occasion had been advertised far and wide, and every mode of getting to the city was utilized to bring in the pious pilgrims. At first I thought I should buy tickets in advance for the whole three days; but second thought suggested the prudence of a trial before investing the sixty reals necessary for this worthy purpose. The sequel rather justified than put this prudence to shame. We were particularly favored at the Hotel de la Villa de Madrid by having the whole officiating *troupe* in the hotel with us, including the great Lagartijo and Frascuelo themselves, men of national reputation, the Kean and Kemble of the bull-ring. As heroes of the bull-ring they sustain the same reputation among men in Spain as Patti and Nilsson among singers in the fashionable feminine world; strong, stalwart, dark-faced fellows, with sinews of steel, eyes quick as light, and step agile as a cat's. One of the *camareros* of the very dirty hotel (the best, however in Valencia) informed me of their presence with no little awe of manner. They were his Shakspere. The dinner-table was crowded with their suite, and the usually so stagnant Spanish hotel life, even in bright Valencia, had roused itself to something like energy. How the waiters danced about their distinguished guests, pointed out this or that one to admiring strangers, whispered among themselves, laughed at the *bon mots* of the arena, and envied the most enviable of mortals who had tickets to the heavenly entertainment! I made one of them infinitely happy by presenting him with a ticket, and telling him in national phrase, '*Vaya usted con Dios.*' His eyes sparkled, and that day I noticed my room utterly neglected (he had previously attended to it) and the transported waiter absent,— no doubt gloating in the summer sun over the huge ellipse of the *plaza de toros!*

It is of no use to talk of bull-fighting being on the decline in Spain; it is not, and it cannot be. The hair of the Spaniard has not deeper roots than his love of it. Talk to Spaniards of average intelligence about the matter, and they will all agree with you that it is horrible, but they will every one go, and that every time they have a chance. This is not the worst of it. Perhaps the most ardent upholders of the custom are the women, from Isabel II.— whose head seems hardly fit for anything but a debased Spanish copper — to the graceful girls of saloon life, and the poor washer-woman who is fortunate enough to have saved up two pesetas to buy a place in the sun. On the day of the fight the ring outside is surrounded by a crew of boys crazy to get in, hanging there in the fascinating hope that somebody will sicken and come out and give them a ticket. Pictures of it are on every fan, in every shop, before every imagination, on the great day, — generally a day of incomparable brilliance, of thin, warm air wherein everything is marvelously still and statuesque and sweet, a day when no palm waves or yellow gold of acacia-hedges trembles on the mute Spanish plains. The season lasts from April till November, the beautiful summer being from one end to the other trailed in blood. Being the intense people they are, — each one of them is a revolution, a charge of gunpowder, a human torpedo in himself, — the Spaniards must have excitements of a peculiar kind. They have always used dirks and poniards freely; they gamble inordinately in lotteries, at *rifas*, and in the name of alms and Holy Church, they are devoted to cock-fighting, and give up Sundays and Thursdays to it; they have a sort of Irish nature, deeply stained with the ardors and irritations and exaltations of the South; unpractical, isolated, ignorant, and imaginative, their language is a trope, their light is a taper before the shrine of the Purissima Virgin, their blood is a scarlet fever, their pleasures are torments. As a nation they were born under the star Sirius. They live, move, and have their being in an air of flame; the wine is a sweet fire that climbs instantaneously to the brain, an alcoholized syrup which melts ice like a liquid blaze, beautifully colored with the *tinto* and *blanco* of the wine-merchant ; a bottled treachery to him who knows it not and drinks and drinks the amorous fluid till he is suddenly giddy — and the wine laughs. Millions of animals and animal passions shut in from the time when Cæsar defeated Pompey's sons at Merida till the present day — shut in, save that radiant efflux that went forth to find America and the Indies; rarely traveling or seeing anything of the world but themselves; separated into sharply marked provinces by the high sierras ; in a land of no books ; lying a-bed with priests sixteen hundred years, and having eternal *aves* and *angeluses* rung in their ears; from everlasting to everlasting telling beads on their knees in gorgeous cathedrals that strike emotional chords only in the human breast, — such a life of indolence and unintellectuality could not but blossom out into this evil fruit just as we see it ; and one of the hugest and crimsonest blossoms is the bull-fight. It is curious to what elaboration of detail this national sport has given rise, to what slang, what technicality, what peculiar terms to distinguish your specialist from the ignorant amateur. A whole dictionary of terms and distinctions has sprung up to characterize its successive stages of brutality : the implements used, the costumes worn, the entrances and exits and triumphs and falls. Volumes circulate to give the *aficcionado* due information about each shade of the performance. Boys know it from the time they can say their prayers and their parents begin to take them (which is very early); and they follow every movement of the bull and his tormentors with intelligence. A pretty good Spanish scholar is sometimes at a loss to translate these technicalities, and has to apply to some frequenter of the plaza — that is, to anybody in Spain — to explain them; which is always done with suavity and gravity, for the *hidalgo* is the pink of sad-faced courtesy. If a mistake is made during a performance an incredible outburst of derision, indignation, and hissing is the result, often so sudden that one is involved in it before any reason is discerned, so intense is the general attention and appreciation. If a Naples audience is the severest trial in the world for a singer, send your bull-fighter to Valencia! None but experts can stand before this immense assemblage and hope to escape unwithered by blighting contempt.

The *plaza de toros* stands just at the station and is a large amphitheatre, nearly if not quite circular. Its capacity is eighteen thousand people. In form it greatly resembles the Coliseum; it is built of stone and brick, unstuccoed, is entirely open to the sky and contains a vast arena surrounded by a slope of some twenty-five rows of seats, widening as they extend upward. Above these rise two covered galleries, one above the other, with deep rows of seats, some *al sol*, others *á la sombra* as the phrase is. Three or four corridors for promenading, which look out over the city, extend all around the amphitheatre, and admit to the inside by numerous doors and *vomitoria*. The work is of the plainest and most matter-of-fact description; it means business; and save for the unnumbered yellow-and-red flags of Spain, which encircle the edge of the highest gallery and wave or hang listlessly in the stilled air, there is no ornamentation. The arena is smooth as a piece of brown paper and is sanded and rolled everywhere. It is separated from the amphitheatre by a *valla* or partition about five feet high, made of board an inch or so thick, within which, at regular intervals, there are gates to shut off the bull in case the infuriated beast leaps the barrier. I should have said that the amphitheatre does not abut directly on the *valla*, but there is a corridor six or eight feet wide in between and then comes the amphitheatre, with its partition somewhat higher than the *valla* and surmounted by a rope. Whether the seats here are specially desired or not, I do not know; the holders of them seem often in great danger. The corridor is full of officials, police, people, attendants, and the particularly

favored, who are obliged to keep a very sharp
lookout on the bull lest he leap over and tear
them to pieces.

Of course all Valencia was in grand gala on
the opening day; the station where the incoming
and outgoing trains brought in and took out passengers did not exactly, as the local Diario de
Valencia said, present a magnificent (and common as dirt in Castilian) spectacle, but certainly
a very lively one. Sight-seers came in great
force; the station did not pretend to be long
enough for the trains, and many had to walk a
quarter of a mile before reaching the *salida* appropriated to them. No sooner had they emerged
from the station than they were stopped in the
square adjoining by ticket-sellers uttering loud
cries and immediately collecting a crowd of purchasers around them. I had sallied forth early
in order to secure a ticket, as the sale lasted
from nine till twelve only. To a Spaniard such
a matter is a trifle; but to one unacquainted
with the names, positions, and technicalities belonging to the occasion, purchasing a ticket in
such a multitude of fanning, perspiring, clamor-
ing, haggling bourgeois was no easy matter. I
finally succeeded. On the outside of the wall
encircling the *plaza de toros* stand written in
large letters AL SOL and Á LA SOMBRA; mysterious technicalities, full of importance to the

knower and lover of bull-fights, and occasion of many a heart-rending mistake to the uninitiated. The explanation is this: In Spain, bull-fights generally take place at half-past three or four o'clock in the afternoon, and the amphitheatre is so built (the stars even entering into its construction!) that one side of it shall catch the *sun*, and the other the *shade*. Hence *al sol* means 'to the sun,' *á la sombra* 'to the shade.' From this arises a considerable difference in the price of seats; the *al sol* seats are sold at eight reals, the *á la sombra*, on the street for anything the scamps can get over twenty reals, but are put down officially at thirteen reals and a half, for which doubtless they are seldom obtained, being bought up by speculators. Cries, therefore, of *Al sol! al sol! á la sombra! á la sombra!* meet the puzzled new arrivals, and up and down they go, gazing, country-bumpkin fashion, and wishing either that they were in Jericho, or that they had a friend to explain all this mystery. At half-past two or three the gates are thrown open and from that time till the performance begins, the city sends a thousand rivulets of hastening and hurrying life to fill up the great reservoir before us. Dust indescribable, of course, is the first thing met with; then the gendarmes in their curious one-sided hats; then the ticket-receivers; then comes the search for the special *angulo* or division marked on the ticket, with the accompanying *gree* or round of the slope where the seat is situated; and woe to him who comes late! Such individuals are apt to be greeted by pushing and hard words, for it is next to impossible to get along, so close together are the rounds and so dense their population. Many towns, with all their men, women, and children could get into a great amphitheatre like this, and have plenty of room to spare. Inside, the scene is really extraordinary. On one side blazes the pitiless sun, '*por el amor de Dios;*' hence innumerable umbrellas of all colors, parasols, gigantic fans big enough for Bartholdy's Liberty enlightening the World, each containing a furious bullfight on its sunlit radii, converge into a huge semicircle of brilliant and breathing life. Many of the umbrellas are bright crimson; the dresses are of all colors; everything is in motion; soldiers in glittering uniforms sit together gregariously here and there, forming focuses of accentuated color; gold and silver combs, bodices, mantillas, jewels, the flash of falling light on precious stones, the gay and various-tinted mantas, the velvet coats, wide sombreros, and walking-sticks of the peasants, form one of those mighty combinations such as one sees in the teeming canvases of Tintoretto. Motion, Motion, Motion, is written everywhere in capital letters and is caught aslant from the innumerable twinkle of the fans. On the other side the high walls of the structure cast refreshing shade, coolness, convalescence as it were from the deadly violence of the sun: *sombra*, that sweetest of Spanish words, full as Christmas *bonbonnières* with eloquence and restfulness. Here, too, are the fans, the mantas and mantillas, the velvet coats and ivory walking-sticks, and jewels and precious stones, and mighty sombreros with their umbrella-like peripheries, and *dons* and *doñas*, — light, perfume, loveliness, lustrous eyes, and Spanish grace; but it is of the better class, the class that can throw away a *duro* on the savage scene, and go home glad of the privilege. Everybody has lunch, skins and bottles of wine, pockets full of bread and peaches, bottled lemonade, tortillas and sandwiches, for the performance lasts four hours, and will not be over till the poor, gay, long-suffering *al sol* people feel how delightful the shade of descending night is and their sun-shades are furled. Nothing is in stronger antithesis than this munching, eating, drinking multitude with their popping bottles and wild laughter, and the scene they have come to witness, — doing all this, too, in the very thick of it. Nothing seems to pall or appal the appetite of a Spaniard. There were refined-looking women sitting in front of me who ate during some of the most frightful massacring of the afternoon. Perhaps human nature could not have stood it otherwise. And I, crouching behind my fan, in a cold sweat all over, sick, self-loathing, and unable to extricate myself from the crowd, sat in a sort of stupor for four hours, trying not to look, but every now and then irresistibly drawn to peep over the fan down on the hideous doings below. The Valencian who sat beside me hated and despised my chicken-heartedness and asked me if I should come 'to-morrow.' My other neighbor, a fat, funny old peasant in hempen sandals and knee-breeches took off his coat and sat the whole time talking aloud to himself, with eyes fastened on the arena and lips now and again uttering something wonderfully funny, as I judged from the laughter he caused: naïveté itself, in a frame as big as the picture in the Vicar of Wakefield. He did not fail to break out into ferocious cries, like everybody else, when there was the least sign of vacillation or blundering. The Spaniard will have everything *selon règle;* and his bull-fight must be as thoroughly well done as his *puchero* or his *gazpacho.*

A word or two about the order of the entertainment. First of all the fanfare of trumpets is heard precisely at four, when one of the *vomitoria* opens and out march in procession fifteen or twenty brilliantly dressed men who are to bear the brunt of the evening. The two far-famed *maestri* headed the procession, which marched to slow music across the arena to a position in front of the alcalde or mayor's box, where they stopped and went through the pantomime of asking the permission of the town authorities to begin the fight. This being graciously granted, another flare of trumpets, and out springs the *llave*, or man bearing the key to the *toril*, as the *vomitorium* whence the bull is to leap forth is called, on a splendid gray charger. He is dressed in black, with cocked hat, black gloves, and waving black cloak. He is received with acclamation at first, then, if he lingers in the least, with stormy impatience; he prances back as fast as he came, after having made his bow before the alcalde, who is called *el presidente* for the occasion. Then come a moment or two of intense expectation. A little behind the first procession, which is on foot, came in a troop of *picadores*, or men armed with long pikes, on wretched steeds called *arrés* (the word so often used for get up!); they go up to the alcalde's *palcon* and then trot around the arena as gayly as their miserable animals will allow,—poor beasts, doomed to the most horrible of deaths before the evening is over. (A sad substitute are both men and beasts for the true knights and noble steeds who in former days came down into the arena and fought.) The procession consists of four classes of men : the *espa-*

das or swords, so called because it is their business to dispatch the bull at the end of the performance; the *picadores*, or men with pikes, who open the performance by stationing their horses, four in a row, with intervals of some yards between, near the *toril;* the *chulos*, or men with large cloak-like pieces of exasperating red, yellow, and purple cloth, to flaunt before the bull, madden and blind him, and then foil his terrific onslaughts; and lastly, the men with darts (*banderilleros*), instruments called in bull-ring slang 'ear-rings,' 'wasps,' 'appendices,' consisting of pieces of thin wire about a yard in length, prettily ornamented with light fluttering ribbons, with a sharp barb in one end, the design of which is to sting up the relaxed animal by plunging them two at a time into his shoulders; an operation requiring infinite delicacy, tact, and quickness. The men who did this literally seemed to fly like butterflies, insert their intolerable barbs and then spring backward like winged Mercurys. It is done just as the bull lowers his head to toss his enemy to the sky.

Bull-fights might be tolerated were it not for the first act of the sanguinary drama, — the poor horses stationed in dumb show, bandaged over one eye and perfectly unconscious of the exquisite cruelty to which they are to be subjected. The human part of it, though full of danger and excitement, is somewhat extenuated by the admirable dexterity shown in foiling and eluding the bull, keeping him at bay, annoying him by darts and blinds, flying at him or from him. Strength, nimbleness, self-possession, and courage are all required and shown in an eminent degree. But to pick up twenty poor old horses out of the streets and stand them up blinded, to be gored to death by a savage brute, is an unpardonable crime. One loathes and hates the Spanish people and government for allowing it. And what is to be said of the fathers and mothers who flock thither with their young children and teach them to gloat over this ghastly drama? Ought they not every one to be put on bread and water for the rest of their lives? And the strange part of it was that a large part of the proceeds were to go on this occasion to the poor of the Santo Hospital, and the newspapers breathed the pious wish that the attendance might be large as the money was given for a good purpose! The clergy often occupy the best seats, and priests hurry through masses to get to the ring in time. This devilish scene is perpetuated that the 'poor' may be helped and the streets be further thronged with every species of lying and hypocritical mendicancy. Every town of a few thousand inhabitants has its ring, its advertisements of *toros de muerte* ('bulls of death') hanging on the street corners, its local *espadas* and *banderilleros*, and its churches and hospitals to be helped. This freak of diabolism, this amphitheatre dedicated to the devil, is, in Valencia, just behind a church, — indeed out of one into the other!

A bull that will not fight is greeted with inextinguishable hissing; cries of *Vacca! vacca! fuera! fuera! fuego! fuego!* resound on all sides; and darts having barbs with explosives attached are plunged into the hesitating beast and goad him on to desperation. There was no occasion this special evening for the fire-darts. Eight magnificent bulls leapt into the arena like tigers, one after the other, all showing fight, all with wild eyes, mighty horns, splendid heads and shoulders, and slender flanks, — incarnations of daring and dazzling strength. As soon as the *toril* was opened, out bounded a grand tan-colored fellow, a four-footed Hercules, and flew on the first horse with the ferocity of a hyena, goring him frightfully, and hurling him, rider and all, to the earth; then he tried another; then a *chulo* flapped his long, blinding cloth before the bull's eyes; then a mad leap first at one man and horse and then at another; then another horse instantaneously killed and trampled to death; then a *banderillero* made a hair-breadth escape as the flash of the formidable horns came close upon him; then another *picador* in long, yellow buckskin breeches, gold or silver vest, and wide, brown sombrero, with blue or scarlet plume and scarlet sash, stationed his trembling beast before the insatiable monster; then another torrent of blood, and a poor, disemboweled, wretched creature trotted all around the circle, treading his own bowels to pieces; then exulting and thundering cries from fifteen thousand spectators as the winged darts, two at a time, were inserted till the bull was covered with blood and rushed round in agony; then a flare of trumpets; then the *espadas*, resplendent in green and gold (Lagartijo) and purple and gold (Frascuelo), stepped forth with long, thin, steel swords, each having a gorgeous cloak which he flashed in the eyes and over the head and nostrils of the bull till he foamed with futile rage; then as the bull lowered his head to dash his pursuers to pieces, down like a ray of light fell the sword between the creature's shoulders up to the hilt; staggering, falling on one knee, with blind and dying eyes still haunted by unhallowed fires, gasping, faint, bleeding, more and more uncertain in step as he moved, transfixed with the deadly blade, whose hilt bore the sacred sign of the cross, blood issuing from mouth and nostrils, staggering, fainting, falling, dead!

A wild uproar ensues as the huge corpse rolls over in the dust; the band breaks out into delicious strains of music; everybody springs to his feet, laughs, talks, congratulates, lights a cigarette, eats, flirts; opera-glasses without number are turned upon the victorious *maestro;* cigars, hats, cigarettes are rained down on him, which he acknowledges, returning the hats to the enthusiastic owners, bowing and saluting, not a fleck on his unsullied silk, proud of step and bold of eye as he looks up around the great amphitheatre like a minute speck standing in the crown of an immense hat turned upward; then out of the *vomitorium* dashes a span of four beautiful grays with waving plumes, gilded hoofs, and crimson, gold, and blue caparisons, dashing round the arena with their drivers after them, till they reach the stricken bull; a rope is attached to his horns and he is ignominiously dragged out, again to triumphant music; the dead horses have the rope put around their necks; the wounded ones are sent to the *infermeria* to be put in the hands of the veterinary surgeon, who treats them, sews them up, and trots them in again, again to be savagely torn, and killed; then the sharp snarl of shrieking trumpet, universal quiet; the *toril* is opened, and out leaps apparently the self-same splendid tan-colored fellow as before. Slaughtering of horses; fluttering of cloaks and *banderillas;* flinging and fixing of flinty darts; leaping of the *valla* by the bull, and general flight of those standing there, all escaping; cries of *Arre! corre! madre-deu! caballos! caballos!* (On! run!

mother of God! horses! horses!); oaths, execrations, shouts from the audience, inconceivable jeers and hissing when the alcalde makes a mistake and orders the *espadas* to their work a little before the time; blood flight, tumult, hideous disemboweling, falling over of *picadores*, who are lifted up hastily, with their ribs stove in, by the attendants, and their dead or dying horses stripped of saddles and bridles, — victorious music, after the sword had sent its silver subtle flash deep into the vitals of the bull; wild trample of inrushing horses and lifeless thud of dead ones being dragged out, — eating, drinking, fanning, coquetting, lemonade-bibbing, laughter, and delight, — such is an epitome of this national sport. Add for details that eight bulls and fourteen horses were killed; that the bulls were all blooded, and had each his special name (Saltador, Pimiento, Pie de lievre, Azafrancro, Currito, Escribano, Fusilero, Carbon); that baskets of dirt were shoveled up and thrown over the fresh blood spilt from time to time; that the *espadas* received hundreds of cigars; that the bulls jumped the *valla* four times, and twice got hung and fell back, while the corridor was full of people; that here and there people might be seen with antique skins of wine picnicking in the blood-warm, brimming air; that the bulls and the people grew wilder and fiercer as the evening advanced, until the day culminated in the ferocious onslaughts of an enormous black *toro*, with all the difficulties, dangers, bloodshed, dexterity, and horror accompanying his final defeat and conquest; then, with an almighty flare of trumpets the bull-fight was over! '*Vivan los toros!*' And all this in bright, battlemented, social, charming Valencia! One can well understand the etymology which attributed the name *Valencia* to Baal, the god of fire. It is a country of intense shade and light.

V.

> I think of thee, — my thoughts do twine and bud
> About thee, as wild vines about a tree
> Put out broad leaves, and soon there's naught to see
> Except the straggling green which hides the wood.
> Yet, O my palm-tree! be it understood
> I will not have my thoughts instead of thee!
> *Sonnets from the Portuguese.*

WHAT a skip from the city of bull-fights to the city of sherry — from blood to wine![1] All pleasant things must have an end; so Valencia, the city where the Cid died, the city of palms and cypresses, of fairs and regattas, of romantic midnight interviews from the balconies between señoritas and their waiting lovers, of oleander, acacia, and thatched huts, of great, island-like churches rising out of a white sea of low, surrounding houses, all *patio'd* and tiled, of the five graceful bridges with their quaint legendary figures under canopies and pious inscriptions, which span the Turia, — now utterly dry, a spacious parapeted avenue where herds of bulls graze in the great golden sunlight, and *lavanderas* wash clothes where pools of clotted water have been left behind by the vanished river to rot in the sun, — all this, I say, had to be left behind.

[1] This chapter was written in Xeres.

Valencia, with its beautiful port and blue water and busy ships lying in it and on it, bewitched by the warm Spanish yellow haze ; its huge, homely cathedral, where excommunication *major* is pronounced upon whosoever walks about during service ; its trim botanic garden, its statuesque beggars affixed to street corners and church-doors like advertisements of famine in a land of milk and — blood ; hooded, ragged, impudent, delightful creatures, incarnations of petrified and perambulating disease, picturesque in its very ugliness, — well ! Valencia had to be left, and with it the hotel full of bull-fighters. Ah me !

Again the railroad floats out as it were on a lake of rice-fields, speeds through the orange forests of Carcagente, and seems unable to unwind itself from the oasis-like *huerta*. It was evening: green and purple sierras loomed in embattled masses on the distance ; the weltering light of midday had melted into an exquisite sheen ; everything, sunflower-like, turned to bathe itself in this clear radiance, and crags and towers caught it, like a rich antiphonal song, till all the south became an illumined poem. This was Spain indeed, — such as one reads it in the soft dream of Irving's pages, in the volumes of Fernan Caballero, in the poems of Becquer, in the paintings of Murillo.

This is all of such Spain that one gets — from Gerona and Barcelona to the leagues beyond Valencia; the rest, except in the neighborhood of towns and cities, is a Siberia in winter and a Sahara in summer. Late at night we arrived at Alicante, a small, dull Mediterranean town, lying off the general route, but interesting from its proximity to one of the lions of Spain — Elche, the city of palms. Absolute aridity seems to have enveloped this blazing spot — the sun has leapt like a tiger on everything and burnt it up; *glare* is the one word that expresses its shadeless solitudes and desolations. Alicante is a beggar by its rich sea — and an unwashed one, too. The sole tolerable moment in its eternal tedium is the stroll in the evening along the alameda, which faces the harbor and is planted with date-palms. Women in long, floating summer dresses sweep up and down the plaza in search of they know not what — eternal confession, perhaps, of inconceivable sin; the yellow *calesas* drive to and from the station in a cloud of fire and dust, like Spanish Elijahs; even the sea refuses to lap the land and stands off, a sheet of mirror-like, motionless blue flame. The market-place, with its low, white-washed arches, mosaic smells, and chaffering Israelites, is the single region which the sun has not paralyzed and turned into a dormitory for this somnolent and long-suffering people. In the hotel and out of it is alike a weariness. Only when night has quenched the glare can one's brain creep into anything like clearness about the place, its ancient history, the splendid crag beside it, the dispute of the antiquaries about the origin of its name, the life and the loveliness of its middle ages, may remember even the two or three ships that run in here annually by chance, and then come, as it seems, to everlasting anchor in the glassy water. Its inhabitants are dead souls doomed to a purgatory of calcined air, living light, and bitumen pavements. Could one harness the innumerable flies to draw the *colèches* and curtains, row the boats, fan away the great spots of stagnant air, and keep the lids of one's eyes open, the life might be tolerable. 'There is refreshing shade under the palms at Elche,' sounded sweet to tired ears. Who could help thinking of Heine's lovely poem, 'Ein Fichtenbaum steht einsam,' or of Bayard Taylor's 'Arab to the Palm'?

At four in the morning, while the moon was still bright, the *calèche* called at the Hotel de Bossio, and we 'pilgrimaged,' as an old English version has it, toward the peace and the shadows of the palms. A singular sight; miles on miles of plumy, airy, arabesque-like palms, with their sudden fountain-like foliation at the end, their bunches of rich-colored dates contrasting fantastically with the trunk and leaves, the imbricated trunks themselves like closed pine-cones, standing thick together as the pillars of a cloister, overhanging turreted Moorish houses without blinds, and with ancient wells and water-wheels; groups of long-eared asses whisking their tireless tails; and visions and recesses of self-withdrawn and overarching shadow! What an Eastern picture! There was an Eastern salutation in everything; the very houses said *Salaam*, — peace. A high bridge crossed the river, then palms. The old cathedral, with its summer swallows and its gilded shrines and its kneeling women and ministering acolytes, seemed, in its groined ceiling, its marble pillarets, and its shooting lines of delicate tracery, to be but a continuation of what you saw outside in the groves of palms. See the picture: a low house — one of the lowest — and thick wall; behind, and springing up with joyous unexpectedness, a group of regal palms waving to heaven in sunny strength and power. Then a court-yard and fountain overshadowed by palms. Then plantations of palms, near and distant, where straight trunks and scimetar-like trunks, trunks perpendicular and trunks bending in every conceivable, delightful curve, till the thing became an imaginative panorama, full of plumes and tossing things, laced and interlaced into an intricate horizon of lovely shapes and forms. Palms by the river, palms in the plain, palms afar, palms

near, palms male, with the leaves tied up to be
blanched for Palm Sunday, and palms female, in
all the glory of full expansion and fruit; palms
in trenches where the water can percolate the
sandy soil and refresh their roots; palms interspersed with purple-clustered grapes, with immense aloes and Indian fig; it is as if one had
gone to sleep and awakened at Damascus. How
all these lovely forms floated on the air and filled
the heart with longing for the verses of Saadi!
The air seemed full of the pinnacles of a Berber
palace. Two palms on opposite sides of the road
bend over and form an exquisite arch; three
stand together and make an oriel window; in a
sunny spot they herd together voluptuously and
form the flying buttresses of a cathedral. Yonder
is a Gothic vault ornamented with the graceful
rosettes and foliage-wheels of the ends of the
palms grouped together; here are a dome and
pinioned arches; there a baldachino, yonder a
crypt, then a heaven-y-pointing campanile in the
shape of a transcendent lady-palm straining upward. We see the elements of the Gothic architecture, and its lost secret is found again. Here
they are in solution, loosed from the stained
windows and incense and priests, dancing in the
air with elfish grace; isolated pillars, bearded
towers, filigree spires, antic gargoyles, and all;
Seville Cathedral dissolved by some magician's

wand and celebrating its Walpurgis night in the groves of Elche.

All this is very singular, and the effect is heightened by the desert through which you pass to reach it, the filthy *posada* where you are obliged to put up, the astonishment of the native population to see a *forastero* in this out-of-the-way place, and the entire absence of all life about the place itself. It is a slice of Syria; the very dogs bark Arabic; the town-pump calls down the blessing of Allah, and the muezzin will call to prayer in due time, saying this : 'The Empire is God's, all is His.' As usual, flies and beggars, the only active members of society, — '*por el amor de Dios, por el amor de Dios,*' — at every step. The phrase has given rise to a curious Spanish word : *pordiosero*, a man that says '*Por Dios*' (for God's sake). An ass, with his brace of water-jugs steps gravely by on his errand of furnishing water to people too lazy to get it for themselves ; a little bread and meat and fruit in the market-place furnishes sustenance to the drowsy blood of the place ; a few old, worm-eaten cobblers sit in the cool doorways and mend *alpargatas ;* when there is a shirt or a sacque, it is as open in front as Dr. Johnson's or Lady Mary's ; the same Iberian type universally, with the intense eyes and hair, orange complexion, and slender grace, adding for this special place a slouchy, indescribable gait and languor born of the air and the East. Such is a pen-reproduction of Elche. To have a perfect idea, however, of its air, its palms, its helix-like streets, its slumber-smitten houses and priests, its Andalusian sombreros and portentous donkey ears, its scarlet paint of pomegranates a-blow, the stone seats and fountains of its alameda, with the maroon plains flooding about the town, and Alicante gasping in the distance,—it is necessary to have been there, to have seen and felt all this. In the common run of Spanish towns Elche is unique. It is off the sea and the railroad, in a situation of its own, and the traveler will have to seek it if he desires to get there, having first undergone a course of very early rising and (for Spain) very unusual fleecing. The visit can be made from Alicante in six hours.

From Alicante a long and fatiguing journey brought the train to Cordova, changing at Alcazar at three in the night. Even at that hour I found people drinking chocolate and eating sweet-cake at the station buffet — a habit not at all favorable to good health, but much indulged in by the Spaniards. The Arabs left behind a great number of words in Portuguese and Spanish, signifying *sweet*, *sweets*, and the like, which both nations have amply utilized. The love of sweets is universal. Perhaps this accounts for the word *Dentista* written in gilt letters on so many Spanish houses. Beaumarchais, too, in his inimitable Figaro, touched a national chord, for every other shop is a barber-shop. To these add the *sastreria*, or tailor-shops, and the *estancos nacionales*, cigar-shops monopolized by the government, and one important aspect of the Iberian streets may be kept in view, — the passion for clothes, tobacco, and gossip.

6

VI.

> O Nineveh, was this thy God,
> Thine also, mighty Nineveh?
>
> D. Rossetti.

WE are just leaving for Malaga and the great bay of Gibraltar is a scene of singular magnificence. The rock resembles, when seen from the Cádiz side, a titan's slipper, — toe, instep, heel, and all, and is all the more striking from its almost vertical lift out of the water, with no apparent connection with the adjacent continent, to which, however, it is joined by a low and long swan's-neck of land. There is such a wealth of tropical color about Gibraltar that it is a joy to see — superb blues, silvers, browns, and great spots of iridescent water, within which lie the ships, — 'a painted ship upon the painted ocean.' Across to the southwest loom in blue and silver the great masses of the Atlas Mountains, cloud-capt. In every direction lie thin-lined mountain forms, — skeletons clothed in light which at this early hour is extremely pure and luminous. Gibraltar is a little world in itself, intensely prosaic, intensely poetical. East and West, North and

South, jostle each other there in every variety of costume, language, and custom. The streets and their promenaders are *en masque*, — a crowd of every-day carnival people who have forgotten to lay off their masks and are bartering, chaffering, banking, attitudinizing in their carnival dresses. An element of intense commonplace is seen in the characteristic English names seen everywhere, — Waterport Street, Tukey's Lane, King's Bastion, Prince Albert's Front, Cathedral Street. Add to this the wooden figures which the names call up, — the pompous flunkey, the stiff English girl with 'Soho Square' written all over her, the broad-shod and broad-cast cockney flinging arms and legs affably in the wind, the h'odds and h'ends of Downing Street and Spitalfields with visages reminiscent of beer and ''alf-and-'alf;' the English hotels with all the horrors of 'domesticity,' commercial rooms, 'home comforts,' bottled stout, and obsequious 'boots,' — put all this commonplace amid the most enchanting surroundings, picturesque to the point of the incomparable, and a tolerable vision of Gibraltar may be called up. As we steam around the rock it changes shape, and all the lines of confluent mountains adjust their angles to it. Far in the distance to the east the Sierra Nevada rises, with all Andalusia nestled about it, where mountainous Spain outdoes herself, and, as if conscious that here she must cease, rises to giddy heights and dazzling precipices overlooking the sea. Light, the fertilizing principle of everything, has not accomplished its mission here, certainly. These mountains, with all their beauty, are bare; they would require to be re-forested before the rain will fall abundantly and Spain become that Hispania Felix which she seems to have been in ancient times. The Spaniards, like the negro races, have a most inexplicable repugnance to trees. When one looks over this yellow, desert, luminous country, and reflects on the possibilities which its soil and people contain, hopelessly undeveloped, the reflection is not agreeable. As soon as a stream or a fountain is unlocked, there blossoms perennial verdure. All that is needed is water, that life-giving essence known in all its fruitfulness to the Arabs of blessed memory and applied by them to the conversion of Spain into a paradise during their seven hundred years' occupation. The Vega of Granada and the Huerta of Valencia have remained to this day inexhaustible monuments of Moorish culture and foresight. They have the sun, the perpetual summer, the balmy climate and atmosphere, and a vast system of water-sheds; but water! water! We know, for example, how our alkali West effloresces as it were at the magic touch of water. At Cordova a great river (the Guadalquivir) flows

by at their feet and yet the surrounding lands
have a steppe-like sterility. At Seville the same
river has made a delightful pleasure-ground of
fields and orchards. The languid Spaniard waits
for the ripe fruit to drop into his mouth, and if it
does not, 'charity, that holy child of God,' as he
poetically calls it, extends an untiring hand and
importunes the much-enduring neighbor.

At Gibraltar (occupied since 1704 by the British) English rule has introduced much that is
commendable. Other things strike an independent observer as mean and petty. English prices
and English extortion prevail; everything is a
'shilling' where before and elsewhere in Spain
it was half a peseta. There is sharp practice in
pounds and cheating in pennies. Fees are expected and demanded. English is the language
of the place. Wine, that child of Spain and the
sun, elsewhere so lavishly given and so little
thought of in the bill, — being in fact the invariable accompaniment of every dinner and breakfast, however humble, — is here withheld and subjected to a hotel tariff. It is doled out in half
glasses, as it would be over a London counter,
and thrust into the account as if to remind the
visitor that 'England expects every man to do
his duty' — by paying a wine-tax. The shops are
abominable: Moorish wares (made in Manchester); Turkish cutlery (from Sheffield); photo-

graphs of African and Mediterranean scenery 'taken on the spot' (Oxford Street), abound in these haunts of Morocco Jews and cross-legged Berbers. Never go into a shop and dream of giving the price first demanded. You will by so doing simply subject yourself to the wonder and contempt of the shopman. Give one half or one third of what he asks, and he will be satisfied. If a shilling is asked, give *dos reales* (two reals). Pay no attention to exclamations and attitudes. The whole thing — buying and selling — is a tableau of the Orient which must be looked on calmly, weighed, and considered with due reference to the hyperbole of the East. In Gibraltar shopping does not, as at Constantinople, positively amount to proffering of coffee, benignant salutations, and a sitting down to discuss prices for half a day or half an afternoon; but the influence of the adjacent Africa is felt, and demands must be quartered or halved just in proportion to their unreasonableness. A good rule of three for a Gibraltar shop would be, take the sum demanded, divide by four, and the quotient will give the amount expected (and gratefully accepted) by the *dueño* or lord of the counter.

Chaos reigns among the coins, too, at Gibraltar; the place is a centre for counterfeit money, clipped valuations, and depreciated currency. Spanish money, in contact with Old England, is undervalued, loses its intrinsic value (which is greater than the French), and is made to redound to the benefit of the Gibraltese in every transaction. Spanish centimos, escudos, and dollars circulate side by side with Victoria pennies, half-crowns, and sovereigns. The steamers come to anchor out in the harbor and are met on their arrival by the usual fleet of welcoming boatmen, with whom, as in the Ægean, a bargain must absolutely be made or the passenger will be the worse for it. It is not pleasant dancing about on this beautifully green water half an afternoon trying to come to terms with a refractory boatman. A friend gave me an experience of two gentlemen who had engaged a boat for the neighborhood at two dollars, but the current, which flows through the straits at the rate of two and a half miles an hour, carried them over to Tangier. Night was approaching; they were nearing a strange coast, and landing was necessary; but the two boatmen refused to land the passengers unless they paid five dollars, at the same time emphasizing the demand by drawing their knives. The gentlemen therefore both drew revolvers, which they fortunately had with them, and told the fellows with equal emphasis that they should take the two dollars and land them, or —— a convenient blank was left here to intimate certain possibilities to the oriental imagination which it had not taken into account. This anecdote is related as by no means typical, but as an extreme example of what *may* happen in Mediterranean Europe, from Syria to the gates of Hercules, provided due caution is not exercised by travelers.

The fortifications of Gibraltar are something stupendous and well worth seeing. The six miles of circumference which the rock embraces are a net-work of tunnels, galleries, mines, powder-magazines, shell-rooms, concealed communications, and military works of every sort. Ten years ago England had already spent $250,000,000 on the defenses, which have been greatly elaborated and strengthened since. The soldier who accompanied me through the galleries said there were at present six hundred mounted guns, among them (though not yet all mounted) three eighty-one-tonners. One sees in every direction heaps of shot and shell, pyramids of case-shot and cannon balls rusty with age or just piled up with mathematical precision and all the pomp and circumstance of expected war, in perfect order and readiness. The donkey-ride to the galleries and signal station is (leaving the donkey out) charming. The road, which is macadamized up to a certain point, gradually ascends to the guard-station, where the pass to see the galleries, previously obtained by application to the colonel commanding, is demanded. A red-coat then takes you in charge and you enter one long tunnel after another, cut through the limestone rock and mile-stoned at every few paces by enormous cannon, which look out through embrasures on a landscape of exquisite loveliness. Here and there open terraces have been arranged, where the visitor descends from his donkey and enjoys the unparalleled panorama at his feet, — Spanish Sierras, lofty peaks of Morocco, the Atlantic ocean and the Mediterranean, Andalusia, the kingdoms of Fez, Mezquinez, and Morocco, the town of Gibraltar beneath, with the bay alive with boats, steam-launches, lighters, and ships of every nation, the low peninsula, with the 'neutral ground,' the Jewish and garrison cemeteries, the 'Spanish lines,' with far-vanishing curves and sweeps of jagged and serrated mountains; Algeciras, with its pretty women; San Roque, with its cork-forest and bull-ring; Tarifa and its Moorish towers; Malaga, among its muscatelles and pine-apples, and Trafalgar, with its light-house and glorious memories, all near. St. George's Hall is the name of a beautiful Gothic cavern excavated from the rock, with outlooks in two directions, and connected with other works by long and dimly lighted corridors. Picnics take place here among the cannon; and through the windows, out of which peep formidable Armstrongs, there is another series of unrivaled views. Sea-gulls float below on the sea like winged lamb-fleece; one catches sight of unromantic buzzards floating over the Jewish cemetery, in which the men are buried on one side and the women on the other; steamers creep into view out of the illuminated haze on the water, and the lovely coast with all its lace-like points and indentations throws its serene outlines effulgently into relief. From the galleries, before passing which one comes to the ancient Arab castle on the hill-side, admission to which is no longer granted, the journey continues up the rock to the signal-station, one thousand four hundred and fifty feet above the sea. If the views from the bull's-eye of St. George's Hall were fine, those from the signal-station were still more so. The air, after the sultry heat of Gibraltar below, was delicious. The station is a small platform, with a tower, bastions, and parapet, from which the encircling seas and continents as they melt into each other, like the colors of an enamel, can be studied as on a map. The refreshments, licorously described by the guide-books, consisted of a visitor's book, a dirty table and two or three chairs, a few bottles of Bass's ale, and John Bull in the person of a stalwart private. The officers we saw were amusing themselves turning their telescopes on the outgoing or incoming steamers. The descent is in another direction, towards Europa Point, which is at the west end of the rock — another mass of bristling and embattled fortifications, as indeed the whole side where the town of Gibraltar lies is. This west-north side is the only weak side, the south and east sides being by nature nearly, and by art absolutely, inaccessible. The result is that engineering skill and military science have exhausted themselves in strengthening the weakness of nature and making this side impregnable. Huge cannon look out through masses of cactus, palmetto, geranium, and pine-apple. Stone-pines lift their emerald umbrellas here and there, affording a frame for the tropical pictures below. Monkeys chatter among the dwarf palm on this end of the rock, — 'the primitive inhabitants of Gibraltar, respected alike by the Spaniards and English.' Teeming vegetation is descried between garden walls, where immense figs, peaches, and grapes and airy almond-trees scatter scents and sweets; the coloring everywhere is more pure and passionate than unkindled northern eyes are acquainted with, and amid it all the great forms of silent Sierras watching by the sea, sphinxes of eternal expectation, forms poetized by this perpetual air, not nocturnes nor arrangements, but irradiated harmonies whose key-note is transparence, fantastic grace, and weird stillness.

VII.

> Pale in the green sky were the stars, I ween,
> Because the moon shone like a tear she shed
> When she dwelt up in heaven a while ago,
> And ruled all things but God.
>
> MORRIS.

> Je propose des fantasies informes et irresolues, comme font ceulx qui publient des questions doubteuses à desbattre. — MONTAIGNE.

ONE'S first impressions of Granada are certainly delightful. The train from the south arrives in the night, so one goes to bed full of the dreams and expectations of the morning, which are more than realized. Already the cooling air, as the train winds up the long valley from Malaga and the sea, announces the presence of the snow-tipt Sierras — a gradual ascent out of glowing tropical air, all a-tremble with heat and perfume, into the continual spring of this favored haunt of the Khalifs. Bare, absolutely bare, are the mountains, gorges, and ravines through which we pass after leaving the fruitful *huerta* of Malaga, with its edging of sunlit sea, its interminable vines and oranges, and the bright vision of tinted and tawny mountains which frame it in on three sides. Two or three whitewashed Andalusian towns are descried amid groves of citron, fig, and olive; two or three stations are passed, where herds of donkeys stand loading or loaded; a lazy diligence or two awaits a sleepy passenger, and Malagueño peasants in wide sombreros sell melons, or look over the fences wistfully at the train, some with fowling-piece and dog, some with fishing-rod and basket. Nothing is in any special hurry except the fussy little train, which, once started, makes haste to be as slow and exasperating as possible.

The engineering work on this road is of considerable importance and difficulty, and there are many bridges, trestles, and tunnels. At Bobadilla trains meet and passengers change, some for Cordova, some for Malaga, and some for Granada. As we meandered on up the Sierras (Granada is nearly twenty-five hundred feet above the sea), the mountains became infinitely purple and rich-tinted, aided by the silvery effluence of the half moon which — the glorious symbol of Islám — hung over the gray-and-crimson altitudes as their eloquent exponent. The roseate and orange tints gradually melted into indistinguishable umber till the last steel-gray of the moonlit Sierra became immerged in amber-enameled night. Delightful freshness filled the air; the presence of glaciers, snows, and icy torrents is felt all through the languid frame relaxed by the oven-like heat of the plains. The train stops, and a *calesa* receives and deposits you at one of the three or four hotels in this city of seventy-eight thousand inhabitants, the capital, bishop's see, and cathedral city of one of the eight provinces into which Andalusia is divided. I selected the Washington Irving Hotel, not only on account of its associations with the charming historian, but on account of its being in the Alhambra grounds, on one of the four hills on which Granada is built, and commanding glimpses, through tall elms and over flowering terraces, of the *Vega;* and I have not regretted the choice. The city lies below, half a mile off, blazing with heat, sunshine, whitewash, and dust, while we are enveloped in magnificent elm-walks, delicious shadow, moisture, sweetness, and verdure. The spirits of the lost sultanas return every spring in the song of the nightingales that throng these woods; Moorish music is heard in the tinkling and ear-titillating melody of rivulets, unlocked from the abundant Sierras; long arcades of overarching trees radiate from the hotels to the Alhambra and the town; expressive quiet reigns everywhere about this famous domain, and through the night glitter of hastening water may be seen in the moon. Altogether, it is the most charming place I have visited in Spain.

It is almost impossible to write of Granada satisfactorily on the spot. The strange and tender air, the richness of the plain, the monumental masses of the Sierra Nevada rising eleven thousand feet above it, and the mingled histories and poesies of the place, all put description at a disadvantge, and render an effort to reproduce them almost impertinent. The white, gray, and yellow masses of the town would be uninteresting enough were it not for the transcendent scenes enacted among them, — the gorgeous Khalifate, the tournaments, sieges, battles, and assassinations; the ivory and mother-of-pearl loving Moor rearing his fabrics beside the ponderous arches of Rome, to be succeeded by the cathedral-loving Spaniard with his domes and pinnacles, imagery, and civic splendor. The place is an architectural palimpsest. One life and civilization lies upon another. The keen blade of the antiquary is necessary to run in between, pierce, penetrate, and separate these lives, and bring forth the elements to clearness and intelligibility. Much of the glory of 1492 has departed. How much hatred, prejudice, and ignorance are buried in the leaden sarcophaguses of Ferdinand and Isabella! Splendid cenotaphs are raised above them, to commemorate their mighty triumph in the conquest of Granada, the expulsion of Moors and Jews, the beginning of the cathedral in whose Capilla Real they lie, and the work of grace accomplished in the capture of the puissant city.

Their wooden, marble, and painted images smirk from every corner; their coats of arms are emblazoned on every side; the arrows of Aragon everywhere mingle with the yoke of Castile; scutcheons, bas-reliefs, reliquaries, canvases, celebrate and perpetuate the most Catholic sovereigns. A sudden loathing at their work seizes one, and an immense desire to escape the eternal F. and Y. intertwined. Even the beggars that crouch around the archbishop's palace become more tolerable as they wait the daily alms, and stretch themselves in attitudes of monumental indolence about the pavement. Charles V. and Philip II. at Madrid, San Ferdinand and Don Pedro at Seville, and Ferdinand and Isabella at Granada; such are the continual torment of the unhappy tourist, who is forced to see, hear, taste, and smell them at every step, from the jabbering of cicerones to the drivel of guide-books.

One advantage of a residence on the Alhambra Hill is that it is too quiet for the beggars; only five or six buzz among the elms and molest the dreaming and meditating promenader, — one blind beggar who can see, and three or four seeing beggars who are blind. Two or three Americans, an Austrian, a few English, and one or two Spaniards, constitute the summer boarders at this, of all the places in Spain the most fascinating. Whoever cares for tranquillity, umbrageous walks, a serene and tender sky, perfect associations, and the ever-brooding spirit of gentle and heroic memories, will come to Granada and walk in its shady alamedas, among the oleander and jasmine of the two rivers, in and out of the old Moorish streets, and along the twilight avenues of this haunted hill. Never mind the cooking, the greasy *comidas* and ill-attended *almuerzos*, — never mind the fleas and 'domestiques' of the night, the lack of concerts, cock-fights (!) and theatres, the drowsy shops, whinnying asses, and washer-women chatting at the fountains! there is a fund of quiet enjoyment in the dilapidated old place, and one will go away laden with precious souvenirs, — 'in the name of God, the merciful and compassionate.' 'Perpetual Salvation' was written by the poetic Moor all over the walls of his Andalusian palaces; 'There is no conqueror but God,' is the continual cry of the traceries of the Alhambra. Grace and praise are continually ascribed by him to the creator of this wonderful region where a Damascus of lace and fretwork and stalactite carving was enchanted by dexterous chisels out of the womb of the Sierras. There is no lack of attraction of many sorts about the place. There are charming excursions in the neighborhood to Alhama, Lanjaron, and Santa Fé, the city built by Isabella during the siege. Alpine climbers have magnificent sport in the peaks and gorges that rise on all sides. The forests abound in sweet-scented medicinal herbs. Fifteen hours bring one to Cordova, eight to Malaga, and twenty-three to Madrid. The hotels are quite tolerable in comfort and price; living is cheap, and one can fancy few lives more endurable than such a summer passed among such surroundings. The elms planted by the Duke of Wellington — whose estate, presented by the Spanish government, lies near here — are singularly slender, tall, and thick, festooned with ivy, and forming verdurous glooms and obscurities through which the sun hardly breaks. The poetic tenants of the opposite hotel played the guitar delightfully last night; and as one glanced upward through the long reed-like poplars and elms, the most brilliantly pure moonlit sky became visible, and the mellow masses of the abutting walls of the Alhambra looked weird and remote. The Hotel Washington Irving fronts the road which leads up to the Generalife and its fairy gardens, belonging to the Pallavicini family, and famous for its cypresses, rushing fountains, tower, and view. The back of the hotel, which is for three or four stories one vast *mirador* framed in glass, looks down on terraces and fountains, and orange-trees full of golden fruit of last year's growth. The air possesses a piercing freshness unknown elsewhere in summer, so that the upper story of the hotel, nearer the sun, is far the most agreeable. Last year's newspapers, some old music, a hideous book on anatomy full of colored plates, a cracked piano, two or three ancient inlaid cabinets, and a wall hung with daubs, grace the *sala de lectura*, where nobody can or does read. The long, Last-supper-like upper chamber, which serves as *comedór* or dining-room, is almost devoid of guests, save the Austrian geologist, the American and English artists, and the English vice-consul. Nothing can exceed the beauty and fruitfulness and verdure of this spot. Yesterday evening an immense number of people came trooping from Granada to see the corpse of a poor *majo* who was murdered the day before. The long *navaja* — a huge knife, very fashionable among the lower classes of Spain — did the work. The *reino* of Granada is said to rank second on the list of provinces most fertile in homicide. The people are quick-tempered, passionate, and impulsive; and scenes of bloodshed, sudden reconciliations, and unexpected outbursts of affection or hatred, quite characteristic. The fire in their eyes is like the fire in their wine, — evidence of the slumbering heat that may spring to the surface in an instant, and do deeds of unpardonable violence. If, as Alfieri said, the crimes of the Italian people were a proof of the superiority of the stock, what excellences must be attributed to their Spanish brethren.

While the crowd was trooping by, the American artist amused himself pelting little Enrique, the beggar boy, with melon rind, peaches, bread, and cake, all of which he devoured greedily, whether falling in the water of the gutter or not. One is saluted quite regularly of a morning with '*Buenos Dias, Señorito,*' or '*Vaya usted con Dios,*' by the little flower-girl, who is the dragon of this Hesperides, and lies in ambuscade under the elms with unfailing punctuality. If you answer — as the Spaniards do — '*Mañana*' (to-morrow), or '*Esta tarde*' (this evening), she will impatiently exclaim, '*No, ahora,*' or, '*Siempre mañana*' ('No, now,' or 'Always to-morrow'). As she has a poor little basket of flowers as her excuse for begging, one can tolerate her importunities. That is so much better than the continual '*Tengo hambre,*' or '*Por Dios*' of the wretched professionals!

Brilliant masses of crape-myrtle, laurel, box, daphne, geranium, myrtle, plumbago, and fire-plant, illumine the summer darknesses of the Alhambra gardens and hang their blossoming flame over the ruined walls and towers. Bright-feathered martlets sport among the tops of the poplars, and the whole inclosure is a labyrinth of interwoven light-and-shadow arabesques. On the façade of the hotel opposite is a tablet with this inscription: 'FORTUNY habitó en esta fonda desde el 10 de Junio de 1870 al 30 de Octubre de 1871.' Fortuny was a young Spanish painter of extraordinary genius whose Moorish and Oriental pictures with their dash, individuality, strangeness, and superb coloring, were the talk of the artistic world of Paris for some years, and whose untimely death was a cruel loss. Hans Andersen lived in the same hotel. Of an evening — these infinitely soft, spiritual Spanish evenings of the Sierra Nevada! — all the señores, señoras, and señoritas of this hotel come out and sit before the door, and nearly every evening they have music. There is a beautiful terrace full of arbors, urns, walks, and tables, where one sees the ladies sitting at their work in the shady forenoon, delightfully deshabillés like all Spanish ladies in the morning, and the pleasant murmur of the melodious Castilian comes over to our grilled and curtained balconies, which wall in the other side of the street. A great dry fountain lies in the way below, and before it chairs and benches and a little stand where a busy, dark-eyed Granadina dispenses all sorts of highly-colored refreshments out of cut-glass tumblers and decanters. Again and again one is enchanted with the eloquent peace and beauty of this spot, — the very donkeys laden with huge wicker-work hampers, the *majos* in their velvet jackets twirling the invariable *vara* or cane, the comfortable two-horse carriages awaiting customers, the blue and sunny vistas up and down the avenues, the lazy song of the locust idealized by distance into a sweet suggestiveness of patient and evanescent existence: all is so tranquil and so lovely.

A walk down into the town brings you into a totally different set of feelings. The mental habit is completely changed. In Granada itself, tiles, dust, turreted houses, parapets full of flowers, old churches full of mellow and pleasing coloring, full of famous ashes, images, and pictures, Arabic-looking streets and alleys where the houses nearly touch, and where tiny shops nestle in cuddies and corners innumerable; all is different. The principal street is the Zocatin, which looks more like a blind alley than anything else. Singularly picturesque is the *Albeiceria*, or quarter of the silk mercers, divided up into narrow passages crossing at right angles to each other, and full of marble pillars, horse-shoe arches, and dainty traceries in the Moorish style. It is a bit of antiquity which you come upon suddenly and find alive with antediluvian shops, fantastic figures, and Eastern sentiment. Then the old houses, with long, projecting, two or three storied wooden galleries in front, curiously carved and outlandish, form a peculiar feature. My artist friend was delighted with an old Arabic house with three turrets, tiled roof, and arcaded windows which overhung a public square.

Then we came by an ancient building in whose wide-arched doorway stood a group of crimson-trousered Spanish hussars, in deep Rembrandt-like shadow, while beyond them a fire glowed, throwing weird and fitful illumination on the walls and figures. Presently the street debouched on the Vega, where we found vast gardens inundated with water for purposes of irrigation, while suspicious looking *contrabandistas* with their short guns with down-turned muzzles, coats slung over their shoulders, and oriental sash, sauntered leisurely along in the gathering shade. We soon lost ourselves in the unknown streets, and finally took refuge in a café with resplendently frescoed ceiling, knots of Granadinos and Granadinas sipping *horchateria* and puffing cigarettes, and an infinity of marble tables. On the return the artist was struck by an effect of blinding moonlight striking a wall up a deep shadowy lane, — so fantastically white that it seemed more like calcium light than the delicate splendor of this Spanish moon. Then a long walk up through the mysteriously illumined elms, by marble seats and fountains, through the aisled and nave-like shadow exquisitely broken in upon by a remote silvery sky.

From the Alhambra terraces one looks down over the tree-tops upon the Vega, a most fertile and highly cultivated plain, where the rivers Darro and Xenil flow down from the Sierras and form a wonderful oasis. It is a little kingdom in itself, and every stone of it speaks eloquent Arabic. It has been said that a journey in Spain is a continual funeral procession in the footsteps of the Moors. One comes on their splendid traces — their cities, mosques, arts, evidences — everywhere, and finds that whatever of best and noblest Spain possesses is due to them. So it is with this heir-loom of irrigation, by which they transformed so many deserts into orchards. The savage want of unirrigated Spain is the truest tribute to Moorish intelligence. You feel certain that the king of the fairy tale who remained a king only so long as he did not see water would run little risk in this kingdom.

I have heard of five or six murders taking place in the short time I have been here. Several of them were from the most trivial causes. At Malaga and elsewhere the prevalence of an intensely exasperating wind called the *levante* is regarded by the judge as an extenuating circumstance in many cases of crime, and criminals often escape by alleging its prevalence. Justice seems lax enough here, for I have not heard of any one of these being severely punished. It is forbidden to carry knives and — everybody carries them. Formidable-looking things they are, too.

VIII.[1]

>   El dorado techo
>   Se admira fabricado
> Del sábio Moro, en jaspes sustentado.
>   FRA LUIS DE LEON.

THE monuments of the Alhambra seem scattered in a certain disorder as if thrown there by chance, rising in picturesque confusion, extending among spacious gardens, the most notable and splendid buildings for the kings alternating with the less elegant ones dedicated to the favorite women, the numerous sons, and the courtiers of the Khalifs. The Alhambra palace, in particular, expresses the culminating point of seven ages of culture, and, what is most worthy of attention, the transition from the puritanism of the Koranic schools of the Orient to that ideality and freedom which characterized the Moorish Renaissance of the thirteenth century. Science, literature, the heroism of passion, the chivalric militarism that has struck such deep roots in Spain, political toleration, the respect shown the wise, the poetic,

---

[1] Many details of this chapter are taken from Contreras' unique monograph, *Estudio Descriptivo de los Monumentos Arabes de Granada, Sevilla y Cordoba.* Madrid, 1878.

and the valiant, the predilection for art, and the love of popularity which plunged the Moorish magnates into splendid crimes of vanity or ambition, — whatever, in short, can reveal the development of the civil power as the beginning of progress, — all is more or less clearly indicated within the walled inclosure of this half ruinous, half restored construction, on which the labors of four centuries have exhausted themselves in efforts to recover a lost splendor. This palace is not simply an enchanting system of capricious ornaments whose originality arrests us, but it reveals the secret of the last two ages of Arabic domination, explaining by what artifice the ruin of the Saracen power could not be consummated in Spain immediately after the conquest of Seville, and why the victorious arms of the Spaniards quailed, if they did not absolutely surrender, before the brilliant ascendency of the Granada dynasty. This dynasty, though confined within an insignificant region and besieged by the Christian forces, yet by its very grace, culture, and refinement dictated peace to its enemies and commanded the admiration of the world. Strange scenes and centuries — proclaiming the power of that people who cherished the very sons of the princes against whom they fought; celebrating tourneys with them like gallant friends; offering them their arts; presenting them with the beauteous products of their luxurious industries in silk and needle-work, and inviting the powerful captains who were besieging them to gorgeous hunting-parties, where, in cultured rivalry, their arms, vestments, and accomplishments shone emulously!

The Alhambra rose, like all the classic edifices of antiquity, at that culminating epoch from which begins inevitable descent and decadence; an epoch of **abounding talent,** in which delight in architecture verges on extravagance. It might be called the descending apogee of civilization, which we must surprise as it were in the very act in order to recognize its progress, without giving way to the enchanting intoxication which it evokes or perverting our taste by too ardent a contemplation of its masterpieces.

He who ascends through the study of the Moorish monuments of Cordova, Toledo, and Seville, finds an unsatisfied void in his mind and involuntarily remembers Cairo, Tunis, and Fez, arriving by successive deductions at the mosques of Constantinople, the tombs of Afghânistân, and the ancient pagodas of Delhi. These oriental monuments are all reflected in the Alhambra, — are the architectural annotations to this exquisite volume which the Moorish kings have opened for us under the radiant skies of the Sierras. And though at first sight its outlines seem scattered among towers, walls, and gardens, the slightest investigation of the precious remains of the Alhambra will display symmetry and regularity. There is more than the conception of mere gaunt, right lines; there is convergence of objects all referred to the same point, whose plan and method, maintained with superstitious rigor, make us admire what we were inclined to believe the chance product of the fantasy or the insomnia that produces a fairy tale.

During the mania for classicism which dominated Europe at the Renaissance, efforts were made to explain the Alhambra by an exclusive system deemed, even by the most brilliant disciples of the academies, synonymous with the just and beautiful. The Spanish artists, not being able to view with indifference a monument which awakened more curiosity than those of Seville, Toledo, and Cordova, sought with sudden tolerance to respect what the emperor Charles V., by the advice of Italian artists, had left for the admiration of posterity; interpreted its inharmonious appearance according to their classical education; sought to fit their theories of beauty and suitability into the remains they encountered at every step, and by dint of looking through a prism manufactured for the exclusive use of the reasonings of the schools, persuaded themselves that they had found the key to the importance attributed, out of Spain, to these monuments. From that time the Alhambra ceased to be called a barbarous edifice; the academy of San Fernando ordered a work illustrating its artistic treasures to be published; the famous Jovellanos explained its beauties and its history; and thereafter writers of more or less note devoted themselves to celebrating its glories. Why, when academies respected pagan antiquity alone, did they stop to admire this 'semi-barbarous' Alcázar, relic of a domination which they would so gladly have wiped from their memories?

Well, the Alhambra palace could be squared! The lines which, according to the academy, had disappeared, could be restored! The original plan could be found again! A central axis was sought; courts and naves were traced arbitrarily to suit the preconceived system; the same towers were imagined on both sides; the same gates; equal altitudes. Delightful uniformity, on a par with the heroics of Pope, the avenues of Versailles, or the yardstick of a mercer's clerk!

It almost seems as if the genius of antiquity were uncomprehended in the decadence of the Renaissance. Is there not a strange conformity between these Moorish edifices and the houses of Pompeii and Herculaneum? In the gipsy quarter of Granada, when we penetrate into the few houses that remain, is there not a distribution closely akin to the Roman and Greek? If we look to the arrangement for baths, we see not resemblance, but absolute equality. Oriental civilizations both; both inspired in one and the same origin. What the Spanish academicians thought they discovered was not the special merit of the Alhambra; it was the mistaken interpretation of its character and symbol.

Recent excavations demonstrate beyond the possibility of a doubt the misconceptions of the academy. 'No parallelogram is possible,' says Contreras, 'whether from the configuration of the site or — a more certain proof — from the uncovered remains.' There are no lines of cement which would prove the truth of the imaginary parallelogram. The uniformity and symmetry demanded by the situation exist, it is true, but elsewhere than was imagined by these erudite speculators.

In every Arabic[1] monument the entrance is by an advanced tower or between two towers, except in edifices serving for family purposes, when, as is still often seen in Andalusian houses, they are replaced by a small square ingress. A long narrow hall cuts the axis of the edifice perpendicularly, and from this point the distribution of the two wings departs. Where the two axes cross is usually found the entrance, giving birth to

[1] Contreras.

those fantastic perspectives so often observed in Oriental constructions. Then behind the door of ingress follows a court, or *patio*, with a tank and fountains, light and graceful arcades at the two ends or sides (for these courts are square), and beyond the second gallery, following the same central axis, parallelogram-shaped naves succeed each other till the final one is reached, where the finest nave is found rising majestically above the edifice and mirroring its cupolas or minarets in the long undulous reflections of the waters of the tank. The other apartments of a house of this description were placed in little pavilions ranged along the sides of the courts or *patios* as irregularly decorated as the booths of a Turkish encampment.

This plan — so closely resembling a long cross cut at various distances by perpendicular arms parallel to each other — is entirely classic; the Spanish Arabs did not depart from it, and enriched or simplified it according to the special exigency. Renaissance art of course brought in a flood of ornamentation, — grotesques, frontispiece-like balconies, and other slight deviations; but note, ever the same plan, the Moorish origin, a principle of enchanting, classic simplicity, that makes us to-day admire and envy, for it would be admissible, even now, if the spirit of Spanish society would permit of its introduction, slightly modified.

Such is the regularity of the Alhambra — not what the classicists of the last century, with their façades, angles, and quadrangles, believed. The ruins that remained, the rubbish so often disdainfully abandoned by an age which deserves to be forgotten, lent themselves to the most absurd interpretations. The very cement used by the Arabs harmonized with this misinterpretation, and by its peculiar hardness and quartz-like formation so closely resembled the natural crystallization going on in this soil, that the two were often confounded, and imaginary lines of buildings were discovered which precisely fitted in with the square and parallelogram theory.

The approach to the Alhambra is by a tunnel-like avenue of elms, which runs along one of the terraces into which the hill is cut. By an architectural paradox the access to this luxurious home of Oriental despotism is — of all imaginable gates — by the Gate of Justice. Everybody has heard of the mystic key and hand sculptured over the inner and outer door about which such charming romances have been written. Some fancy that the Arabs had such ideas of their power and trust in the law that they were persuaded this Alcázar would not be opened to the enemies of the faith till the hand grasped the key. Unfortunately the same key is sculptured over other portals, and a less poetic and more rational interpretation is found in a passage of the Korán. There we read: 'God delivered the keys to his elect with the title of *porter* and with power to give entrance to enemies.' The key, therefore, like the cross and key of the Catholic, was the principal symbol of the Moslem faith and represented the power of opening and shutting the doors of heaven. It is also certain that the hand was a blazon of the Andalusian Moors, used on their banners and standards from their entrance into Spain, suggestive of Gebel-al-Tarif or Gibraltar, 'Mount of Entrance,' as possessor of the key that opened its gates. According to the Moslem astrology, too, entangled as it is with their theology, the hand conjured away evils and exorcised demons. It was a species of talisman, or amulet, used for ages by Moors and their conquerors, and even down to the present day. The Egyptian hieroglyphics figured the hand as it is found here as the attribute of force; the Arabs believed it to be the *hand of God*, and compendiously explained the Moslem law by the hand as a unity; the five fingers representing the five principal precepts of their code, and the joints representing modifications of these precepts. This key unlocks for us the enchanted dwelling-place of the Moorish sultans, and the hand gives a hospitable welcome to its poetic solitudes. The Moorish kings, according to the Oriental custom, sat in this gate and administered justice to their subjects. Well might the key symbolize Paradise, and Paradise on earth, for such was the Alhambra. Everywhere on its walls is the silent and splendid cry of the Korán: 'God is one; God is eternal; God neither begot nor was begotten!' The same uniqueness, perpetuity, and unknown origin may, almost, be ascribed to this clustered and fantastic mount. No other king's palace is like this; its fragile ornamentation seems eternal, and its architects are unknown. It rose like a dream, a chiseled exhalation, the creation of poet and prophet, the first and fairest poem of the Arab bards. Of the three well-recognized periods of glory which Arab art developed in Spain, the purest, most typical, and glorious was that exemplified within the noble precincts of the Granada palaces. In them we find the inspiration under which the Moors wrought concrete; the style is harmonious; the form has become regular; and one of the few supreme efforts of human genius takes its origin, urged on by the sentiments, beliefs, and habitudes of an infidel golden age. Nowhere else in all the Spanish territories is to be found so complete an example or so classic a proof of the wondrous elements at work to show the civilization which eight centuries of constant progress had attained. Hence, none deserves such consideration, and none has attained in the world's eye the **exclu-sive** renown which it enjoys; neither the Arabic civilization of Egypt, Persia, and Turkey reached the refinement and beauty of the Granada Alhambra, nor are the glories of the reconquest symbolized in any Spanish monument more perfectly than in this great bulwark of Mussulmandom, so obstinately defended and so heroically won.

Situated on the top of a hill, which was chosen as a secure and defensible place for the use of the state, it remained isolated and girdled by a line of strong walls and robust towers which flanked its gates. The steep declivities were clothed with frondage. The water taken from the Darro by means ingeniously adapted to bringing it to that height and causing it to feed the tanks, baths, and underground cisterns, flowed everywhere down the natural incline of the mountains, and produced these fantastic forests so celebrated throughout the world. Within the space contained in the walls rose the Alcázar, the mosques, the harem, the public offices, and the opulent habitations of a numerous court; between the fortresses and their battlements sprang up airy minarets; precious arabesques were lavished on all sides, and the luxury of convenience and delight gave a magic charm to this singular sum-total.

Its whole space, with its forests and gardens, is sown with the spoils of twelve hundred years, and rendered beautiful by art and nature, where both elements have combined marvelously to produce a contrast inviting to meditation and study. Under the formidable frown of its forts and ramparts it nestled like some dragon-guarded princess. Placed on the summit of a mountain, like the feudal castles which thronged Europe during the Middle Ages, it had all the simple spaciousness of the Oriental castles, with the added beauty of lying in the most delicious spot Spain could offer, — a fact to which, perhaps, it owed the elegance of its construction and a peculiar style of ornamentation, unrivaled among the innumerable palaces built by former khalifs. Here one may look in vain for the inflexible lines of the Greco-Roman monuments, the symmetry of the Escorial courts or the quadrangles of the Renaissance ; and yet there is a peculiar felicity and fitness in both site and system. In the house of the Arab his life is reflected, his desires are suspected, his wantonness is shadowed forth ; a life as various in its forms and proportions as it was fickle in its enjoyment of a refined sensuality. There is nothing like the splendid majesty of Roman courts : tiny rooms, tiny vestibules, slender, icicle-like pillars, narrow passages, obscure entrances, unostentatious exteriors : it requires a peculiar divination and instinct to penetrate into his perfumed life and analyze its strange reserves. The heroic and majestic Arab, the musing Arab, the tender and gallant Arab, the cruel and tyrannic Arab: for every virtue and for every vice of his existence there is a form, an urn, a divan, an altar, on which rises the ruby and diamond flame of perpetual desire. A sword, a poem, a perfume, — such is khalif-life on the altitudes of Granada. In the Alhambra all its mystery and luxury lie revealed; titillating waters, scented vapors, rare silences and sunlight, glitter of marble and tremor of rose-gardens under morning-light, haunting music from upper cupolas, flash and flight of silver-throated rivulets through the baths and *patios*, singing birds and whispering women. Such is one aspect of this fierce and tender race.

The present Alhambra is an agglomeration of three distinct palaces which, together with the palace built by Charles V. up against the Alhambra walls, and for the construction of which priceless portions of the Moorish building were torn down, made four palaces within a space perhaps not so large as the Luxembourg Garden at Paris. All around rose beautiful towers literally bedewed, within, with the imaginative illustration of the Arabs; the Vermilion Towers, the Tower of the Infanta, the Tower of the Seven Portals, the Tower of the Vigil, the Tower of the Beaks, and twenty others, each melodious with some Moorish romance or legend. It was through the Tower of the Seven Portals that Boabdil, last of the Moorish kings, left the Alhambra, and it was his last request to Isabella that no one might ever again be permitted to pass through it. The wish of El Zogoybi — the Unlucky — has been fulfilled.[1] The arch remains, but huge stones bar the entrance, which is half hidden by mounds of earth and ruins — impassable since the day that the luckless Moorish king with his band of cavaliers sadly and silently rode through its gate, whilst distant shouts of triumph told them that the Christian hosts had entered the Alhambra by the Gate of Justice. Boabdil halted on a rocky height, — his mother and wife were already there, — then, turning to take a long, last look at his loved city he burst into tears, saying: 'God is great; but when did ever misfortunes equal mine?'

'You do well,' exclaimed his wrathful mother, 'to weep like a woman for what you failed to defend like a man!'

This hill is still known as 'La Cuesta de las Lagrimas' — the Hill of Tears — and the summit of the rock, where Boabdil bade farewell to his home is still called by the sorrowful name, 'The Moor's Last Sigh.'

[1] Tollemache, *Spanish Towns and Spanish Pictures.*

Does not this story recall another King, another Hill of Tears?

Just before you enter the Alhambra there is a broad open space, parapeted on several sides, with a booth in the centre. Beneath is the great reservoir for the water of the Darro — that water which, Gautier tells us, was the night before a streak of silver among the snows of the Sierras: such water as gods might drink and no longer remember their ambrosia. In that brilliant sunlight — λαμπρὸν ἡλίου φάος, — and white day — λευκὸν κατ' ἦμαρ — which Æschylos loved (Agam. 645), how prodigally must this beauteous waterstreak have shone as it spilt its silver down the mountain sides and emptied into this Stygian reservoir, thence to be drawn like jeweled mist to the light! It is ice-cold water, having in it strange refreshment. Happy pilgrims, who can thus drink the Sierras under the towers of the Alhambra!

There was a strange stealth in the Arab nature. The gorgeous palaces which he reared were entered unostentatiously; a small door — purposely small, to avoid the Evil Eye — led into his Aidenn. So with the Alhambra: no one would imagine its fountained and filigreed interior from the homely outside, the mean little side-entrance through which one comes suddenly on its quaintly serene picture. Its rooms and courts are a series of visions.

The first is the Court of Myrtles, where the sunlight is so golden that it seems the distillings of centuries, — a scene that at once transports you from Gothic Spain to the Orient. There is a tank in the centre full of lustrous water, rimmed by myrtle-hedges that for hundreds of years have fed on this shining air: water through which the light trickles and lights up the backs of thick-crowding gold-fish: water that seems to pasture on the lovely, uncertain shadow-pillars and shadow-cupolas, that dance on it from the neighboring walls. The pavement was of white-and-azure tiles, and the classic style of the court at once attracts the eye of the archæologist, because in it every detail of the Arab's most intimate life is before us. The richness and seclusion of his voluptuous tastes are foreshadowed in the great variety of doors and decorations and combinations which meet the eye. Numerous portals conduct to different apartments, whose use may be divined without entering; precious divans, narrow sentry-boxes, sumptuous porticoes, two elegant cloisters, whose arches very nearly, in their curvature, resemble Roman arches, filigree doors, elegant upper galleries exquisitely ornamented in their tympanums with translucent arabesques, rhomb-shaped, interlaced with ribbons, leaves, shells, and rude but delicate pine-cones. The patience of the artists who wrought these dainty windows is seen in the fact that each one of the blinds that close them is a mosaic of fifteen hundred pieces. The work is Meissonnier-like, delicate, infinitesimal. A star not much bigger than a button is a combination of thirty pieces. Everywhere one sees the sweet and sinuous curves of the Gothic line twining along the plinths of the opposite sides, among arches which, for the harmonious proportions of their archivolts, and the admirable turn of their columns, with capitals in azure and gold, are among the most precious objects of Mahometan archæology. The tranquil and shadowy cloisters at each end were the favorite lounging-places of Arab voluptuaries. They were lavishly ornamented with quaint and devious conceits, and each has a stalactite roof covered with brilliant lapis lazuli blue. There were once places for bronze candlesticks, arms with enameled hilts, and jars of perfume. Imagine, then, the sheeted shimmer of water, the green wall of myrtle, the fantastic colonnades, the strange grace of the window-tiers, the tranquil irradiation and summer silence of such a spot!

All over the ends are scattered salutations and thanksgivings from the Korán, and in one place is a beautiful poem of twelve verses in Tamil metre, which breathes most eloquently of the impassioned East. It begins: 'Blessed be he who gave thee command over his servants, and who exalted by thee Islam perfectly and beneficently!'

This parallelogram-shaped court, in its entireness, grace, and delicacy is a jewel-box from out which leaps a sunny picture of Moorish life. Mellifluous sadness reigns amid its silence: the greater part of the scenes which, from the time of Muley-Hacen, hastened the downfall of the Moors, took place in this court, says the legend. The monarch *Zagal* rested under these light and lovely galleries, and, surrounded by his women, is said to have lamented the misfortunes which were to come upon the Moors in the far future. Standing in it, a tide of thronging and poetic memories floods upon you: a dainty pathos broods about the place; the open blue sky above looks in tenderly, and dwells pathetically upon the enamored water-mirror: gently move the myrtles; gentle are one's thoughts in such a perfect spot. The poetry of languishment, of desire, of secrecy, of many-colored passion, of fantastic imagination, of a voluptuous code, of a chivalric sensibility, of brilliant danger and audacity, of strange and tender vicissitude, has gathered here into such beauteous form as the world will not willingly let die. In these three or four rooms Moorish history is epitomized and crystallized. One hardly knows which way to turn: to the right is the Court of Lions, at the end the Hall of Ambassadors.

The Hall of Ambassadors is the most spacious, and the most celebrated in the Alhambra. The Arabs excelled themselves in its amplitude and elevation, recalling the achievements of the Romans. For splendor of decoration, boldness of construction, and whimsical ornamentation it is unrivaled. It is entered by a long vestibule, boat-shaped, with exquisite arches and niches for water-jars, with the word 'liberality,' found everywhere through the palace: a word which, in the Arabic usage, signified the desire to supply with water, for which manifold ledges and alcoves, ablutionary jugs and clay drinking-vessels, were placed here and there, — a reminiscence of the desert. The curves of an ellipse are seen in the roof of this vestibule, which is full of stars and geometric designs, once covered with blue and gold. The arch of entry into the Hall of Ambassadors is like a piece of goldsmith's work, with its minute ornaments and delicate traceries, full of perfectly executed inscriptions. There are two wonderful niches, with arabesques inside, and tiny roofs of ebony and alerce-wood, one on each side. On one side is read: 'Praise to God: I take refuge in the God of dawn.' 'The stars of the Zodiac bend down in love to me.' On the other, among other inscriptions, this: 'He who approacheth me wearied with thirst will find water pure and fresh, sweet, and without any mixture.' Here they hang like dainty ear-rings, each on its side, each with its song of praise and salutation, a sort of pendant to the grandiose arch beneath which they are placed, — an arch of simple, slender curvature, with inner pencil-border and microscopic details. As you enter, the upcast eye catches sight of three balconies in each of the sides opposite the entrance, which, owing to the extraordinary thickness of the walls, form nine little alcoves, each with its own wonderful roof, traceries, and borders, and looking out into the domed Hall of Ambassadors through suites of *ajimez*, or double windows, with their open-work crystal ornamentation, now gone. Imagine the bouquets of flower-like faces flitting about these shadowy balconies, while the gorgeous ceremonials of the East were going on below, — large-eyed, silken-clad apparitions, accompanied, peradventure, by pulse of perfume or throb of cithern. The roof is designed to represent the starry heavens, with the orbs constellated in groups, — a series of inclined planes, facets, and polygons, blending in the peculiar roof called *artesonado*. Over one hundred and fifty sorts of traceries are discovered on the walls of this apartment, — the Comoreh of the Moors, — not to mention the precious, almost invisible details in azure and black, which to-day would cost immense sums to reproduce with the same skill and precision. The name of the Sultan Abul Hachach, and the name of Yusuf, dwell among the happy spaces of these heavens; and the value set upon the hall is seen in the inscriptions: 'On my part, morning and evening, lips of benediction, prosperity, felicity, and friendship salute thee.' 'I am as the heart in the midst of the members, for in the heart dwelleth the strength of the spirit and of the soul.'

Here took place the council, presided over by Abu Abdillah XI., in the presence of all the magnates of the realm, when the surrender of the palace was agreed upon, and here the haughty Muza, knowing the secret intercourse of Boabdil with Ferdinand, taunted him with it, and departed to Africa to avoid the humiliation of imprisonment.

'Unhappy he who lost such a possession!' exclaimed Charles V., beholding the beauty of the landscape disclosed from its outer windows, when his chronicler, Guevara, recounted to him the legend of the Moor's Last Sigh. 'If I had been he,' cried the emperor, 'I should rather have chosen this Alhambra for a tomb, than to live outside of it in the Alpujarra!'

Columbus once visited this apartment, says tradition, when he came before the Queen Isa-

bella to expound his plans. 'The King Chiquito
(Boabdil),' says the veracious continuer of Hernando del Palgar's chronicle, 'held counsel with
his mother, who was called Seb, of Christian nation, and who was a captive when the Moors
plundered Cieza, which is a city of the kingdom
of Murcia; and as, at the time, she was but
small, she became a Moor through flattery and
other means, and turned out beautiful and good;
and the king, Muley Buasen, married her, because among the Moors it was held good that the
king or other cavalier should marry a damsel
who from Christian had become a Moor. Of
this marriage was born the King Chiquito, and
this queen was of great and valiant soul, and op-
posed with all her power the King Chiquito, her
son, intriguing with the Catholic kings, or con-
certing with them, and bade him hope for pros-
perous fortune, and die a king; and owing to
this, the King Chiquito was on his guard lest his
mother should know he was treating with the
Catholic kings, to deliver over to them the realm.
When the capitulation was concluded, his mother
suspected it, and dissembling it, it is said she
took him by the hand, and entered into the tower
of Comoreh, which is the spot where Granada's
grandeur most lieth revealed; and after having
led him around the tower, and to the window,
pointing, she said: '*See what thou surrenderest,*

and remember that all thy forefathers died kings of Granada, and that the kingdom ends in thee!"

At the side opposite the entrance arch is an alcove with arched windows and pillars between, from which all that Seb's words so eloquently suggest is grouped before the eye; immense depths below, green with climbing trees; the Darro, hedged in by quaint walls, and spanned by quainter bridges, with towers at intervals; Albaicin, the gypsy quarter, with its strange population of human beings burrowing in the hillsides; the variegated roofs and architectural groups of the ancient city of the Khalifs; the luxurious panorama of the Vega of Granada, filled with towns, forests, and wheat-fields; last, but not least, the mighty Sierras, with their pink and lilac heads, surmounted by a dazzling comb of snow, and stretching to the skies. Well might the last of the Moorish kings shed bitter tears over such a scene.

One may go over and over these beautiful legends as over some priceless rosary, and still they seem ever fresh.

No sooner have we read this dainty poem of the Court of Myrtles and the Hall of Ambassadors, than one still daintier rises before us, after passing through a narrow passage — the Court of Lions. It is one of the most beautiful and elegant structures of Mussulman architecture.

There is nothing finer in all that the glowing imagination of the race of Hagar has reared, whether in or out of Spain : transparent arcades; groups of columns so clustered as to uphold their fragile burdens of ethereal arches and canopies like caryatides ; seven fountains perpetually murmuring amid the solitude of the place ; two sumptuous galleries advancing at each end from the cloisters beneath ; four cupolas exquisitely lifted to the sunny air by reed-like marble pillars slight as flower-stems, and eleven sorts of arches surpassingly decorated ; the whole forming a picture of delight, even after the ruin of seven centuries.

The Court of Lions is the acme of the Alhambra. As the returning Agamemnon was to Klytæmnestra like summer in the winter-time ; so is this court the most cherished possession of the Arab palace. Without tanks, or gardens, or statues, or the ideal wealth gathered from painting or sculpture, its simple self produces the most enchanting effect. No race of barbarians could have fashioned so perfect a place. Whichever way the eye looks, a varied combination of different and yet symmetric arches presents itself, blending in the distance and producing an elfishly beautiful perspective ; and whether contemplated from the sides or angles, each of its decorations offers a diversity of multiple details so harmoniously distributed that they do no prejudice to the utmost regularity of form. To deprive the tiled roofs of the sombre symmetric aspect of squares suspended on such delicate colonnades, the Moors raised cupolas, shaped like half-oranges, with their Eastern minarets interlocked with the ornamentation of the galleries and ceilings of the adjacent halls. The plan is one of perfect regularity and simplicity; a parallelogram formed by two **perfect squares**, including the vestibule. Here if anywhere in this charmed palace breathe and flute the voices of the East, Bagdad and Damascus, Ispahan and Cairo. Where was this transparent architecture invented — a palace of point-lace through which moonlight is pouring? The galleries of its four sides are unequal; the innumerable arches are not absolutely uniform; the columns are not grouped together symmetrically; the portals are not alike; there is no such constant repetition of the same lines and heights as constitutes the chief charm of other architectures; and still the whole spot breathes pregnant and subtle charm. Unity dwells in diversity; compare arch with arch, roof with roof, one cluster of capitals with another; and identity is not found in the *act*. But take in the whole labyrinth of structures at a glance — each one falls harmoniously into line, and at a proper distance the effect is as perfect as any strophe of a poem.

What a magic system had the Arabs of converting their ceilings into stalactite grottoes! The effect is quaintly and curiously beautiful. A passage in the Korán throws light on this peculiar mode of architecture, unknown before the advent of the prophet. The legend runs that it is a reminiscence of the Cave of Tur, when the spiders with their webs, the bees with their honeycombs, and the doves with their nests covered the entrance of the cave and concealed the hiding-place of Mahomet when he was fleeing to Abyssinia from the Koreysh.

The vision of crystallized, trickling water is realized in these apartments. Looking up, one seems to be in the multitudinous sparkle and exfoliation of a crystalline chamber, as if long, light, fulminant showers had been caught and transformed into wavy sculpture. There is a tremulous beauty about such ornamentation that befits the emotional and imaginative character of the Arab. Nothing can be more full of grace than an entrance arch thus ornamented. It is like walking underneath waving grasses and ferns chiseled into undulous masses out of the white heart of this Macaen marble. It was in 1377 that the Arab artificer Aben Cencid began this court, which is neither Persian, Assyrian, Greek, nor Roman; and yet time has but little impaired its beauty. The elegance of the pavilion roofs, composed, as they are within, of thousands of different pieces, has never been equaled.

In the centre is the famous fountain supported by twelve lions of antique form — the sole imitation, save certain problematical pictures — of any living thing to be found in all the varied embellishment of the Alhambra. It was an ablutionary fountain designed in accordance with the prescriptions of Mahometan law, and though now empty, was once full of water. There is a certain rigidity in the limbs of the lions, which was purposely designed to give them a more architectural form; and, according to the best writers, inspirations drawn by the Arabs from the ruins of Persepolis and ancient Persia are observable in their monumental attitude and expression.

Though an empty basin, the Fountain of Lions flows with a perennial stream of persuasive and fascinating legends; here took place the marriage of Abu Abdallah Yusef and the lovely Záhira; here feasts were given in the Castilian fashion, and the Christian ambassadors of Castile and France were invited; here the last of the Abencerrages was beheaded; and many another romance of life and death was enacted. As I wandered about its spaces, there reigned everywhere what I might describe as gorgeous stillness. A glorified calm seemed to distill from the liquid Spanish sun, and rest like a benediction on its marble pavement. A spell of beauty enveloped the spot, and enthralled the idle feet as they tried in vain to leave this pathetically lovely precinct. Nobody was near; I was alone; the intense poetry of the place struck me with redoubled force, and its delightful melancholy was like the dainty trouble of sweet music.

Among all the salutations, eulogies to the Sultan, and *suras* from the sacred book with which its walls overflow, none is so rich in voluptuous hyperbole as the inscription which is sculptured on the border of the fountain-basin. Its concluding line, which I applied involuntarily to the Court of Lions, is : 'The peace of God be with thee evermore ; thy pleasures be multiplied ; be thy enemies cast down!'

Opening off the Court of Lions, to one side is the Hall of the Abencerrages, entered by a rarely ornamented door. Many traditions converge on this spot and throw their radiance on the mind of the spectator. According to one, the Abencerrages formed an influential tribe that possessed palaces in the Alhambra and at the foot of the Sierras, and they favored the cause of the last king, persecuted by his father, Abul Hacen. This monarch had become enamored of Zoraya (the Isabel de Solís of some legends), and separated from his true wife, the Sultana **Aixa**. The favorite instigated the king to have Aixa's sons beheaded; so that the Sultana feared for their lives, and saved them by letting them down from the windows of the Tower of Comoreh. She fled to Guadix and threw herself under the protection of the Abencerrages, while the triumphant Zoraya lived and reigned in the Alhambra, adorned with the jewels of the mother of Boabdil. Again, in the time of Hernando de Baeza, secretary to the last king of Granada, this apartment was called the Chamber of Blood, and the Moors told how the seventeen Abencerrages, while going through a narrow passage, were suddenly warned by a female slave **not** to proceed farther, but disregarding her warning, they were all beheaded near the Fountain of Lions. Spots of blood **are** still shown to mark the locality of this tragedy — spots **less** romantically explained by the porous nature of the Macaen stone, which absorbs moisture readily, though it is far from improbable that blood, too, may have been absorbed by it.

This chamber is one of the most elegant of the palace, rising in three perfectly proportioned bodies, and lighted by sixteen airy windows opened in the star-shaped roof. A sweet and tranquil light streams through these windows; and the spacious alcoves that open at their sides, by means of four arches full of scarlet and azure ornaments, seem waiting for the luxurious divans that have disappeared, where the odalisques passed hours in amorous meditation. The everflowing fountain in the centre; the brocade-like ornamentation in vivid relief around the walls; the fantastic censers, encrusted with silver, for exhaling perfumes and giving light to this weird apartment, with their niches; the quaint pertinacity of lines and colors that exhausts itself in inundating these walls; the flicker of the polished surfaces and the witchery of the thousand-fold arabesques; — all this must have communicated a unique grace to the Hall of the Abencerrages and made of it something more than the vision of phantom architecture we see to-day. During the Renaissance of the sixteenth century, the alcove roofs were filled with paintings and reliefs. The ornaments of the entrance door are subtle beyond description, and the eight-pointed star of the roof, with its prismatic triangles and complicated geometric traceries, is a masterpiece of some inspired mathematician. The same stalactite incrustation is richly used in this boudoir-like hall, whose small dimensions are in such striking contrast with the exuberance of skill lavished on it. First come two rows of horse-shoe arches; then a tier of alcoves with their clustering columns and stalactite vaults; then a row of sixteen windows with their converging radii; then an intricate half-circular, half-conical roof with its many tints, — blue, brown, red, and gold.

An Arabic chronicler says that Bulhaxix invented alchemy, and that, thanks to the gold men made by it, they were able to embellish the palaces, surround the city with a triple rampart, and build the Alhambra with walls of gold and precious stones. The fabrication of gold and the discovery of pearls and amethysts in the Alhambra walls were not necessary to make us conceive the effect which this construction must have produced on the Eastern imagination. Vestiges of colors and gold are seen everywhere, and in the Hall of Justice nearly all the ornaments show them. The Hall of Justice is a nave with three lofty and five smaller domes, flanked by three elegant doors which communicate with the Court of Lions. It is divided into seven compartments or divans, where the Khalif sat and administered justice, and there are stalactite arches and literally a world of fine, fanciful ornamentation. Its seventy-five feet of length must have shone like a bed of flowers when the colors were fresh. The recesses in the side of the hall have ceilings filled with paintings on skins nailed to the wooden roof. They are of unknown origin; and as they are full of representations of men, animals, and living things, contrary to Mahometan law, it is conjectured that they are late additions.

But —

> 'Allons, bel oiseau bleu,
> Chantez la romance à madame,' —

the true poem of the Alhambra — I have been hitherto describing its prose — is the Hall of the Two Sisters. It is a young girl's dream — a reverie from the inner circles of one's daintiest imaginings — a picture of airy fragility and luxury, through which all that the Moors were and hoped to be floats like music. Here one comes upon something pure and perfect — an Arab idyll breathing the long distances, the sunset palms, the muffled cadences of the desert; the stopping-place where his imagination halted before it took off its sandals to enter Paradise, the sweet core of his many-colored longings as they gazed a-sea from the portals of Smyrna and Morocco, and shifted and shaped themselves on the exalted horizon. The first word spoken is by the lovely *azulejo* socle, whereon, in four-and-twenty verses, this poem is engraved in Arabic : —

> 'I am the garden that appeareth in the morning decked with beauty: contemplate my beauty carefully, and thou shalt find my rank explained.
> In glory complete, for the sake of my lord, the prince Mahomet, with the most noble of all that is past and to come. . . . .
> How many delightful spaces offer themselves to the eyes! The spirit of a man of sweet condition will see realized in them his dreams.
> Here often in the night the five Pleiades seek their rest, and the noxious air dawneth sweet and delightsome.

And there is an admirable cupola that hath few equals. In
  it are beauties occult and beauties manifest.
The constellation of the Twins extends its hand towards it
  in sign of salutation, and the moon approacheth, for
  secret converse.
And the shining stars would abide in it and not keep their
  courses fixed in the celestial vault;
And in its two galleries, like the youthful slaves, would
  hasten to render the same service with which they
  please him.
It were not wonderful if the morning stars left their altitudes and passed the limits fixed.
And they would await the orders of my lord, for his service
  most high, winning more lofty honor.
Here, then, is a portico of such beauty that the Alcázar hath
  in it what excelleth the arch of Heaven.
With how many ornaments hast thou increased it, O king!
  Among its adornments there are colors that put to
  shame the precious vestments of Yemen.
How many arches rise in its roof on columns bathed in
  light!
Thou wilt believe that they are planets revolving in their
  orbits and obscuring the clear glories of the coming
  dawn.
The columns possess every sort of marvel. The fame of
  their beauty flieth and hath become proverbial.
And there is lucent marble that sprinkles its clearness and
  illumines what was left in darkness.
When it shineth sunlight-smitten, thou wilt believe them
  pearls by reason of their size.
Never have we beholden an Alcázar of more lofty appearance, of more clear horizon, or of more fitting amplitude.
Never have we seen a garden more delightful in flowers,
  more ambient in perfume, or more exquisite in fruits.

It payeth double and with ready money the sum which the
    Cadi of beauty hath bestowed upon it.
For from the morning the hand of the zephyr is full of coins
    of light that contain the wherewithal to pay.
And the rays of the sun fill the precinct of the garden and
    its branches, leaving them beautiful.'

The Arab imagination has reached its utmost refinement here. The stalactite roof is made of five thousand separate pieces and is a network of tiny domes and vaults. The *azulejo*-tiles of the basement are of great elegance, most difficult in combination and outline, and there are shields and medallions bearing the arms of Ibn-l-Ahmar on the wall. All is peace, whiteness, passion, stillness, in this inimitable spot; a fountain flickers in the centre; aerial *alhamies* or alcoves lift their latticed windows from out a multitude of frost-like traceries; the dome is of unparalleled boldness and beauty; and so exquisite the geometric proportions that not the slightest detail could be touched without marring their perfection. All the rooms of this hall were the apartments of the favorite women who lived in independence in the same harem. The tradition is that two fair captives dwelt here and that they died of grief and jealousy on beholding from their latticed windows the scenes of love enacted within the garden of the ladies. Others derive the name from the two marble slabs in the pavement. Voluptuousness has here become spiritualized into a fragrance, and the whole place exhales the ardors and languors of an intense life. The apartment is a white rose; its illuminated elegance is unknown elsewhere in the world; its serene spirituality is a thing of angels; its marble spaces are truly, as the inscription says, the dwelling-place of the Pleiades. In no place have the throbbing wealth, the voices and the silences of the Semitic nature come to such articulation. Could a perfume live, its columned exhalations would take form and fire in this shape. A Watteau interior as compared with this is simply vulgar; Pompeii is garish. The Moors seemed to build by moonlight and to breathe through their architecture the plaintiveness, tenderness, and purity of the perennial star. They instinctively avoided discords; all is with them harmony, deep-laden sense of beauty, refinement of detail, mystery, secrecy, spirituality. Clay seemed too coarse; so they worked in spider-web, gossamer, mother-of-pearl. Colors and gold they used lavishly, but with the utmost delicacy. The great vase of the Alhambra is a triumph of their skill in enameling. They loved water and imitated its fluent forms, and they transferred its sparkle to their domes. Exploring the under-world, they brought forth from its darkness this ethereal stalactite-architecture which nature preciously and jealously builds up in her heart; and they hung it in the vaults and arches of their palace-roofs, there to shine evermore. They called in the flowers and winds, and fixed their tints and shadows in their *alhamies*. They did not care for the outsides; these were often rude and homely; and superstition bade them be on their guard. But within, the winding spaces of the desert, the reminiscences of Damascus, the sea with its curves and crests, the beauty of the mirage, the sound of fountains, the grace and airiness of the Bedouin tent, — all found a space. And at the heart of all these sense-forms, surrounded by his odalisques, his censers, his poetic Korán, his muezzin-cries, the veiled and allegorized poetry of his life, sat the Defender of the Faith.

'Mateo spread his cloak for me in the fountain in the Hall of the Abencerrages, over the blood stains made by the decapitation of those gallant chiefs, and I lay half an hour looking upward: and this is what I made out of the dome. From its central pinnacle hung the chalice of a flower with feathery petals, like the crape myrtle of our Southern States. Outside of this, branched downward the eight rays of a large star, whose points touched the base of the dome; yet the star was itself composed of flowers, while between its rays and around its points fell a shower of blossoms, shells, and sparry drops.

From the base of the dome hung a gorgeous pattern of lace, with a fringe of bugles, projecting into eight points so as to form a star of drapery, hanging from the points of the flowery star in the dome. The spaces between the angles were filled with masses of stalactites, dropping one below the other, till they tapered into the plain square sides of the hall.

'In the Hall of the Two Sisters I lay likewise for a considerable time, resolving its misty glories into shape. The dome was still more suggestive of flowers. The highest and central piece was a deep trumpet flower, whose mouth was cleft into eight petals. It hung in the centre of a superb lotus-cup, the leaves of which were exquisitely veined and chased. Still farther below swung a mass of mimosa blossoms, intermixed with pods and lance-like leaves, and around the base of the dome opened the bells of sixteen gorgeous tulips. These pictures may not be very intelligible, but I know not how else to paint the effect of this fairy architecture.'[1]

From the delicate presence of the Two Sisters one passes an ante-chamber with vaulted roof of admirable complexity, and enters a little apartment called in the Arabic, Daraxa, place to enter or ascend; but the poets from the sixteenth century on suppose it to be the name of a favor-

[1] Bayard Taylor, *Lands of the Saracens.*

ite Sultana who passed her days in this delightful chamber, — a tradition based upon the name of the Sultana Aixa, **a name borne** by many queens whose chosen abode this is said to have been. **Hence** the name, Mirador de Lindaraxa, Boudoir **of** Lindaraxa. The entrance arch is a **true inspiration**; nothing richer, more *recherché*, **more delicately simple.** Beyond are the arched *ajimez* windows with the pillar between and a vista of the garden on which Washington Irving looked when he lived in the Alhambra and composed his charming stories, — the 'poet Irving' as the Spaniards most truly call him. Its **walls** are covered with Cufic ornaments. One **part** of this precious structure is crowned by an openwork *tracería* made of wood, and there were skylights filled with many-colored crystals through which sweet mysterious light percolated, filtered of undue garishness and full of the twilight **so** congenial to the Arab. The light from the garden was veiled by daintily wrought open-work blinds, **and the whole** harmonized perfectly with the colors of the walls and **the** translucent roof. The four walls of this boudoir are composed of double and triple **pointed** arches under a common centre; the tile-work is of the finest, and shows labor of indescribable patience; the floor was a carpet of mosaics, and the whole reveals an enchantment and voluptuous mystery unequaled in the palace. The Arabs covered the smooth spaces of the ante-chamber with carpets, worked leather, or woven panoplies of divers colors; and here and there were basket-like cranes for holding clothing, arms, and other objects. The tiny apartment is full of notable inscriptions, filled with that reference to *light* with which the Arab was always intoxicated.

I sat at the window as if spell-bound. Beneath was a fountain, half Arab, half Renaissance; beyond were walls over which dense orange-trees full of fruit were trained; the same ancient yellow sun filled the court as with a pool of gold; and the fountain and garden of Lindaraxa lay beneath it in an ecstasy of stillness and beauty.

This court is inclosed by cloisters and is of the time of Charles V. Through it you enter the Chamber of Secrets, — an ellipse with an acoustic device by which every whisper can be heard.

But it would take hundreds of pages to go conscientiously through a description of the Alhambra. The palace could be put many times over into one of the huge king's barracks of London, Paris, or Berlin; and yet there is such ingenuity, patience, skill shown in it, that Contreras and his father devoted a life-time to studying and restoring it, and its ruins alone have produced a school of Spanish art. What can one weak pilgrim do to recompose this rifled mausoleum of Islám and bring it vividly before an absent eye? With one glance at the Queen's Boudoir — the Peinador de la Reina — the description must end.

What a panorama unfolds from this side-piece to the Mirador de Lindaraxa! the ancient city of Albaicin; the walls constructed by Bishop Gonzalo, running over the far-off hill-sides; the low houses of the barrier of Hajariz; the seminary of San Cecilio, redolent of devout associations; the delightful vineyards; the hermitage of San Miguel above the Aceituni fort, with its long-venerated image; the old Alcazaba-buildings remote on the mountain-top, once the residence of Arabic dignitaries; the Palace of the Generalife on the hill to the right, partly hidden by the adjoining Tower of the Ladies; and beneath and within this rare scene the silvery Salom (now the Darro), which, said Mármol, came from the mountain of the myrtles and ran grains of gold, until it mingled with the Genil and flowed in company with it through the heavenly plain of Granada.

This tower or minaret wherein lies the queen's boudoir was not originally arranged as at present. The corridor surrounding it was then a series of pointed battlements; the windows had translucent blinds; and under the threshold of to-day was the small temple erected to the Sultan Abul

Hachach in memory of his welcome. Its sides were open to the east; in it the emirs awaited the coming of the sun, and in its isolated precinct they murmured the holy prayers of the morning. The inscriptions on ceiling and door, the salutations and Koranic verses on the columns and panels of the hall beneath, all point to the sacred use to which it was put. But the Pompeian paintings, the perfumers in one corner over which the Christian ladies stood, to let the vapor fill their garments, and the traces of Italian pencils of the Renaissance, all point to its desecration and subsequent diversion from this original purpose.

Below this suite of rooms I have been describing are the Hall of Couches and the Baths. In the Hall of Couches are divans, an alcove designed to hold some hidden favorite, and the tribunes where the odalisques recited the *kasidas*, sang, and played their stringed instruments while the Sultan enjoyed his hours of repose. It was an undressing room, in preparation for the temperature of adjacent rooms where no current of air could penetrate. The floor is of glazed mosaic, and the whole place, together with its elaborate appointments, is full of epicurean suggestiveness. But it will be impossible to enter into a description of the Hall of the Grating, the antiquities of the archives, the court of the chapel, the mosque, the abandoned palace of Charles V. (which resembles an unfinished bull-ring), adjoining the Court of Lions, the Tower of the Poniards and of Mahomet, the various wells, the church of San Francisco, or the ancient environs, gates, and alcázars of Granada. On the Alhambra-hill alone there are more than twenty towers, some with decorations and legends of great beauty. Though the Arab palace proper is so small, the whole — terraces, gates, towers, fortresses, walls, pleasure-grounds, promenades, palaces, elm-walks, churches, mosques, stables, and convent — makes a cluster which once transformed the hill into a city.

Of their one book they have made the most, for out of it has sprung the palace of Abdul-ar-rhaman.

IX.

> In hir is heigh beautee, withoutë pride,
> Yowthë, withoutë grenehede or folyë;
> To alle hir werkës vertu is **hir gyde,**
> Humblesse hath slayn in hir al tirannye.
> She is mirour of allë curteisye;
> Hir herte is verray chambre of holynessë,
> Hir hand, ministre of freedom for almessë.
> <div align="right">CHAUCER, <i>Man of Lawes Tale</i>.</div>

ALMOST the first bright speck of flowing water one sees in Spain is the Guadalquivir, the river of the Arabs. Imperishably associated with them, with the ancients, and with Columbus, its arrowy sparkle is a true refreshment, and the great curve which it describes at Seville seems to suggest a grandeur that has passed away. The history and antiquities of this one place would throw their radiating threads over the whole country and bring in contribution the Roman chronicles, the church histories, the Moslem domination, and the whole rosary of Christian kings. It is a singularly interesting spot. The Andalusian type is here seen in perfection. The wit, the jest, the romance, the music of this peculiar people — their infinite knack at rhyming, their proverb-making, their rhythmic and sensuous intellectuality, if one may so speak — are nowhere so ripe and rich as in Seville. Take away Andalusia, and one might look around for Spain; take away Seville, and one might ask in vain for Andalusia. An evening in a square in Seville is a revelation. Life is not an even flow with these people; it is a tumult, a sort of passion. The noisy sunlight, the loud sky, the ringing air, the tumultuous character of land and laborer, bring one's psychologizing to a stand-still, and one is lost in wonder at the freakish versatility, the petulance, the emotion of the Andalusians. Where the air never sparkles with frost, all the sparkle has gone into the people. For a thousand years they have been overshadowed by one great cathedral or another, and their souls have prospered. The Sevillians can put up their hands to their eyes and see Julius Cæsar in the great distance of twenty centuries, anchoring his fleet before the Tower of Gold, beleaguering, conquering, reëstablishing, and leaving behind — as he nearly always did — the autograph of his own name to the re-conquered and re-christened city. As nearly everything in London is Nelson *This*, or Wellington *That*, so in antiquity, *Cæsarea, Cæsarea Augusta, Julia Romulea*, etc., showed traces of what Marcus Aurelius called 'Cæsarized' self-perpetuation. And the bloodhounds of history might, like the Eumenides of Æschylos, scent out the great conqueror by the blood he has left behind.

The first glimpse we get of Seville is a scarlet sunrise. This is no place to go into the wrath and wrangling of Cæsar and Pompey; but throughout Spain, at the beginning of our era, we find them in the attitude of Canova's Boxers. The jangle of their sweet bells out of tune has rung on down to our times, and not a book on Seville can be written, hardly a line on Seville can be read, without interminable references and cross-references to these delectable athletes. Let them anchor their fleets and butcher their tens of thousands, then, in peace; it is none of our business. The Roman patricians who wormed themselves into the highest offices of the place, surrounded themselves with lordly monuments and fortifications, and gave up the light of Rome for the loveliness of Seville, have left behind them the thinnest spider-web of connection with the present. The greatest glory of once glorious Cordova is that she has given her name to the guild of French shoemakers; *Corduba*, the brilliant hearth-stone of Roman poets and philosophers, has become the *Cordonnier* of the Rue du Bac. *Julia Romulea* might have been proud indeed if people had literally walked in her memory, as is the case with her rival. But she contents herself with being the home of the prettiest women in Spain, the seat of a once splendid university, the heir of the mighty sovereignty of the Moors, the city of the strange worship of Adonis and Astarte, and the pink of teeming idleness, indolence, and plenty. The Sevillians laugh at the abounding calabashes and tomatoes of the Cádiz region, and have a story that their neighbors once tried to scale the heavens with their tomato baskets; but they need not talk, there is plenty to scoff at on the Guadalquivir. For example, one would not judge by the rags in which the good city abounds that scores of thousands of people were once occupied there in the manufacture of silk. In the Spanish *romanceros* the grandees are always clad in silk, with mottoed Toledo blades, steeds of fire and wind, and shirts of mail like the ringed meshes of Beóvulf. They stalk up and down the ballads after the fashion of the old heroes of the boards breathing fury and verse. You wonder where they got leisure to do their doughty deeds, so milliner-like is the cataloguing of their dress. The most celebrated armor of the most celebrated captains of the Middle Ages may be seen in the armory at Madrid; and precious little of it seems to have seen any service. Historic doubts seize one in the very presence of Don Juan of Austria's sword and under the very edge of Don Jaime's rapier.

From a remote time the people of Seville have been the same; they wept and wailed in the train of Venus, commemorating the lost Adonis, as they now weep and wail in Holy Week, commemorating the lost Redeemer. Their customs, fairs, festivals, household gods, have been touched with the chrism of the new religion, but remain substantially the same; only, as Gibbon would say, they have accepted with alacrity the advantageous offer of immortality. Underneath the great and noble cathedral may almost be heard the strange murmurs of a prehistoric Venus-worship, as in some Tannhäuser-legend, for the exquisite fabric is reared over the ancient temple and smothers as it were the cry of those ancient times. One is quite sure that just such conversations as Matthew Arnold has so daintily rendered from the Greek of Theocritus may be overheard any day, even now, under the arches and cloisters of Seville Cathedral. There is something quite inextinguishable in the strain of southern nations; their characteristics have always been the same. After the Moors had made Seville so splendid, it is sad to read of their overthrow and the vanishing from the face of the earth of all their elegance and grace. The soft flow and fantasy of the Arabic verse have captivated the world's ear and made it listen with sympathy to the legends of the Khalifs. Spanish hidalgos get little justice beside the glittering squadrons of Abdul-Aziz and the Almohades. There is something incredible in the story that Seville was once a dependency of Damascus. It is necessary to look into Gibbon's record of the sudden spread and prosperousness of the Osmanlees before thorough acknowledgment of the truth of history is made. In his noble story of Mahometan conquest we see the splendor of their achievements, the spread of their intelligence, the superiority of their arts and sciences, and the gifts and gallantry of their leaders. It seems as if they civilized the Spaniards and taught the most passionate of Christians the true doctrines of the cross. Seville under them became a star which shed the light of their glorious khalifate over the surrounding nations. A single relic of their dominion — the Giralda Tower — surpasses all Christian belfries, even Giotto's, in beauty and harmony. They had published encyclopædias when the barons of England had yet to learn how to write their own names. Chemistry was to them a science when to the rest of Europe — even to Dante — it was a black art. Aristotelian philosophy was preserved in the deep wells made by them when abject illiteracy had befallen the heirs of the Greeks and Romans. And yet the roaring beef-eaters of St. Ferdinand and Ferdinand and Isabella — 'the flower of Castile and

Leon'—drove them out by the hundred thousand and made the country the wilderness it deserved to be.

No change of dynasty, however, could change the conformation of the country — the beautiful mountain lines, the valleys green with cork-trees, the everglades along the rivers, the mountain streams falling like a crystal bath down the cliffs and precipices, and the orchards that mingled their perpetual bloom with undying olive and oak. The cypress-loving Moslems had left behind them this constant mourner over their lost sovereignty. Their great, low, jewel-lighted mosques were torn down or incorporated with the structures of the new faith. Their schools of learning became a hissing to the Catholic archbishops and all the light of their poetry and romance seemed to go out in the darkened land. The city of Pleasure became the city of Superstition; no more Castilian princes came to the Arabic universities to learn the civilization and the refinement of the East. What an utter sunbeamless twilight succeeded the rich day!

For a town of some one hundred and forty thousand inhabitants Seville has a very varied life and an unusual variety of interesting objects. Apart from the psychological features of its gypsy and Andalusian population, the bright Eastern *patios* wreathed in flowers and filigree, the spacious chronicles of its legendary and poetic history, and the conservatism of its habits, it has had a very distinct literary and artistic significance in the peninsula. The most famous of the Spanish painters came from Seville. 'Difficult and diffuse would be the task of citing,' says a Spanish author,[1] 'all the illustrious men who in sacred things, in arms, in arts, and in sciences have shed distinction on this city by their birth.' The poets Herrera, Aleman, Urquijo, La Cueva, Jáuregin, Alcázar, Rioja, Carvajal, Reinoso; the painters Murillo, Velazquez, Zurbarán, Cespedes, Herrera, and Roelas; and archbishops, patriarchs, generals, bishops, mathematicians, captains-general, men of science and adventure, actors and dramatic authors, presidents of the Junta, publicists, prose writers, like Fernan Caballero, and the translator whom Spanish hyperbole calls '*el sublime traductor de los Salmos*, came from Seville. After such an enumeration one may well be prepared for a *Te Deum Sevilliam*, and is not at all astonished to find mention of the town in the dusty volumes of Mela, Pliny, Ptolemy, and Strabo. We are told that one of the triumphs of Christianity was the conversion of the temples of the Sun, of Hercules, of Mars, Bacchus, and Venus, at Seville, into 'parishes' such as

[1] *Sevilla, Historica, Monumental, Artistica y Topographica.* Sevilla, 1878.

Santa Marina, San Romano, San Ildefonso; and
it is added that so illustrious a city could not but
receive the evangelic light as it poured forth from
the capital of the world. Seville in Roman times,
in Vandal times, in Moslem times, and in Spanish times, has a series of physiognomies quite as
varied and astonishing as those attributed to Gar-
rick. It lived on in successive stages of loss of
identity down to the times of the 'Serene Sirs,
Dukes of Montpensier'—called in Spanish *SS.
AA. R. R. los Sermos Sres. Duques de Montpensier*
— who established their august court there in
1848. One would no more undertake to disentangle these successive civilizations than to unwind the historic skein which bears so prominent
a part in the curious coat-of-arms of the city. A
quaint gleam is cast on the history of the place
by mentioning the titles it enjoys: *Very Noble,
Very Leal, Very Heroic*, and *Unconquerable Seville;*
each one of which, as it was successively added,
forms a chapter in its history.

In character and manners the Sevillian type is
the most decided in Andalusia. Their exaggeration of language has become proverbial: 'Child
of gold, and child of silver, and child of pearls,
and child of carbuncles,' is a specimen of the pet
language applied by a great Spanish writer to
a fair young gypsy girl. They have all the characteristics of the South vividly concentrated:

sensibility, imagination, gayety, promptness and fertility of invention, vehemence of expression, rapidity in perceiving relations, and metaphors, epigrams, and quips enough to make the fortune of several Lopes. Great aptitude for painting, poetry, and the fine arts exists among them; great inaptitude for the abstract, speculative, metaphysical side by side with it. Indeed, a glance at the brilliant physical environment in which their lives are set — the sky, the landscape, the sunny voluptuousness of air and out-door life — will go far to explain the fullness of their imaginations and the emptiness of their understandings. They recoil from meditation; they take a book to church, and read out of that; they listen to beautiful music and have little taste for analysis. They have the repute of being lazy and inert, — qualities no doubt engendered by the languor of the Andalusian climate, the facility with which the means of subsistence are obtained, and the somewhat easy accumulation of property. Northern people who establish themselves under this fervid sun soon become as loose-limbed as the Andalusians themselves. What particularly strikes an Anglo-Saxon is the religious enthusiasm of the people. Seville has always been celebrated for sumptuous *funcciones* — gorgeous religious ceremonies in Holy Week and at Noche Buena, which rival those of Rome under the irresponsibles, and even to-day combat with the bull-fight in attracting visitors. Alms-giving is certainly an invention of the Spanish Catholics, for nowhere has the growth — fungoid or otherwise — attained such luxuriance as in Spain, and nowhere in Spain such luxuriance as at Seville. Every pillar, post, and chancel railing in a Spanish church is peppered with alms-boxes of every description, from those purporting to be 'for the edification of this holy church' to those purporting to be for the refreshment of souls in purgatory. They are a lavish, wasteful people. The crowded taverns, clubs, and cafés show the devotees of piquet and ombre (which Catherine of Braganza introduced into England) in full passion; among a party of friends each insists on paying for what has been ordered, though he may have in his pockets not more than the single coin which is the dinner-in-the-pocket-book of a whole family. True and counterfeit indigence abounds: a fact which seems to spring from the impressionable nature of the Andalusians who cannot bear the sight of misery, but must needs help it upon its legs again; sturdy legs enough, too, which do not fail to walk forthwith into the Spanish purse with the Seven-League Boots. The streets are filled with itinerant venders of every dye, who form a class quite dangerous to society; they have a peculiar faculty of investigating each other's entrails with *navajas* and getting up a tragedy in the streets at a moment's notice. The artisans proper are lively, 'smart,' active, energetic, and noisy, but honorable and diligent. Nowhere in Spain are there so many enamored swains, love-lorn bachelors, and jealous husbands. Balcony interviews are frequent by day and night, and courtship through Venetian blinds has become a science. The women of Seville are slight, intense-looking little things, as vivacious as a canary, as pliable as wire, as agile as a cat. They pride themselves on airiness of figure, brilliance of eye, enchanting conversational power, small feet, and enormous passions. One had as well touch an electric eel as an Andalusian woman. I cannot vouch for their constancy in love, their carefulness and neatness in family life, their tender solicitude, their purity, and their sweetness; every Sevillano, however, would instantly challenge you to deadly combat if you doubted in the least that each and every Sevillana possessed each and every one of these traits.

It has been well said of Seville that from ancient times the arts have had constant occupation in building, rebuilding, and preserving churches and monasteries; the 'gentility,' as the Spaniards quaintly call the Gentiles, abounded in temples; the Christians, under the enlightened administration of the Moors, were permitted to erect and retain houses dedicated to their own worship, side by side with the overshadowing elegance and richness of the Saracen mosques; and the Saracen mosques, at the re-conquest, were converted by a sprinkle of holy water into Catholic churches.

The glory of Andalusia — perhaps the most elegant thing of its kind in the world — is the Cathedral of Seville. It is broader than St. Paul's at London, but not so long by more than a hundred feet; while the Giralda Tower, built nearly a thousand years ago, would come within a few feet of the cross which surmounts the vast and ugly pile of Wren. It is one of the most eloquent voices of the Dark Ages speaking to our generation of a faith that is lost. It has the advantage over St. Paul's of standing in a large square, whence the incomparable details of the exterior — tower, buttresses, pinnacles, courts — can be seen in perfection. Think of a great Gothic mountain three hundred and seventy-eight feet long and two hundred and fifty-four feet broad before you, with a glorious sentinel tower three hundred and fifty feet high standing beside it, upon a raised terrace reached by encircling flights of stairs. It has been compared to a grand vessel at sea in full sail, with all its pennons flying, high-pooped, massive, and filled in every detail with the harmony of artistic proportions. You can enter by any one of nine doors, the most beautiful of which is beneath a splendid horse-shoe arch, and leads into the Court of Oranges, thence to the Cathedral. Five aisles fill it with a forest of pillars, which spread out as they touch the roof into the lovely, fan-like radiations of a grove of palms, the symbol of peace. All these lock and interlock, forming a groined roof of sixty-eight compartments. All the gardens of the Goths shed their leaves over the central pillars, and round the screen of the high altar. Imagine the radiance streaming from the ninety-three painted windows, five of which are wheels as full of glory as the windows in the Eve of St. Agnes! Here are the Scriptures dyed blood-red, purple, and amaranth; it is an incarnation in flesh-tints; it is a Pilgrim's Progress and a martyrology in colors. There is awe upon you as you enter and look up. The choir, as usual in the Spanish cathedrals, has been pushed forward nearly to the centre, and grievously interrupts the calm and magnificent flow of the spaces. There are one hundred and seventeen stalls in it, beautifully carved, surmounted by a sort of cornice of turrets and statuettes. The lectern is very rich, and there are many mass books, admirable for their miniatures. What shame these noble organs, mellowed by the harmonies of hundreds of years, cast on our wretched little *vox-humana* boxes with their feverish squeak! A good organ, like a good violin, improves with age, and gathers about it an intensity of sweetness which seems to proceed from constant use.

In the centre of the nave lies the memorial slab of Ferdinand Columbus, son of the great navigator, with the well-known inscription: —

> 'A Castilla y á Leon
> Nuevo mundo dió Colon.'

The High Chapel contains a tabernacle for the elements, of silver gilt, unique in its kind. The usual reliquary contains the usual Virgin Mary, — or what are called relics of her. The Chapel Royal glitters with gold, silver, bronze, and crystal, and contains no end of sceptred ashes. The sword of the Holy King Ferdinand is kept here: quick-footed lads dart about with tapers, and take you here and there in this pantheon of decayed notabilities, — kings, queens, coffins, and banners. You are always looking for something, and never see it; then you are summoned out; then you pay. Such is the Chapel Royal, in brief. The sacristan would go on till doomsday, till your very soul chattered kings and queens, if you would let him. Not that he or any of his tribe know the slightest of Spanish history: it is a sort of idiotic talk, which perpetuates itself in European cathedrals, as much a part of the whole as the petrified patriarchs and prophets that grin around. If every one of the cicerones could be safely urned and coffined, — here especially in Seville, where they pounce upon you from behind every pillar, — the relief of the traveler would certainly be great.

Clouds, angels, thrones, and saints people the huge canvases that light up the obscurity of many of the chapels, the most interesting of which is the Chapel of the Baptistery, containing the most lovely Saint Anthony of Murillo. On Guy Fawkes' Day, 1874, a thief cut out the exquisite figure of the saint, who is represented on his knees, gazing in ecstasy on a vision of angels. Some months after, it was purchased in New York by a picture-dealer for two hundred and fifty dollars and handed over to the Spanish consul. It is now again in place, so perfectly restored that no one would ever fancy that it had gone on so fantastic a journey. 'Near him is a bunch of lilies, placed in a vase, and so true to nature, that birds (perhaps the doves we had noticed flying among the arches) are said to have come and pecked at them.'[1]

An idea of the wealth of this cathedral may be gathered from a few statistics concerning it.[1]

[1] Tollemache, *Spanish Towns and Spanish Pictures*, p. 182.
[1] De Amicis, *Spagna*, pp. 336, 337.

Twenty thousand pounds of wax tapers were annually consumed in its illumination; every day five hundred masses were said at its eighty altars; and eighteen thousand quarts of wine were used in the sacraments. The canons were served like kings, and drove to church in splendid carriages drawn by prancing horses; while they celebrated mass, clerks fanned them with jeweled fans,—a privilege that has been preserved down to the present time; and the pomp of the ceremonies was little, if at all, behind that of the Holy City itself.

The most singular thing about the whole foundation, however, is the sacred *Dance of the Six*, which takes place in the church every evening about dark, for a week, during the *Corpus Domini* feast. The church is dark; only the High Chapel is lighted; a throng of women on their knees crowd the space between the chapel and the choir. Priests sit on each side of the altar; on the steps in front a carpet is spread; two files of boys, from ten to twelve years old, clad like Spanish cavaliers of the Middle Ages, with plumed caps and white trousers, are drawn up before the altar, one behind the other. At a signal given by the priest, mysterious music of violins floats softly along the gigantic aisles and sends a thrill through the profound stillness of the church, and the two files of boys move in a quadrille step, divide, interlace, fall apart, unite again, with a thousand graceful turns; then suddenly the whole band break out into a gentle and harmonious chant, reverberating through the air like a choir of angels; then they dance again, accompanied by drums and chants. It is impossible to describe the effect of this strange ceremony, — the silence, mystery, and melody of this dance. Two centuries ago, says the account,[1] an archbishop of Seville tried to stop what he considered a piece of irreverence; but a tumult arose: the people clamored; the canons roared; the archbishop appealed to the pope. The pope, full of curiosity, desired to witness the dance with his own eyes, in order to judge of its impropriety. The boys, clad as cavaliers, were conducted to Rome, received at the Vatican, and made to dance and sing before his holiness. The pope laughed, refused his disapprobation, and decreed that the boys should continue the ceremony until the costumes they wore should be worn out; after which the ceremony should be considered abolished. Archbishop and canons doubtless laughed too, for they annually renewed a part of the garments which, as a matter of course, never wore out, and never will.

There is a sacristy full of the inimitable canvases of Murillo, where the painter's genius

[1] De Amicis, *Spagna*, p. 338.

breathes on wall and altar with a true Andalusian pomp. Jewels without number in gold, silver, and precious stones, of rare workmanship and great age, are treasured here; the rich vestments belonging to the clergy are kept in chests of drawers; and various much reverenced relics are now and then displayed to the faithful. The circular chapter room, built in the Ionic and Doric styles, and full of fine works by Murillo, Céspedes, and Pachecho, is shown to one side. There is a sixteenth century monument in the church, before which one hundred and fourteen lamps (eighty-two of them silver) and four hundred and fifty-three tapers burn on special occasions, making a marvelous scene. The dainty jeweler's work, the rare Flemish glass, the profusion of carving and statuary, the beautiful retablos, and the vast proportions of this cathedral make it perhaps the most elaborate church ever built, the most harmonious and impressive pile in Spain. A single one of the church articles is enriched with twelve hundred diamonds. The wealth of ages has poured into its precincts, and all has been received and welcomed. If there is nothing here to make one's 'very feet move metrically,' as old Fuller says of Westminster Abbey, there is much that throws a profound spell over the imagination, and stirs the deepest and sweetest channels of the heart. A beautiful court-yard, with Arabic portal, and a group of mighty orange-trees, opens from the cathedral door, and admits you to the delightful sunlight and perfume, amid which the Giralda lifts its pinnacle in gray and gold. It is a work — a muezzin-tower — of the Arabs. What can one liken it to except to a gigantic spike of golden wheat flashing into the air for twenty-five miles around? There are lovely arabesques, balconies, and frescoes outside: a cluster of superb bells hangs in the belfry, to which you ascend partly by inclined planes, partly by steps, — and the first bell-clock put up in Spain is there. A man on horseback might ride almost to the top. Faith, picturesquely on tiptoe, whirls with every change of wind from her perch on the bronze globe; hence the name *Giralda*, weather-cock.

'What keeps you here?' asked the sacristan of Murillo one day, whom he found time and again in absorbed contemplation before the Descent from the Cross, of Campaña. 'I am waiting till those holy men have finished their task,' said the painter, pointing to the figures of Joseph and Nicodemus, who are engaged in taking Christ down from the cross. Murillo's epitaph — '*Vive moriturus*' — is not quite so striking as Wren's in St. Paul's, — '*Si vis monumentum, circumspice*,' — but it is full of meaning. There is an old hospital in Seville which is enriched with the creations of his pencil: perhaps the finest Murillos in the world are in the Seville Museum, if we except the unrivaled collection at Madrid. I was taken to see the humble room where he died, and found — a bright group of Spanish women at work. We were received with grave courtesy, and a glance at the inscription commemorating his death explained to them the purpose of our visit. A pretty little square outside, all intense sunshine, acacia-trees, and seclusion, bears his name.

No little astonishment is created by one's now and then passing beneath the arches of a stupendous aqueduct which gallops over a part of the town rough-shod, and has been doing so since the time of the Romans. To see one of those great vanishing lines of arches tapering off into the distance, and jumping one house after another as they approach a town, is one of the most picturesque sights in the world. What exquisite bits of looped sunlight and landscape flash through the arches of Nero's aqueduct at Rome! and how the grand lines of the aqueduct of Alexander Severus lift themselves over the tawny shoulders of the pagna, and form a long-seried gallery of lovely pictures! Here at Seville the town itself seems puny in the presence of this great work, as it does still more at the thought that Trajan, Hadrian, and Theodosius came from a little village in the neighborhood. It is hard to think that this massive yellow structure has a silver torrent at its heart, — an inextinguishable column, driven by its own silvery force into the very heart of the old town, — a pure flood of precious water distilled out of these maroon hills, and affording never-failing refreshment to the townspeople. One would like to know how many of the four-and-twenty thousand Spanish proverbs collected by Juan de Yriate apply to water.

A fine bridge crosses the Guadalquivir at Seville, and from the number of donkeys that make it a thoroughfare, the famous Pons Asinorum would be no inapplicable name. It connects Seville with Triana (a corruption of Trajana), its gypsy quarter. Here, if anywhere, would be the place to find out whether it is true that the gypsy muleteers pour quicksilver down the ears of their donkeys to quicken their pace! I am sure, if I had known the fact at the time, I should have laid in a supply of the article. The dogged determination of these beasts has filled the Spanish language with picturesque oaths, and enriched it with many a saw. Couplets innumerable celebrate the virtues and vices of the faithful *burro*, friend in life, and companion in death of the wandering peddler. It is the only thing in Spain that seems to have ears, — for surely waiters and chambermaids have none. The squalor of Triana and the long columns of twinkling asses' ears did not leave a favorable impression; but the cheerful beauty of the river, with its sail-boats and steamships, the animated quai, the long reaches of glassy water, and the great heaps of juicy *sandias*, — the water-melon of Andalusia, — gave an element of charm, to counteract the unfavorable impression.

One of the funniest of experiences is to take a turn through the vast tobacco manufactory of Seville. The building is nearly as long as the Great Eastern, and is a hundred feet broader than St. Peter's. Here is the source and centre of the everlasting fumes of Spain; five thousand women are at the bottom of it, who work here, one might say, day and night, to keep their lords and masters in something to do. They are paid by the number of cigars and cigarettes they make, and form a very distinct guild in themselves, — piquant, saucy, sparkling-eyed creatures, in all stages of dress and undress (the weather was hot). De Amicis, in his book on Spain,[1] gives a charming account — for Italian readers — of his visit to the factory. What struck me most was the nastiness of the whole thing, — women, tobacco, babies, paste, lunch-baskets, cast-off clothes, perspiration, and impurity of every sort mixed in inextricable confusion. It made no difference whether they were married or not, — all the

[1] De Amicis, *Spagna*. Firenze, 1878.

women seemed to have babies: all rocked them with their feet, and made cigars at the same time. The walls were lined with unmentionable garments, hung up till their owners became their occupants later in the evening, when they depart peacefully to their homes. It really requires a great deal of moral and physical courage to walk through this gallery of temptations. A tobaccophobe is safe; but woe to the man that follows Charles Lamb. If his imagination be active, let him keep out of this International Exhibition of low-necks and short sleeves. The great building is as strong as a fortress; there are no less than twenty-eight courts within it; and it has stood a siege. Tobacco manufacture is two hundred and fifty years old in Seville: even while the very Pilgrim Fathers were starting on their western mission the abandoned Sevillians were beginning to manufacture the weed. One of these nimble-fingered women can, I was told, make a hundred (?) packs of cigarettes in a day. They smoke with the utmost *sang froid*, and there is a great ebb and flow of conversation all the time. Many were asleep, resting their heads on their naked arms, and supporting these on the paste-beslimed tables in front of them. The babies were as guilelessly unclad as any cherub of Correggio.

The great literary glory of Seville is, or was

a few years ago, a lady. Cæcilia Böhl, author of the numerous novels which pass under the name *Fernan Caballero*, is justly celebrated. Her books have been translated into nearly all the languages of Europe, and are known in this country. They are admirable pictures of Andalusian manners, and abound in faithful description, warmth of feeling, grace, and intense religious fervor. There is very great beauty in the sweet spirit of Christian charity which pervades all her works, and it has been well said that Fernan Caballero would die for her faith with the strength and serenity of Loyola. Augustus Hare[1] pays a graceful tribute to 'the inexhaustible wealth of beautiful word-pictures which may be enjoyed in the stories of Fernan Caballero, which collect so much, and reveal so much, and teach so much, that it is scarcely possible sufficiently to express one's obligation to them.' Many of her stories have exquisite pathos: they are invaluable to the student of folk-lore, village superstitions, and quaint observances of the olden time. There are stories of hers in which the conversation for whole pages is carried on in proverbs, proverbs so intimately interwoven with the very woof of Spanish life that they cannot be got rid of, and fall every moment from the lips of the people, so that one can believe — if one cannot read — the

[1] *Wanderings in Spain.* London, 1873.

three epistles of Blasco de Garay, which are said to be composed of a continuous narrative of one thousand proverbs. Her special study has been to illustrate every phase and aspect of popular life and manners: her industry in gathering and utilizing material has been unexampled: the Grimms themselves could hardly excel her in this respect. She repels with indignation, in one of her prefaces,[1] the notion that the homely custom and immemorial habit of a people are matters to be held in contempt. She delights in collecting the beautiful Christmas customs and carols of her country, the couplets and refrains, the catches and snatches of popular poetry that have gathered about the holy festivals of the Church: and all these are skillfully introduced into her stories, and made to yield a rich pleasure to the reader. 'What charming pictures,' she says, ' might we have now of Gallicia with its heavenly scenery, its handsome race, and its picturesque costume, now of Valencia the garden, and its light and airy inhabitants; of grave and solemn Señora Castile; of Catalonia, Aragon, gay Navarre, — in a word, of all; for what province is there that is devoid of beauties, of peculiar physiognomy, of special character and traditions, that its children do not love, that its poets do not feel

[1] *Cuadros de los Costumbres Populares Andaluces.* Sevilla, 1852.

and sing of?' She sets to work, therefore, with a love that is real genius, to do what she can toward making her countrymen know their own country, and indirectly she has done a great service to foreigners. In Seville, she is venerated as a saint. She was, I believe, born there, married very young, and was three times a widow. Her last husband was Spanish ambassador to London: he committed suicide, I think, and his wife mourned for him as long as she lived. When Amicis visited her she was nearly seventy, and enjoyed a reputation for much beauty. Her father, a man of great culture and benevolence, — to which she pays a feeling tribute in one of her books, — instructed her in various languages: she was said to be a profound Latin scholar, and spoke Italian, German, and French to perfection. She ceased to write in her old age, though tempted by very large offers. An insatiable reader, still she was always knitting or embroidering, for she made it a ruling principle of her life that nothing should interfere with her ordinary duties. Without children, she lived in great seclusion, and gave up the greater part of her house to an indigent family, while much of her means was spent in alms. A curious trait of her character was her devotion to animals: she had a houseful of canaries, cats, and dogs; and her sensibility was so great that she could not bear to ride in a carriage for fear she might see a blow given to the horse. At one time she was in high favor with the Montpensiers, who treated her with distinction: the most honorable families in Seville vied with each other in showing her attention; but toward the end of her life she lived entirely with her books, and a few female friends.[1]

It speaks well for the place that there are so many establishments for public instruction and so many scientific and literary societies. There is a university of Seville which, after many vicissitudes, survives creditably to-day, and furnishes instruction in numerous branches. An institution for secondary instruction is situated in Love of God Street, not to mention others of less note. There are numerous archives belonging to the mayoralty, the captain-generalcy, the cathedral chapter, and the palaces of the ancient nobility, which are of great interest and value. The magnificent archives of the Indies, overflowing with documents pertaining to the discoveries and conquests of Columbus, Cortés, Pizarro, Magellan, and others, have been concentrated here in the Lonja or exchange. The jewel of the collection is a petition in the handwriting of Cervantes praying the king to appoint him to one of four vacancies which had occurred at the time.

Seville is very rich in libraries too, both public

---

[1] Vid. De Amicis, *Spagna*, p. 364.

and private. There are fifteen besides the famous Columbine Library, the University Library, and the remarkable private collection of Señor de Alava. The son of the great Columbus was a sort of Pestalozzi in his way; he had a passion for founding academies, libraries, and schools, which would have done immense good had he lived to carry out his plans. At his death he bequeathed his twenty thousand volumes to the cathedral, and they now rest under the shadow of the Giralda tower, that work of grace planned by Gaver, the inventor of algebra. The beautiful face of the old navigator, more like a saint's than a sailor's,—hangs on the wall and casts a sweet and serious tenderness over the ancient library. Curious old vellum-bound books, parchments, illuminated works, and rare manuscripts, peer out from behind the glass doors where they repose in everlasting sleep, in superb mahogany and cedar-lined cradles. What a curious light does his epitaph throw on Fernando Columbus's character! The Latin distichs read as follows: 'What availeth my having bathed the whole universe in my sweat, having traversed three times the New World discovered by my father, having embellished the shores of the tranquil Bætis and preferred my simple tastes to wealth, to gather around thee the divinities of Castaly's Fount and offer thee the treasures accumulated of old by

Ptolemy; if thou, passing this stone in silence, givest not even a salutation to my father nor a fleeting remembrance to me?'

Nowhere, however, is that mysterious perfume of the East which Victor Hugo has translated into Les Orientales, more potently felt than in the Alcázar of Seville. Even Hans Andersen,[1] who was so absorbed in versifying and balladizing on what he saw in Spain that he saw nothing, breaks off his lyrical intermezzos to describe this sparkling palace of the houris. Here, if anywhere, the sun-like eyes, the dawn-like smile, and the paradise of love, ascribed by an old Spanish verse to the women of Malaga, —

> 'Una muger malagueña
> Tiene en sus ojos un sol,
> En su sonrisa la aurora
> Y un paraiso en su amor,' —

might be imagined peeping through the faint glooms of this many-chambered palace. In some respects it is more beautiful than the Alhambra and quite as ancient, but the tender melancholy of the Granada palace is missed in this most gorgeous structure. For hundreds of years it was worked on by Moorish and Spanish kings, each adding a court or a wall or a tower, until it stood forth a miracle of beauty and voluptuousness. Its walls sing with colors, run wild with intricate

[1] Hans Andersen, *I Spanien.* Kjöbenhavn, 1878.

Moorish ornamentation. One of its courts — the Court of Damsels — is, perhaps, the most exquisite thing in Spain. Intense sunlight plays upon its fifty marble columns, its trophies and escutcheons, its lovely cabinets, *azulejo*-tiles and mosaics: intense silence reigns amid the pillars, light and silent as an exhalation. The whole fantastic tradition of Moorish architecture seems here followed out to its utmost strangeness: no minarets, no fountains, no pomegranate belfries upheld by pillarets dainty as spun glass: simply a cloister, rimmed in on all sides by delicious arches, with pillars dropping like cobwebs to the ground; then another story built on this, with pilasters, pointed Byzantine leaves, capricious combination of Arabic, Gothic, and plate work, infinitely delicate in execution. The airiest *alhamies* are perceived on one side, with their minutely worked blinds and translucent spaces, and on another there are communications with the seraglio. The lucent, limpid marble of many of the palace floors, — the tiled floors of others, — the elegance of the curves, the richness of the decoration, the blaze of color and gold kindled over these half-dawning walls, — no language can describe. Here, too, there is a Hall of Ambassadors, filled with delicate columns and arches, Arabic curves, friezes, windows in beautiful series, geometric designs, walls luxuriously illumined with colors and gold, open balconies: over all there is a spherical cupola, with decorations in star-work, designed to be filled with painted glass, and to stain the white or golden light a thousand dyes, as it fell on the groups below. Cufic inscriptions and Koranic verses ribbon the walls, and there is great intricacy of interlaced leaves, pine-cones, palms, and shells, through which, like long delicate serpents, twine fantastic, geometric threads; then these gather about a portal or a window, and wreathe and twine and crinkle into a delightful frame-work. The purest fancy displays itself everywhere in this building. The Court of the Muñecas is one of the loveliest examples of Moslem art, — an oblong, filled with great and small arches, as slender-curved as the spiral of a shell. Over the whole palace the ornamentation forms a dissolving view: constant transformations take place, — Protean combinations and re-combinations; human toil pervaded by dreams and dainty imaginings, wavelets of strange influences, half rhythms in ductile stone, precious recollections of half evolved reveries, — form the strange aliment of these stranger architects. The whole thing is an emblem, an allegory, a piece of luminous soothsaying by the artists of the East, 'a silence between the flute and the drum' into which Moorish fancy has crept, filling the whole with Koranic passion and similitude. The palace is a confused symbolism, a tangled ratiocination in color and stone, a Dantesque legend interpreted by infidels. The very wealth of mosaics, inscriptions, columns, capitals, tile-work, has, like the overflowing notes of some commentator, overlaid and confused the text. The beautiful simplicity of the Egyytian, Syrian, and Persian palace-structures has here been invaded by a torrent of imagery: the Alcázar is a carved and painted metaphor. To me, it is delightful to walk in, whatever it may be to specialists of purer taste. Secret, sensuous Araby — desire in its labyrinthine windings — pleasure near to tears — pain embalmed in perfect phrases — grace that coils about life like a passion-flower, and gives the last light to its dying eyes: such is the Alcázar.

I think there is nothing at Granada quite so lovely as the Alcázar garden: to walk in it is to walk in other centuries. Here you may see in perfection box and myrtle cut into coats of arms, initials, imperial eagles, *fleur-de-lis*, crowns, and maps; lemon, jasmine, rose-bays, and orange clustering and clustered: a garden, the whole of whose graveled walks, by an admirable system of water-works, can be put under water, when up spring, as if by magic, isles of honeysuckle and magnolia, splendid clumps of daphne, water-girt, tiny Ithacas and Islands of the Blest, amid the surrounding bloom. Great urns lift their basins out of the green; rollicking fountains play; flakes of lemon-blossom snow the ground; and every sweet-smelling herb exhales under this potent heat and moisture.

All this beauty, however, is stained with blood; a Newgate Calendar might almost be compiled out of the archives of the Alcázar. But I will not go into the amours and ferocities of Don Pedro the Cruel and the Doña Padilla: the task would be irksome. Doña Padilla — an ancestress of Bloody Mary — lies in the neighboring cathedral, and nothing remains of her but her gentle memory and beautiful eyes. Don Pedro is the ogre of Spanish annals, and peeps out of many a legend with the lineaments of Blue Beard. The singular beauty with which such wretches knew how to surround themselves, — the palaces, gardens, and seraglios in which they knew how to enshrine their voluptuousness, — the elegance and harmony of everything to which they laid their hand, — form a chapter of curiosities not yet explained by the student of psychology.

Another visit of great interest may be paid to the House of Pilate, — a structure of the sixteenth century, built by the Marquises of Tarifa, in imitation of the imaginary house of Pilate at Jerusalem. Imaginary or not, nothing could be more rich than this mass of wavy sculpture, fringed arabesques, painted glass, and precious marbles. The principal court, in its dazzling whiteness and daintiness, is like a crystallization of frost, and nothing can surpass the loveliness of the transformations it undergoes as you look on the airy Saracenic architecture through the many-colored glass of the rooms contiguous. A grand staircase, full of emblems, traceries, and legends, crowned by a half orange dome, admits you to the apartments above: but the whole is one of those low, gorgeous, Oriental piles, whose chief luxury is in their ground-floor apartments; and whose spaciousness, absence of toilsome ascents, and proximity to gardens, more perfectly reveal the poetry and lassitude of the East than the most heaven-climbing Arabian towers. Over the whole palace there is the finish of a Pompadour fan: magnifying-glasses are almost necessary to trace out the flowing continuity of ornamentation which has passed over these walls. It is a legend of the Holy Land, beautified by the most reverent Spanish art.

Famous stories, too, are told of the magnificence of its owners, the poets and painters they entertained, and the discussions in art and science which took place there in Cervantes' time. It would be hard to find a better type of the semi-oriental Andalusian life than the Casa de Pilatos.

I cannot enter into descriptions of the many fine palaces belonging to wealthy noblemen; of San Telmo; of the Tower of Gold (where the first gold brought from America was deposited) and the Tower of Silver; of the environs of Seville; the gay and fashionable streets; the gates of the city; the great bull-ring; the theatres, private collections, and gypsy balls. The *Street of Serpents* is Seville epitomized, — hung with awnings, full of bright shops, crowded with silent women and sauntering men, — short and vivid as Andalusian life itself, and with an intensity of local coloring such as hardly any other street in the town possesses. Since the thirteenth century Seville has been celebrated for its fairs, its religious pilgrimages, its brotherhoods and processions, and its numerous vigils. Holy Week here is like one of the vast canvases of the Doge's Palace reanimated, and many curious customs accompany the religious celebrations of that week: the door of the Giralda tower on Palm Sunday is struck with a cross to commemorate Christ's opening of the doors of heaven; a veil is rent amid loud thunders on Holy Wednesday; the burial of Christ takes place in magnificent pomp; there is blessing of baptismal fonts, Paschal tapers, oil, etc.

A trait rather characteristic of the place is that one of the principal theatres is built on the

site of the Hospital of the Holy Ghost. The
O-shaped bull-ring — a graded amphitheatre
within — has fourteen thousand seats, and the
people remark with pride that the royal person-
ages who have assisted at *funcciones* here were
Charles IV., Ferdinand VII., the Dukes of Montpensier, Isabel II. (said to be a passionate lover
of bull-fighting), and Alfonso XII.

A scrap from the Danish of Hans Andersen [1]
will add another association to Seville — the Legend of Don Juan : 'Don Juan Tenorio,' says the
legend, 'was a young, life-loving Seville noble-
man, proud, intellectual, and frank to excess ;
he seduced the daughter of the commandant,
killed the father, and sank into an abyss of un-
godliness.' Another Spanish legend names him
Don Juan de Maraña, and calls him one of the
wealthiest noblemen of Seville, who led a gay,
wild life, passed his nights in bacchanalian or-
gies, and, in his excessive wantonness, even bade
the Giralda weather-cock (the figure of Faith)
come down from the tower and visit him one
night, and she moved her mighty copper wings,
that whistled in the air, and came down with
heavy feet, like those which were afterward given
the marble commandant. But one midnight
when he was going home through the desolate,
lonesome streets, he heard music all of a sud-

[1] *I Spanien*, p. 166.

den, long-drawn wailing tones; he saw shine of torches; a mighty funeral procession approached; a corpse lay in silver and silk on the open bier. 'Who is being buried to-night?' asked he, and the answer rang: 'Don Juan de Maraña!' The shroud was lifted aside — and Don Juan saw his own form dead and stark on the bier. A deadly fear shot through him, he fainted, and the next day he gave all his wealth to the monastery of La Caridad, entered the order himself, and became one of its most exemplary members.

'The Spanish poet Tirso de Molina was the first who dramatized the legend and wrote The Seducer of Seville, or the Stone Guest. The name of Don Juan Tenorio was retained though the family was still living. The piece called forth many imitators in France and Italy, but Molière gave it the finishing touch; then it was re-written as a text for Mozart's Don Giovanni, whose immortal music carries the legend of Don Juan down the ages and generations. Already in Tirso we see the dramatic conclusion as we now know it. The commandant's marble form comes from the grave; knocking is heard; the servant hesitates to open the door; Don Juan seizes a silver lamp and goes to the door himself and lights the Stone Guest in, who, with heavy marble tread enters the dining-room. The corpse is regaled with ice, merry songs and profane questions about the other world. On his departure he invites Don Juan the next night to supper in the mortuary chapel. At the precise hour Don Juan meets his frightful host; a Satanic meal has been prepared, — " scorpions and serpents;" "the wine is gall." The Stone Guest's hand-shake initiates the seducer into the flames of hell. Don Juan sinks down into the earth with the corpse. The horrified servant creeps on all fours to the foreground of the stage, where he breaks out : " Great God !"' etc.

In the La Caridad Church, where Don Juan Tenorio once intoned pious hymns with the other monks and prayed for his own oppressed soul, his picture is seen on the wall ; passion and penitence speak from every feature ; a red cross glitters on his black habit. Under his picture hangs the sword with which he slew the commandant Don Gonzalo.

Perhaps the only addition to be made to this account is that Hans Andersen could never have read Molière's Festin de Pierre ; a more stupid and soulless composition it would be difficult to find.

Another interesting association admits you to another glimpse of musical life :

> 'Numero quindici
> A mano manca !'

This is the number of the Barber of Seville, whom Rossini has so delightfully embalmed and whose gayety is so associated with the rippling harmonies of Mozart's Figaro. Beaumarchais' verse, too, gives him to us genially, and there is no lack of allusion elsewhere in literature. Over the door may be seen the brass basin, with a large slice cut out on one side for the thumb, which is the sign of the Spanish and Portuguese barbers, apropos of whom John Latouche tells a good story:[1] 'The Portuguese, like the Spaniard, is never full dressed unless he is well shaved, and, unlike the celebrated De Cossé, Duke of Brissac, he never shaves himself; and, in truth, I would not undertake to say that the admirable motive which drove the aforesaid peer to his daily task would, under any circumstances of high rank or idleness, have similar sway with the lazy Peninsula. "Timoleon de Cossé," the French noble was often heard to soliloquize of a morning, with the open razor in his hand: "God has made thee a gentleman, and the king has made thee a duke. It is, nevertheless, right and fit that thou shouldst have something to do; therefore thou shalt shave thyself."'

The reader will excuse me from attempting an analysis of the Murillo gallery in Seville. A painter reduced to his chemical elements is no

---

[1] *Travels in Portugal.* London, 1878.

part of my plan, and nothing can be drearier than the usual dish of art criticism found in books of travel. I shall be original, therefore, in leaving out this well-thumbed gallery and refer the reader himself to the place. Before each picture there sits a worshiping and adoring artist engaged in translating into his own daub the rare tints and tenderness of the originals. There they sit, day after day, hoping that inspiration will come and brush its ethereal wings across their palettes; hopeless Hindoos clasping the sacred lotus-flower till their arm withers to a stick. No more melancholy exhibition is to be found than a peep over the shoulder of the artist who is engaged in the work of form and color translation. In the various galleries of Europe you see the divinest masterpieces in all imaginable states of composition and decomposition as you move from one copyist to another and glance from their easels to the picture on the wall. Here in Seville smoking goes on gayly in the picture-rooms — which accounts probably for the dinginess of the copies made. A very striking similarity exists between Murillo's female types and the Spanish women of to-day. The only difference is in the golden hair now somewhat rare in the Peninsula, but so abundantly introduced by the painter into his pictures. The fine Andalusian type — the type of aquiline noses, small limbs, large, lambent black eyes, hair like Milton's 'raven down of darkness,' and serpent-like grace in the women, — smiles from his canvases quite unchanged and might be verified any night at the Zarzuela. Murillo was a conscientious detail worker, in spite of the depreciation now cast upon him as a poor draughtsman. I once heard an artist say that he always felt as if Murillo's women had all sorts of diseases!

To show the painter's fidelity to details, the following instance — interwoven by Fernan Caballero into one of her stories [1] — may be given. Murillo painted a picture of the patron saints of Seville, Santas Justa and Rufina, who were earthenware-makers. At their feet lie specimens of their wares so perfectly painted that they resemble in every stroke the earthenware of to-day.

The immutability of earthenware types is remarkably illustrated by the present shapes found in the great Triana manufactory of Seville. The objects made to-day are exactly like those of three hundred years ago as seen in Murillo's picture. There is historic evidence to prove that the manufactory had existed for thirteen hundred years before his time, and is far older than the famous manufactories of Sévres, Saxony, St. Petersburg, La Granja, Delft, and Chelsea. So

[1] *El Ex Voto*, p. 263.

that there is truth as well as humor in the anecdote of Marshal Soult, who, on his entry into Seville, passing before a heap of what the Spanish call 'extremely domestic products of the Triana works,' said, in imitation of the Little Corporal: 'Soldiers of France! sixteen centuries are looking down at you!'

My stay at Seville was considerably enlivened by a guide who, far more voluble with legs than with tongue, walked me all over the place, lost himself and me several times in the tangle of streets, plunged into churches regardless of siesta-time, and emerged at palaces and cathedrals in a manner (topographically) astounding. I see the poor fellow now, dissolved in perspiration, which seemed to unglue the terminations of his French verbs and nouns, trying in a sort of wild waddle, to guide his employer, wiping his streaming countenance, darting into little Spanish drinking-shops for a *gaziosa*, or dropping his mouth benignantly to a pump-spigot, and letting the cool stream dart (apparently) down to the very tips of his toes. He was that singular phenomenon, a silent guide. He volunteered little information and maintained a Pythagorean reticence, not even saying 'beans' once. He was gray all over, and wore a threadbare gray suit whose shabby gentility had a touch of pathos in it. A shovel-hat surmounted a head — or rather,

I should say, a cheek — in which two little gray eyes blinked out at the passing world, and I think he twirled a cane and had a pair of toes that turned most delightfully inward.

With this apparition at my heels I went the rounds of Seville, now in a carriage and now a-foot, pursued rather than led by my indefatigable mentor, whose feet were the only part of him that expatiated, and who might have been under the vow of eternal silence for all evidence that he gave to the contrary. In the cathedral his presence saved me from the English sparrows that dart out from behind every pillar and wage baleful war on the Peregrines of that nationality. A kick is the only conjury to which some of them will yield. The raised eye-brow, or the sign of the Evil Eye, said to be so efficacious in Italy, are of no avail with the hankering hidalgo. As it was, we flitted from chapel to chapel, and crypt to choir, 'sweet as summer,' undisturbed by the acrimonious tongues of the church guides. The fair and mighty twilight of that great cathedral will dwell with me, associated with the lifted lodestone of its noble tower, the centuried sunlight of the Court of Oranges, the great Mudejar Gate, and the pealing sweetness of the high-hung bells.

X.

> Wir kommen erst aus Spanien zurück,
> Dem schönen Land des Weins und der Gesänge.
> *Faust*, 2206.

A PEEP into old Cordova is not the least agreeable of one's experiences among the Spanish cities. Age, mellowness, tranquillity are its characteristics; and for all the life it shows it might in Castelar's phrase, be compared to one of those 'Homeric battles where all the combatants, crowned with laurel, have died on their chiseled shields.' The town, crowned with laurel, as it doubtless is, is long since dead, and though there are no chiseled shields to protect or support it in its desolation, there are two or three relics from the general wreck which are most worthy of a glance.

Nowhere is Andalusian life seen on a more *petite* scale. Cordova is a honey-comb of the tiniest habitations, minute in every sense. Imagine a huge bride-cake cut into rings, with an endless meander of intersecting streets and alleys: each street and alley filled with miniature dwellings, low, flat, whitewashed, and windowless; each plazuela, a hive of human beings issuing from these dwellings; each dwelling a sort of raindrop under a microscope, seething with animalcule life; and over the whole, such icing as an Andalusian sun can give as it ricochets from all this whitened surface; such is Cordova. If you are interested in such matters, you may see the women with toothpicks in their mouths all day long, or eating fish with their fingers, or cultivating the natural affections and family life, for which the Spanish women are so celebrated, or showing that righteous abhorrence of 'select boarding-schools' exhibited so comically throughout the Peninsula. As for intrusting their children to such places, immediate invocation to Heaven and all its saints would take place the moment it might be mentioned. Cordova is just the place, however, to see the beautiful small charities in which the Spaniards abound, how they help each other and stand by each other in weal and woe; what great respect they have for individuals, whatever imprecations they may call down upon them collectively in times of excitement and revolution; their 'incapacity for either inflicting or bearing an insult;' their great good humor and gentleness in crowds; and the magnanimity, candor, and docility that lurk beneath their ferocious gesticulation. Vanity is the national vice, and even here, in slumberous

Cordova, where one would think the sun had drunk it all up, its smoldering fires may be kicked open by any clumsy foot.

It is easy to believe the Arab poet who called Cordova the 'pearl of the West,' a city whose renown was like that of Bagdad and to which poets, scholars, enthusiasts, and pilgrims flocked in thousands to drink knowledge of its immense libraries, to worship in its three thousand mosques, to wander through its thirty districts, and to pay court to the myrmidons of its splendid khalifate. It was a source of memories and poesies to the poets of the East. Affluence, knowledge, culture were spread among the three thousand villages of the province. There was a busy and voluptuous multitude at work on its palaces and in its places of amusement. It was the third among the Andalusian cities which for so many centuries after the treachery of Count Julian governed the best part of the peninsula in so regal a way, and extorted, even from the intensely patriotic authors of the Romancero del Cid, frequent tributes of praise and acknowledgment. One half detests Seneca for making but a solitary mention, in all his voluminous works, of his birthplace. The poet of the Pharsalia was from Cordova; and a constant stream of rabbinical and Aristotelian philosophers, from Averroës and Maimonides on, flowed from its schools.

The Guadalquivir has a noble breadth at Cordova, so that there is little difficulty in believing the tale of nearly a thousand baths that formerly existed at the place; while the shocking illiteracy of the present population is a sad commentary on the hundreds of thousands of volumes that once filled its libraries. A solitary decent inn does duty for the six hundred khans of the olden times, and the abounding public schools where the theology, history, and poetry of the Arabians were expounded by poetic and impassioned teachers, have dwindled into a few wretched communal and parochial schools, richly flavored with an obsolete Catholicism. In Cordova you feel a strange geographical remoteness from the rest of Europe; at all events certain habitudes of mind are rather violently upset after a certain degree of intimacy with the Orientalism all around you. I never had the word *still* so impressively thundered at me as in Cordova: a word in which all the meditative tranquillity, all the reserve and reticence of the cautious and contemplative East are concentrated. It seems as if never a passion, much less a revolution, had ever entered these enchanted gates; nothing but a sigh, and that of the gentlest regret. 'Fire, sun, and health are the highest goods,' says the High Song in the Edda, in the code of rules it establishes for the wanderer, the guest, and the lover of home;

'one's own hearth is the best.' Each one of these pregnant blessings is written in light over the Cordovan doors. The town crouches between its hills, and only here and there ventures to send up a timid pinnacle in token of its conversion to the Christian religion. One verily believes half the people are still Mahometans at heart. Hence there would be no surprise in seeing the Berber magnate in our day making the pilgrimage of the great Mosque of Cordova, seven times, on his knees, beating his breast and weeping that his kindred had lost so fair a possession. The tone of the place is elegiac: 'great Pan is dead,' comes floating over the sea, and startles the sailors.

The approach to Cordova is in the familiar track of Cervantes: La Mancha, spiced with Quixotic recollections, is traversed by the railway —a province famed in spring for the vividness of its wayside flowers, and its great masses of convolvulus, blue-bells, poppies, and aloes.[1] The country is touched off inimitably in Doré's illustrations to Don Quixote, an artist who has drawn out into lines and shadows all the pregnant underplay of the book. The train stops at Argasamilla de Alba, the very place where the knight was born and died, and where Cervantes himself was arrested and imprisoned in a house said still to exist.

[1] Vid. Elwes, *Through Spain by Rail in* 1872.

On arriving at Cordova do not be shocked if you find yourself suddenly among quaintly named streets — 'Jesus Crucified Street,' for example, or if you find yourself lodging in the 'Street of Paradise;' it is as much to be expected as the 'gate of pardon' possessed by every church and through which anciently only the specially privileged could pass. It was a belief of the Moors that the paradise of the Korán hung over the Vega of Granada; one is tempted to believe that the other place hangs over the pebbly streets of Cordova. Spenser's

> 'Buskins he wore of costliest *cordwain*,'

brings to mind an ancient association of the place. In the word was perpetuated the name of Cordova itself as characteristic of one of its chief manufactures. Leather of specially excellent quality was called *cordwain* (cordouan), and to tan and prepare it the pomegranate was planted through the country and the bitter rind of the fruit used in the processes. The 'sweet cane from a far country,' the palm, and the damask rose followed in its train, and stand now as the most enduring memorial of Moorish sway; but certainly the fantastical repugnance[1] the Spaniards have to riding mares (!) is not of similar origin, for the Bedouin Arabs at least have no

---

[1] Vid. Thiéblin, *Spain and the Spaniards*, 1875.

such repugnance. The charm for the Evil Eye of the Moor is represented in nearly all Spanish churches by pictures of St. Christopher, whose image by some twist of memory or association is supposed to avert malign influence; hence almost the first thing you lay your eyes on in entering the Andalusian churches is a gigantic likeness of the Christ-bearing Saint. A glance at his figure insures safety for the day. The same tenacity of tradition was shown by the Jews of Toledo who built the rafters and beams of their great synagogue of the cedar of Lebanon, a wood said to be so bitter that no insect will touch it; hence the apparent indestructibility of structures into which it enters. For a somewhat similar reason Westminster Hall is called the 'cobwebless hall,' because, being made of Irish oak, spiders cannot live in it.

The merest walk in the venerable city of the Sierra Morena suffices to start a throng of such legends and souvenirs; the whole place plays with the thirty colors of Charlemagne's magic sword. If you like you may drop in at one of the low long coffee-houses and taste the real Manzanilla wine, — a canary-colored fluid, flavored with camomile blossoms; or in the same resting-place of dreamy Spaniards call for some of the delicious twists of bread from Alcalá de los Panaderos (of the bakers), a village not far off, where there are hundreds of flour-mills supplying half Spain with the finest wheat-flour in the world; or a peep into a sinister-looking old church may bring before you a sentence like this: 'Whoever speaks to women, either in the nave or the aisles, thereby puts himself in danger of excommunication;' or, if the sacristan insists on showing you the thorn from the crown of thorns which his church inevitably possesses, you may see that this thorn is generically and specifically different from the last sacristan's, and that both are absolutely different from the small-thorned *spina Christi* which is found near Jericho; or, if in the proper seasons, you may watch the boys spreading their limed cords to catch singing birds, with twittering decoys in wicker cages near by.

Externally, like Cádiz, Cordova 'lies white as new fallen snow, like a cluster of ivory palaces, between earth and sky.' Apparently, repelled by the mellow browns and grays of the Castilian and Catalonian cities, the people of the South have gone to the other extreme, and everything is blinding white. This love of whitewash is a distinct peculiarity of the Mediterranean countries. It has frequently proved of great harm to fine works of art, churches, and palaces in Andalusia, and occasionally the total wreck by it of some precious mosaic or fresco-series is proudly commemorated by an inscription and a date.

Hardly a whiff from any one of the seven hundred coal mines of the Peninsula seems ever to have blackened these unspotted walls, while the quicksilver, of which such marvels are told, has certainly transferred itself from the sluggish population of Spain to the mercurial neighbor over the mountains. Figures brown as the Andalusian sheep so well-known in song and story cast flickering shadows on the walls as they pass; and now and then these shadows mysteriously disappear into the recesses of a *venta*, where there are cooling drinks made of iced barley-water, ground-nut milk, milk of almonds, rice, or white of eggs and sugar whipped together, flavored, and dried; or there is shadow-play of quaint tasseled leather gaiters, of sheep-skin trousers, of long knives in waist-sashes, or of slouched sombreros and majestically draped *capas*, as the fancifully dressed herdsmen, or the solemn hidalgo pass by the mirror-like walls; or, if it be Piñata Sunday, the first Sunday in Lent, a glance into a window may reveal to you the pretty custom the Andalusians have of ending the Carnival, when a jar of sweetmeats is hung in the centre of the parlor and everybody, blindfolded, strikes at the suspended *dulces*, until after much ludicrous blundering and universal laughter, the jar comes down with a crash and there is a lively mêlée for its contents. Or perhaps these

shadow silhouettes may bring before you in pro
file a member of the legislative body who, in a
paper on the *recent* financial, social, and commer
cial condition of Spain, goes back to the age o
Julius Cæsar, when he supposes the Peninsula to
have contained seventy-eight millions of inhab
itants! Or perhaps another of these admirabl
reflectors, with a view to attracting wanderers o
uncertain nationality, may throw into relief
sign like this:[1] —

HERE RESTAURATION IS PRACTISED
BY MEANS OF
LARGE JOINTS
AFTER
THE ENGLISH PROCESS.

Or the tricksy light may sculpture in sharp sep
lines a wavering tableau of the *buñuelo*-man wh
stands just in the angle to let the sun catch hi
as he drops his little balls of sweetened doug
into boiling olive-oil and then draws them out
skillfully molded twists and rings. Or 'tho
exquisitely fine blades, which are required for op
erations on the human frame,' described by M
caulay, may dance to and fro in the shadow and
operate but too effectively on the human frame.
In short, what is there which the polished walls
of Cordova may not reflect, as one side of the
street lies in puissant illumination, and the other
sleeps in ambuscaded twilight? One sees that

---

[1] Byrne, *Cosas de España*, 1866.

the calcareous soil of Spain, so friendly to the grape, so noxious to the lungs, in its wind-blown ubiquity, is here put to very effective use, and made to yield a white torment to the eyes. Overcome by the general dazzlement, or fleeing from the ammoniated atmosphere universal in the Spanish cities, you 'walk into a *libreria* and ask to see the latest publications. The *librero* receives you with a stare, and when you have repeated your question, if he be particularly brisk that day, he lifts his still sleepy eyes, and, without rising, or removing the everlasting cigar from his lips, slowly and gravely points to a copy of *Don Quixote!* You shake your head, and try to explain that you want something of more recent date, when he rouses himself the second time, and, inclining his head in the opposite direction, he indicates a *Gil Blas!*'

The sun-burnt faces of the Cordovese bear little evidence of the Andalusian custom practiced by the village children who, on Midsummer Eve, go out to gather field flowers, with which they make a decoction to bathe their faces 'para estar sanos todo el año;' nor is the piety of modern times seen to rival that of ancient, when such numberless votive lamps hung in such numberless niches at street-corners and before house-doors that no other lighting was required at night by the good Sevillanos. Piety and cleanliness are associated by the Koranic Moor, but not by the Biblical Spaniard.

I lay in **Paradise** Street the night of my arrival, in a hotel paved with white marble, along which every murmur rang as in a whispering gallery. A fountain in a marble court-yard tinkled garrulously through the night; and wherever there was light it fell in muffled sheets through curtains or awnings, like a wasp deprived of its sting. On one side was a reading-room comfortably cushioned; on another the long dining-room with tables covered with glass and vases of fruit and flowers long-drawn out; and from the dining-room we could look into the kitchen, with its bright coppers and brasses, white-capped cook, and pleasant cheerfulness. I cannot say, however, for either that night or any other I passed in Spain, that I exactly lay on anything even faintly resembling the blue satin cushion on which the little *infantes* are laid and dressed, 'that their little *altissimos* may not come into too close contact with plebeian flesh and blood;' nay, rather, my experience resembled that of Victor Hugo's mother, who, during her residence in Madrid, describes swarms of certain entomological specimens as coursing up and down the blue satin and amber silk draperies of a certain prince's palace in that city. Perhaps nobody but a Spaniard, or one who has traveled in Spain, can understand the joke conveyed by the substitution of an *l* for an *r* in the word *expurgation*. There is danger, too, after you rise from your bed, of getting goats' or asses' milk in your tea and coffee — a commingling rather frequent than otherwise among the economical *fonda* people of the country; while a little later on, at the eleven o'clock breakfast, you may suffer the further indignity of getting *cow* instead of *beef* in response to your orders, if you don't recollect that *vacca* (cow) is the general term for the Englishman's national dish. In many a place, moreover, — I will not slander Cordova, — you will find relics of an old Spanish custom, now obsolescent, of having restaurants, whither you may bring your own comestibles and have them cooked on the premises. Coffee is extensively adulterated with roasted acorns, while ' as for the parties to whose special troughs this article of consumption is consigned in other countries, they are fed on chestnuts, so that if the prodigal son had followed his porcine occupation in this country, he would not have been so badly off in descending to the husks which the swine did eat.' The exquisite whiteness and delicacy of the Spanish bread, however, kneaded as it is all by hand, and the rich and ropy chocolate, in both of which they excel the world, afford some compensation to the disappointed coffee-lover. I have read in some book on Spain that tea in that country is regarded as a sign of advanced tendencies, and is affected only by the strong-minded. Meanwhile, whether from contrast with other things, or from whatever reason, I, personally, have had many a delicious cup of Souchong in these Spanish hotels. However true it be that though the mantilla may be put on by any one, yet it can be *worn* by none but a Spanish lady, good tea is certainly made elsewhere than in England.

A glance into the market-place of Cordova will show you the truth of the Italian saying that 'the watermelon is for eating, drinking, and washing your face.' There they lie in great green-and-silver heaps, as many-striped as Joseph's coat, many of them carefully dissected and presenting their tantalizing interiors to the greedy eyes of the surrounding urchins. They are handed in and out of car-windows, carried affectionately under the arm of peregrinating working-people, and, with the green-and-crimson *pimientos* (Spanish peppers), the greengages, figs, and apricots, the transparent masses of jellied-looking grapes, and the great barrels of ready-boiled thunny-fish from the Mediterranean, furnish a variety of repast very daintily conceived for lightening the pangs of summer hunger. There is never a moment here, as in Paris, when it becomes illegal to obstruct the street with refuse, though antiquated arrangements are in vogue for going round and picking up what scavengery may remain. There is no life insurance against pestilential odors, and this the Cordovese at least fully understand; for though their houses may be insured against fire and *hail*, there is nothing to save them from the reek of the streets, nor is the place so Moslemized that the dogs may do the dirt-carrying, as in Constantinople. True, parts of Spain are found where dogs are so numerous that an official called a *perrero* (from *perro*, a dog) exists, whose function it is to drive the animals out of the churches; and doubtless no small percentage of the four million dogs, which Byrne tells us an ingenious Spanish statistician lately calculated were to be found in Europe, hang around the street-corners in Spain and do untold scavengering there; but in Cordova the 'woful ballad to my lady's eyebrows' has still to be written, and the animal whose moonlit laments generally accompany that performance is equally absent. Hence he who, according to the East Indian notion, 'goes among the perfumes,' will hardly go to the city of the Gaudalquivir.

A tradition lingers in the old place that it, first of all European cities, had the benefit of paved streets, introduced in the khalifate of one of the Abdur-rhamans. Nothing remains of these paved streets except the tradition: no royal carriage could pass through these gorges and defiles, and the custom of festooning chains above a door where a royal personage had alighted, or even of placing the royal arms over the entry and of assuming certain heraldic colors in liveries, still, I believe, adhered to on such occasions, would be operations of some difficulty. The ten or fifteen grandees who live at Cordova live the quietest of lives; a few carriages rattle through the orange-planted Square *Gonsalvo de Cordova*, at dusk every evening, but there is little occasion, amid the venerable antiquity of the place, to follow another bizarre custom which I may as well mention: when a new carriage has been ordered, it is or was the custom to abstain from using it till it has borne a priest carrying the Eucharist to a sick or dying person. The approach of such a procession is indicated by the tinkling of a bell, when everything stops, the men take off their hats, the women drop on their knees, and everybody mutters a paternoster. If a carriage hitherto unused stands before a gentleman's door and the priest bearing the Eucharist happens that way, he is eagerly invited to seat himself in the new vehicle, and then marches in great state to the house of the sick person. Ever after that the carriage is looked upon as consecrated.

In Portugal I had an opportunity of noticing the existence of considerable wealth in silver and jewels among the lower classes; so in Andalusia

I doubt not that, as George Borrow[1] says, the peasant women of La Mancha can still afford to place a silver fork and a snowy napkin beside the plate of their guest; and one can well believe the same author when he says that you may draw the last cuarto from a Spaniard provided you will concede him the title of cavalier and rich man; but you must never hint that he is poor or that his blood is inferior to your own. An old peasant, says he, on being informed in what slight estimation he was held, replied, 'If I am a beast, a barbarian, and a beggar withal, I am sorry for it; but as there is no remedy, I shall spend these four bushels of barley, which I had reserved to alleviate the misery of the Holy Father, in procuring bull-spectacles, and other convenient diversions, for the queen, my wife, and the young princes, my children. Beggar! *Carajo!* The water of my village is better than the wine of Rome!'

> From heretic boors,
> And Turkish Moors,
> Star of the sea,
> Gentle Marie,
> Deliver me!

He who 'undertakes the adventure of Spain' hath this and many another prayer to keep on his lips. Chief among the insect plagues of Cor-

---

[1] Borrow, *The Bible in Spain.*

dova are the animalcule-like guides that infest the purlieus of the place. These torments are from ten to fifteen years of age, and none of them, one is sure, have ever been stuffed and put in the museums where they belong. They angle for strangers as acutely as the urchins at the Alhambra bait their long strings and angle for martlets and swallows along the Moorish battlements. Here you no sooner step out of your hotel — 'of the kind so admirably described in the wondrous tale of Udolfo' — than immediate assault and battery take place, and you are accompanied almost by force, whether you will or not, by a small edition of the Encyclopædia Hispanica, bent on describing the whole town to you from the time Martial called it 'dives Corduba,' down to the days of Amadeus. And from the general and immediate wreck of everything which these Virgils make in conducting their Dantes through this under-world, and the vestiges of dilapidation everywhere met with on the road, it is open to belief that Andalusia is a corruption for Vandalusia. The Gibraltese designate the tribe by the singularly appropriate name of 'rock scorpions.' Many of them are said to be born of Spanish mothers and irresponsible Anglo-Saxon fathers. Their chatter is frequently of the queerest, and their impudence, obsequiousness, and avarice are quite as unbounded as their communicative tongues. You are positively reduced to picking up stones or making menacing movements with your umbrella-handle before you ultimately succeed in even intimating that you prefer your own company. And the instant you enter the great mosque through the glorious orange-garden trailing with roses of Damascus, they dance about you like so many tarantulas. And then if there is the slightest hole or chipping on the edge of the money you hand them, there is not the slightest possibility of their taking it or of your having rest that day. On them each stranger exerts an attractive force fully equal to the famous loadstone of Madrid which, with its six pounds, can life a weight of sixty. Each one all but considers himself a grandee entitled to remain covered in the presence of the king. Each one can loll as ineffably as any Spanish senator who sits in the House of Parliament at the capital, and refreshes himself with sweetened water; or, during the august deliberations of the legislative body, takes a stick of baked sugar and white of egg, soaks it in cold water, and then sucks the *bâton* to his heart's content! Only bishops and kings may in Spain drive through the streets in a coach and six; but the urchins of Cordova are quite equal to experimenting in the same direction. In a country where brides dress in black, people who marry a second time are outrageously *charivaried*, window-panes are still leaded instead of being puttied, bluish-crimson Val de Peñas is drunk for breakfast, and numerous other solecisms flavor an otherwise tasteless existence, it is not to be expected that the younger population should be entirely free from eccentricities. The poor little wretches all look as if they lived on the oil-cake from which the olive oil has been expressed, and which is both fuel for man and fodder for pigs and cattle in Spain. They skip about every ruin in Andalusia like lizards, or like the sparkling-eyed salamanders you come on in your rides about Seville; and yet, if one of the little fellows is hospitable enough to ask you to his home at meal-time, you will be given the seat of honor, and asked to say the benediction.

The 'velvet and fire' seen by Balzac in the eyes of the Catalonian women are certainly reflected in the 'orbed omniscience' of the saucy Cordubenses. Wherever there are Venetian blinds one is always conscious of a flickering presence behind them, and a little orientation soon reveals a pair of curious eyes looking out on one with Eastern intentness, determined to take in the whole of the precious occasion. Throughout Spain the semi-twilight life of the women has given birth to no end of skillful window-tactics. During the day they are immerged in the shadows of their chambers; the *patios* are marble Walhallas where the shadows fight each other in the amber dusk, and the light dies in the fountains, or is drunk in by the heavy chalices of the flowers, leaving little behind. Hence the universal resort to the curtained intelligence-box of the windows. Still what the architects technically call 'fenestration' is but scantily developed in Cordova, for, as in the East, the windows generally look on the inner court, and if there are outer windows they are jealously grilled and draped. The streets of Cordova are mere blinding streaks of sunlight during the day, and too full of curves and spirals withal, to admit of any great perspective; hence little can be seen, except perhaps your *vis-à-vis* across the street breakfasting on *jamon con dulces* (ham with sweets) and washing down the meal with potations of wine out of a pig-skin coated internally with pitch. As for drinking water without a lump of sugar, or a spoonful of aniseseed brandy in it, that is quite unhealthy!

It is said that the descriptions of Montserrat made so powerful an impression upon Goethe's mind that he deliberately appropriated the scenery for the fifth act of the second part of Faust. It seems most probable that had he seen Cordova, so unique an experience would have found a niche in his West-Easterly Divan. The thyme, the wild flax, the box, the dwarf ilex, the mastic, the masses of purple clematis, and the aconite blossoms that hang in the crevices of the Sierra Morena and spice the air in early summer, would have delighted the great German philosopher, and perhaps have given rise to a 'Spanische Reise,' thus realizing Tennyson's saying that 'a book of travels may be so written that it shall be as immortal as a great poem.' For if ever a man had the elements of a great traveler, harmoniously blended with noble poetic and scientific powers, Goethe was such a man.

While sojourning at Cordova I did not hear the great bell of the cathedral, so I cannot say whether it, as they say of the cathedral bell of Toledo, is roomy enough to permit fifteen shoemakers to seat themselves in it, with space enough to draw out their threads without elbowing each other; but bells big and little I did hear, and in considerable quantity. Kneeling and standing are generally the only admissible postures in Spanish churches; it is rare to see any one sitting. In Cordova the churches are numerous, but they close early and open late, so that visitors who drop in in the incidental way of English and Americans and stay but a few hours are frequently disappointed in their efforts to see them. In one or two of the great Spanish cathedrals there is a little greasy cushioned shelf in a certain corner of the church where the dead infants of the poor are deposited that they may get the Christian burial which their parents are unable else to procure for them. It is then the business of the parish to bury them. In Barcelona I remember frequently seeing huge black-plumed hearses rapidly driven through the streets, while within them, entirely exposed to the view, were fixed tiny snow-white coffins with the remains of deceased children being galloped (!), entirely unaccompanied, to the grave. The shocking disregard of the dead is rather striking in a people so punctilious to the living.

If there are things to shock the sensibilities of strangers in Spain, there are many others which foreign nations would find it admirable to imitate. Capital punishment, while it exists, is extremely repugnant to the Spanish feelings, and many are the criminals that are acquitted on the plea of 'insanity.' They are not, however, immediately dismissed and allowed to rove around till the perpetration of a new crime brings them again within the reach of justice. Spanish ideas are far more precise: the criminals acquitted on the plea of 'insanity' are literally and wholesomely sent to the mad-house!

Their antiquated modes of treading out grapes with the feet, of drawing off wine into huge eight hundred or twelve hundred gallon stone-jars, embedded in the earth, of distilling brandy from grape-skins, of threshing out grain by driving a donkey with a harrow round and round over it, and (formerly) of depositing thousands of bushels of corn in conical holes made in the dry earth where it kept for several years, are simply customs characteristic of themselves, and show little advance in the last thousand or two years. But if they are behind in these things they are before in others. Cordova and other Spanish cities are full of charitable institutions, excellently managed; the people are personally pure, sober, and honest; and though there is more or less 'desecration of dove-cotes,' flagrant vice is rare. Thiéblin, who knows the Spanish people well, speaks of their rare self-restraint, good-humor, and temperateness. They have had more than twenty revolutions since the beginning of this century, and perhaps as little bloodshed as was ever recorded of revolutions so numerous. Books which, like Baxley's Spain,[1] systematically vilify the Spaniards and make them out the most abject nation on the face of the earth, cannot be too strongly reprehended. Miss Eyre, an indignant Englishwoman, and George Augustus Sala, sent similar fictions to their friends at home. 'If English ladies could only imagine what a fearful impression is produced upon a Spaniard when he sees,

[1] H. W. Baxley, *Spain*, 1875.

under his radiant sky, a British home-made dress, a pair of big, " comfortable, solid, leather boots," and a mushroom-like, black straw sun-hat, they would forgive him all the incivilities he might have proved capable of, in a moment when his sense of beauty was so severely hurt.'

One writer will declare that the male population of Madrid is the most atheistic in Europe; another that every individual Spaniard is an ever-active crater of tobacco smoke; another that there is a hereditary deficiency of teeth in the Spanish Bourbon house; and a fourth that the general unreliableness of the Latin race is but one of the natural results of the whole of their historical development. Wallis,[1] Irving, Byrne, Thiéblin, Borrow, Bayard Taylor, Hay, and Hare, are almost the only English travelers who have done the country justice. Miss Kate Field[2] touches off delightfully many of the foibles and frailties of the national character without wounding the susceptibilities of the people. But it is really difficult to find a wise and sober-minded man who can write in a wise and sober-minded way about Spain.

The red, green, and yellow-tiled roofs, and blue, bubble-like domes of Valencia, will be missed in Cordova; but every turn brings out

---

[1] S. T. Wallis, *Glimpses of Spain*, 1854.
[2] *Ten Days in Spain.*

something idiosyncratic : the characteristic fretted balconies and doors admitting into half-illuminated inner parlors ; quaint brass Moorish lamps swinging from the centre of the rooms ; curious bronze door-knockers, representing a clinched fist, or an open female hand with the outside turned back ; lion-heads, with wide-open mouths for letter-boxes ; floors pebbled in mosaic with vari-colored stones, so as to form rude but effective bits of ornamentation ; marble tanks, and garden pavilions wreathed in creepers ; or walks that bend round and round their graveled spaces as flexibly as the Toledo blades, which may be curled up and put away in a box, or even tied into knots, so rarely tempered is the steel. It is essentially a place of details. Shady alamedas take you along the Guadalquivir, where the magnificent bridge ascribed to Augustus Cæsar stands out boldly in the foreground, one of the rarest sixteen-arched bits of bridge structure in the Peninsula. Old Moorish mills beneath chafe the green waters into foam as the sun glints on the bronzed torsos of boys bathing in the stiller pools ; while the scythe-like sweep of the river throws a grandiose arm about the antique walls, and seems to gather them in a wide embrace. You wonder if an offshoot of that wondrous Roman road, described by the historian as more than four thousand miles in length, stretching from Jerusalem to the confines of Scotland, did not pass over this bridge and into the city of Cordova, and on down to ultimate Cádiz. And it would require but little imagination, and less rehabilitation, to fancy the panoply and glitter of Roman legions, as they defiled along the opposite bank, and then, in a long golden ribbon of dust, threaded their way over this bridge. Many a procession, doubtless, with the Virgin as *generalissima*, — so she was proclaimed when Valencia was besieged by the French, — has come with chant and incense along this solid monument of Roman toil, and entered one of the nineteen richly carved portals of the cathedral which stands in front of the bridge ; and, doubtless, on still summer nights, during the great Ramadan ceremonies, the brimming river caught a reflex from the ten thousand lamps hanging in the Kaaba of Spain, and illumining the sanctuary of Abdur-rhaman. What a 'Cloudcuckooborough' there must have been in the water then, and what a medley of twilight muezzin-towers, leaning over and disporting their slender apparitions among the water-lights!

You have seen a great bell of crystal thrown over some rare clock of precious workmanship, and guarding with its ambient clearness every nicest detail from harm ? One is reminded of that in looking on the Mosque of Cordova for

the first time; not that these solid yellow walls
and battlements are by any means transparent;
far from it; but from the perfect picture of Oriental
religious life which they dome over and
hedge in for us. It is the fairy acorn, that expanded
into a pavilion, and grew into a tent, and
covered a whole army with trumpets and banners.
There is a certain hesitation in applying
numbers and measurements to such a structure;
and yet, perhaps, in that way the best idea can
be gained of the ampleness, the vistaed distances,
and the fertility of its interior. It is rich in every
way, — in dimensions, in decoration, in subtle
elaboration of detail, in complexity without entanglement,
in simplicity without any sudden
check to imaginative expatiation as the eye
courses through its thousand pillars, as if gazing
from the centre of some multiple, star-petaled
flower, radiating in every direction. To me, the
mosque was more like a vast, many-aisled chamber,
than a church. The roof is hardly more
than five-and-thirty feet high, while the dimensions
are something like six hundred and twenty
feet long by four hundred and forty feet wide.
Fifty towers garnish the walls, and between them
run serrated battlements, with here and there a
foliated Moorish arch, an elaborate bronze door,
or a pinnacle. Every precious stone that can be
carved into pillars and thrown into perspectives

is here represented in monolith. Jasper, verd-antique, and porphyry, become commonplace before you disentangle yourself from the forty-eight naves among which you are enforested, — twenty-nine running north and south, and nineteen running east and west. Just as if one should insert a silver heart in a beautiful human frame, and expect it to keep up the subtle enginery of circulation: so, just in the centre of this gorgeous and venerable *mezquita*, has been dropped a Gothic chapel which pierces the roof, interrupts the labyrinthine maze of columns, and is altogether out of place. The idea is a prompting from the evil dreams of a Cordovese bishop. To gain the mosque you cross the Garden of Oranges, filled with orange-trees three hundred years old, palms of unknown antiquity, cedar, and cypress. The whole garden, in blossom season, is a solid perfume; there is a great fountain of Abdur-rhaman, 'Servant of the Merciful,' which flickers restlessly under the heated odors, and is surrounded by highly original human figures bearing water-jars: there are two colonnades, arched over, at the ends: there are walks, and there is a noble belfry.

'The roof,' says a chronicler of the wonders of this mosque, 'was entirely overlaid with fretwork, such as the Arabs alone knew how to execute, with a wealth of design, and a precision of detail unrivaled by any other artists, in their wonderful stucco, of which we see such perfect remains at this day. This rich stucco ornamentation was illuminated in colors at once brilliant and mellow, and a value, obtainable by no other means, was given to the work, by the lavish interspersion of gilding, which covered every inch of the material. The walls were of such fine and delicate tracery that they could only be compared to a fabric of lace, the exquisite finish of which was shown by an ingenious system of illumination from behind. The graceful and picturesque Moorish arches were not only gilded, but were enriched with studs and bosses of glass mosaic, wrought with so much skill by the Arabs that they had the effect of rubies and emeralds, topazes and sapphires, and, like golden bows enriched with gems, were supported, as they still are, by columns of marble, alabaster, verd-antique, jasper, and porphyry. Amidst this gorgeous profusion of labor were suspended the countless gold and silver lamps, which shed their brilliancy upon the costly detail, and illumined the remotest corners of this vast treasury of arts.'

A saunter through this extraordinary building reveals the truth of the description. Perhaps the rarest piece of mosaic in the world is in the Mihrab, — the Holy of Holies, where the Korán was kept; within this sanctuary, and the whole spot where it is found, breathes breathless purity, stillness, and beauty. It is pure and perfect as a lily, — this domed recess, with its seven-sided floor, cupola, and wall of seven sides, keeping apart from the garish chapels which adjoin it, as if afraid its ethereal skirts might be tainted with the contact.

The pleasant lingering in Cordova, however, had to come to an end, and the beauty of the cathedral and orange courts left for another day. It is a place that leaves behind many gentle and abiding regrets, many happy memories, many light and spiritual longings.

XI.

> One of those beautiful old cities in Spain in which one finds everything; cool walks shaded by orange-trees along the banks of a river, great open squares exposed to the burning sun; .... labyrinths of buildings all confused together. — KENELM DIGBY, *Broadstone of Honour*.

> Ultimus suorum moriatur! — *Inscription for Toledo*.

THE journey from Granada to the Fontainebleau of the Spanish kings is more interesting than such journeys usually are in Spain. If you come from Granada, the fertile Vega is traversed; orchards, pineries, and wineries are seen on all sides, and you have a chance to enjoy the Moorish city by the light of dawn. The train leaves at five, and it is necessary to rise very early to catch it. To be alone in a *calesa*, traversing a huge wood and many ill-paved and worse-lighted streets, past mysterious-looking people with lanterns picking up things in the street or sitting brigand-like in recessed doorways, under shrines of the Virgin where a tiny taper tells of some faithful heart that has put it there; past groups of chattering washerwomen washing by starlight in the public tanks; past Moorish gateways and beautiful horse-shoe arches, silent churches and towering walls; amid shadows that seem perpetual, and over cobble-stones that resound like muskets with their sharp ring through the soundless night; the most brilliant stars peeping in through the long avenues, and a solitary bell pealing forth the melodious *angelus;* to be alone with a ferocious little Spanish driver, a pair of mighty mules with shaven coats and bells, among the stars and trees and associations: all this was at least romantic, and grew every moment more so, as one remembered the multiplying accounts of recent murders and robberies. However, nothing happened, and we arrived in safety, after an uncommonly long ride, at the station. At intervals during the drive — which, apart from its loneliness, was charming with early freshness and dew — we caught sight of the queer-looking policemen perambulating the darkened streets with a huge staff and lantern, ever and anon crying the hours, and accompanying the cry by a peculiarly sweet mediæval chant: *A-ve Ma-ri-a-a-a pu-ri-si-ma-a-a, l-a-s tres-s-s; se-re-no-o-o.* (Hail holiest Mary, 't is three; clear.) One hears the cry and sees the observance everywhere through Spain, and the sky is so prevailingly *sereno* or clear, that the policeman now goes by that name and is called *el sereno.* The invocation to the Virgin is an ancient usage, and, no doubt, in the mind of the superstitious *sereno,* seems a sort of amulet to ward off peril. The position is not without danger where night is so generally turned into day as in Spain, and the street swarms with overflowing life.

A few miles from Granada we reached the little station of Pinos, where Isabella's messenger overtook Columbus as he was going away to seek the help of Henry VII. of England, after repeated disappointments. At Bobadilla, breakfast and a change of cars: then a long journey through mountains and plains glimmering with sunlight, pink and yellow cliffs, sombre olives, and white hamlets. It was a journey through a kitchen-range. The Gaudalquivir, which we followed part of the way, was hot and sluggish. Very little fruit could be obtained. Water, water, was everywhere (for a wonder) cried for sale up and down the stations, and one's only pleasure was in washing away the suffocating dust by means of a wet sponge. The long day passed more rapidly than usual in the perusal of Contreras' Monumentos Arabes — a feat (I mean the reading) of great difficulty, owing to the frightful roughness of the train. It was with effort that you could keep on the seat at all; sleeping was out of the question, and at every respiration at least an ounce or two of the impalpable Sierras all around seemed to be taken into the lungs. We passed places immensely famous for their wines, such as Montilla, Val de Peñas (the best red wine of Spain), and others, and a few bunches of exquisite grapes bought for two coppers, solaced the torments of the *trajet*. A wave of blue mountains was seen in the distance absolutely covered with timber — a rare sight in Spain. Peasant women brought the peculiarly graceful white clay water-jugs made in this district to the train for sale, which travelers here should never be without; beggars without number promenaded up and down and exhibited their pranks to the delectation of the passengers, and besought the compensation which Providence had denied them. Alcázar was reached at midnight, and everybody got out and took chocolate and sweet cake, already hospitably set out at long tables for the expected guests. At half-past four we reached Aranjuez, and found the vast station almost absolutely deserted — no carriages, omnibuses, or vehicles of any description at hand.

The morning star shone with intense brilliance over the tree-tops and the air had a rare keenness and purity.

A sleepy porter was secured and a short walk brought us to the Hotel de los Ambajadores, Antigua de los Infantes, — more like a calaboose than a hotel, inside and out. The astonished garçon and chambermaid having recovered from the shock given by our early and unexpected arrival, we were conducted to our cell.

Aranjuez is only a short distance from Madrid and in that respect is more like Versailles than Fontainebleau. One gazes on its wide Dutch streets, Louis XIV. architecture, spaciousness, and verdure with astonishment, in contrast with the picture of most Spanish towns, — Gothic or Moorish styles, narrowness, closeness, and aridity. Aranjuez is quite a city of magnificent distances, and according to one is as much of a failure as the city which originally gave birth to that appellation. . But I do not think so. To some it looks like a vast Louis XIV. joke perpetrated on the Spanish people: very broad avenues, very long arcades, very lofty sycamores, elms, and oaks, very trim French gardens, fountains, and statuary. An old château built in 1727, and embellished by Philip V., Ferdinand VI., and Charles III., with tapestried and rococo rooms populous with clocks and gilded furniture, frescoes and tessellated floors, it is simply a quaint old picture of French life in the eighteenth century, such as we see it in Watteau's pictures, and it is quite a lovely spot for one of Watteau's garden-parties — everything, of course, though French, flavored with Spanish taste. Aranjuez is at one season of the year — when the court arrives — a fashionable suburb of Madrid, and then awakes from its drowsy, deserted, eighteenth century look, into the dwelling-place of ambassadors, ministers, court-people, and soldiers. I delight in its splendid planes and elms. The Tagus and the Jarama have their confluence in the palace gardens and form enchanted isles full of dells, bowers, and lover's walks, with the ever-melodious sound of rushing waters and rustling leaves. Many famous scenes of love and intrigue have taken place within the precincts of the Jardin Real of Aranjuez. I visited it just before sunset, when the softest and goldenest evening light was streaming down the long walks, lighting up the river and the giant cork-trees, the many fountains, glades, and arbors. Just below the palace is a large artificial cascade before which the river spreads out into a broad glassy floor, spanned by a graceful iron bridge; beyond, vista on vista of really grand sycamores and elms radiating *en eventail*. All is delightfully spacious, friendly, and characteristic. I was afraid of getting lost in the bushy wilderness, especially as the shadows began to lengthen and the departing sun shed bewildering light in my face, as through some great golden rose window of ancient time. The water-works are most extensive, but the fountains were all dry when my visit took place. Urns and statuary accentuated the all-embracing green of the beautiful wood. In front of the palace was a flower-garden in most abundant bloom, running along the Tagus and overlooking one of the islets. Around Aranjuez, low, snuff-colored hills, calcined to powder by the sun, give one that constant surprise of contrast found in perfection only in this country.

In the morning I took a guide and visited the Casa del Labrador, an elegant palace built by Charles III., more elegant than any lady's dream immersed in reveries *à la Pompadour*. A special permit gave us entrance, which was effected after a walk of about a mile down one of those magnificent elm aisles called *calles* in Aranjuez. *Casa del labrador* means 'laborer's cottage;' but this delicate palace is more like one of the proverbial *châteaux en Espagne* than anything I have seen. Airy lightness, infinite grace of decoration, lavish and fastidious ornament, charming vistas from one room to another, — such is a faint description of this low square building, most uninteresting on the outside, built perhaps according to the Moorish superstition of avoiding the Evil Eye by too great display, but inside, a series of matchless boudoirs fit for a transformed Cinderella. You almost forgive the 'aristocracy of skin' in contemplating the structures reared by their ill-gotten wealth; so much taste, grace, and refinement have been displayed by them. One enters by a staircase whose brass balustrade (hung with cloth) has gold to the amount of fifteen thousand dollars mixed with it. Then begins a suite of apartments where Scheherazade might have told her stories — small, dainty, cabinet-like rooms full of the loveliest German and Italian tapestries, and frescoed by Luca Giordano, Velazquez, Lopez, Maella and others. Marble mantels and tables filled with splendid clocks, for which the Spanish kings had a mania; sets of rare furniture, walls inlaid with mirrors, a museum with fine tessellated floor, full of marbles from the ruins of Italica, near Seville, a many-colored salon with the four points of the compass pictured on the wall, and chairs and lounges, such as one reads of in Madame De Lafayette and Mademoiselle De Scudéry, dying to have one sit on them; a small room wonderfully inlaid with platinum, ebony, and ivory, profusely gilded and chased as any Philippe Égalité snuffbox: — one is lost in the graceful detail of this architectural dream of an *ennuyé*. It is the Palace in the Woods of the fairy tale 'beyond the twenty-ninth land, in the thirtieth kingdom.' When the wonderful clock — which is a music-box, planisphere, and time-piece all in one — begins to play like harmonica-bells, one momentarily expects the enchanted princess to spring forth and dazzle the scene with her Aslauga hair.

The visit to the palace was certainly a pleasant conclusion to the long walk. Altogether, an excursion to Aranjuez is well worth making. My impressions of it would be entirely pleasing, were it not for the drunken guide, who desired extortionate pay for what he did not show me, the exorbitant bill, and the quantity of counterfeit money which I got in exchange for an Alphonse d'or. Spain is literally filled with bad money, especially paper money, and half-peseta and two-peseta pieces. Everywhere, as one walks along, in the hotels and out of them, the ring of money on the stones is heard, — a process invariably resorted to to test the genuineness of coins. The copper money — and not always that — is the only safe money to take. Five-franc pieces, and pieces of twenty-five francs, gold (Alphonses d'or), sixteen-onza pieces, gold four-duros (dollar) pieces, and others, are constantly rejected as false and worthless. A short time ago the very bills of the Bank of Spain were refused outside of Madrid. At the stations, in front of the window where railway tickets are sold, there is always a small piece of marble or stone on which the ticket agent rings the gold and silver to see whether the *timbre* is true. If not, he will reject what is offered. Avoid, therefore, the *cambio del moneta*, or money-changer, as you would the plague. Get no money except from a well-known banking-house; scrutinize the two-peseta and half-peseta pieces carefully, and take no gold in change which you have not subjected to a sharp ring on the stone. Such simple rules will be of great service to a tourist in Spain unaccustomed to such an inundation of counterfeits as exists in that unfortunate country. Many Spaniards are wonderfully acute in detecting bad money. They will reject a piece instantly on the most cursory examination, for reasons often inscrutable to you. The safest plan then is to follow their example and test every individual piece, yellowish-looking fifty centimes pieces, escudos, duros, golden doubloons, and all. An acquaintance of a friend of mine received thirty dollars in gold counterfeits at one time from a *cambio del moneta*, which he afterward tried to get rid of in masses for the soul of a dead friend! The prudent *padre* refused; only good money passing current in purgatory. One often sees *cambio del moneta, bureau de change, money changed*, etc., alluringly figured in gilt letters on plate glass windows, but only absolute necessity should force a traveler into these dens of Jews and money-stealers. I met with a very honorable exception in Bayonne, where I had occasion to exchange a considerable amount of French gold for Spanish. The money all proved good.

But what a contrast between Aranjuez and Toledo! If Aranjuez is all spaciousness, vastness, fertility, light and grace, what shall I say of squeezed up, jammed in, tormenting, torturing Toledo, tied in a Gordian knot to its precipitous hill? Simply that it has been greatly overrated. Of course an American transported from one of his own perfectly new, regular cities to the heart of this venerable town would rub his eyes for a long time over its startling combinations, church-encrusted steeps, plateresque hospitals, and purgatorial alleys; and a guide would have to be taken before he even left the hotel door. But beyond the cathedral Toledo is tiresome. There is endless material for florid expatiation at every step. It is a constant ascent or descent, up or down, in or out, here a little and there a little, the whole livelong time, up against saint this or saint that, along the abysses of the Tagus, over immensely ancient and picturesque bridges, through mauresque portals into fantastic old Jewish synagogues where artists sit and sketch the arabesques, and old women sleep beside *jarras* of water, over their Dorcas-like knitting; Punch and Judy market-places, where heaped fruit, stone colonnades, flies, mendicants, dogs, donkeys, mighty panniers and church steeples combine into a sketch by some crazy Fuseli; then up and down and round and round again as in a dance of dervishes, a thousand miles away from the lovely sunlit *patios* of Seville and Cordova with their marble cloisters, mystery, and filigree. Toledo is simply hideous. The wrench up the hill from the railway station, over the Bridge of Alcántara (in Arabic the Bridge), by the Puerta del Sol with its medallion and horse-shoe arches, is a witch's ride on a broomstick. Toledo turns in every conceivable direction as one wanders on up, now this, now that side of the river, now on the hill-tops, now in the valley, till the plaza Zocodover is reached and the omnibus stops. The whole was like a phantasmagoria to me — the mysterious moonlight, milk-white with dust, falling on groups of half-illumined people standing beneath walls or along battlements or in the sombre market-place; tall mediæval houses with their basements in profound obscurity and their battlements bathed in the August moon; crescent-like streets, with a long curved scimitar of brilliant light above the houses, like a Toledo blade, while they themselves weltered in a darkness wherein nothing could be distinguished; rapid glances from the omnibus into bright cavernous shops full of Spanish figures, to be followed by a quenched state of utter stillness and blackness; then a sharp and sudden drawing up before the Fonda de Lino where we all joyfully descended into light and comfort (as we thought) once again.

In Arabic the word *fondak* means a stable, in Spanish a hotel. The Fonda de Lino preserves many reminiscences of the etymology. The houses are so close together that people are continually looking in on each other at unexpected *déshabillé* moments; hence the infinity of blinds and sets of blinds, awnings and curtains, designed to thwart curiosity. A striped awning, two sets of curtains, a set of lambrequins, a pair of glass doors, and within these folding doors an inch thick, defend me from the feminine population of the opposite windows; despite all which a señora with very red arms was found leaning out this morning and taking a tranquil inventory of me and my room. Furniture of the times of the crusades, tawdry prints and cornice, tiled balcony and floors, a courtyard full of huge omnibuses and stable smells just below the principal apartments; corridors, laid with brick, running round as a mode of communication from room to room, ancient tablecloths, napkins, and omelettes, fruit and beefsteak of by-gone times, wine of peculiar taste, chambermaids and garçons of peculiar smell; a cavernous establishment, excavated as it were out of several jammed in, dislocated houses; garlic, fleas, and all the odds and ends of long-abandoned barbarism in superfluity: such is this best of Toledo hotels. The guide-books will not even mention any other. There is no room for any other. The traveler is abandoned by his guardian genius as he is dropped at this fatal door, and Dante's '*Lasciate la esperanza voi che entrate qui,*' is the handwriting on its wall. Immediately one falls into the hands of a guide, whose unintelligible French is as complicated as the streets; but, however unintelligible, he can at least bring one back to the hotel again, a feat nearly impossible of accomplishment alone. One had just as well try to follow the meshes of a Turkish carpet. Again, the Toledo knife is so dextrously used in this vicinity that it is far from perfectly safe or satisfactory to venture out alone in the evening, especially when the main street of the place is hardly wider than the aisle of a church. The Goth, the Jew, the Moor, and the Christian have all lived and labored here, each one doing his best, and leaving his worst behind him. One would never have suspected Charles V. of having made his capital of this guilty place, were it not for the Austrian arms blazoned here and there over the gates, and the long roll of *memorabilia* recorded by history of his doings here. The whole place is like a monkish carving on the choir and stalls of some grotesque cathedral, foliage, fiends, pigs, fairies, and griffins pouring their grinning imagery over the seats where the old canons used to sit and sleep in the interminable masses. About twenty-five thousand people out of the former two hundred thousand are bewitched in some way or other to inhabit this eyrie, an oven in August and an ice-box in March. Artists with skins that cannot be punctured, stomachs that can digest pebbles, feet and ankles that nothing can pain or sprain, eyes a-thirst for *motifs*, pockets laden with cuartos for the blind, the halt, and the lame at every synagogue, church-door, and Gothic hospital; artists, I say, endowed with all these, added to the patience of Job, the passiveness of San Sebastian, and legs like the Christobalon of the cathedral, might be tempted to linger in Toledo and paint its relics of a triple and quadruple civilization; but surely nobody else. It is a withered corpse surrounded by burning candles, and paper flowers, with, at rare intervals, a kneeling and worshiping figure. The place is all nooks and corners, jaggedness and raggedness. One delights to heap abuse on its low houses, its stern and solemn public buildings, its Saracenic court-yards and once enormous but now departed wealth. Very pure Castilian is spoken in Toledo, perhaps the best in Spain, but how strangely the language of architecture has uttered itself! Toledo is the Canterbury of Spain and holds the primacy among the archiepiscopal cities. Long stories are told of its kingly archbishops and warrior prelates — men like Mendoza, Ximénes, and Fonseca — who possessed as much bigotry as wealth, and power enough to win them the name of the *third* king. The Cid was the *alcaide* of this great city; it was once full of palaces and gardens; an opulent court reveled here in the sixteenth century and an immense and variegated page of history is the page which poor Toledo, now a heap of devitalized brick and mortar, once occupied in the mighty volume of human events. The *calèche*-drive up its hill, which rises terrace above terrace over the Tagus, is enough to disenchant the very Don Quixote of travelers. City of Generations it is indeed, as the Hebrews poetically called it; City of Silences and Tears it might be called now in its desolation. All that keeps it alive at all is the cathedral, to which it desperately clings as its last and only claim to indulgence. Although but a few steps from the fonda, a guide (as said before) is quite necessary to find it; for in spite of a tower three hundred and twenty-nine feet high, full of grand bells, carvings, and Gothic ornamentation, its very existence is never suspected by the unilluminated; such is the way in which this elegant masterpiece of Gothic architecture is concealed by its setting of houses. It was begun just five hundred years ago, and its great heart is heard to beat when the 'Gorda' — a bell weighing nearly fifty thousand pounds — begins to toll. The weathercock may well crown the cross on top of the spire. Toledo has seen many a change in religion and politics. Decidedly the most interesting thing about the cathedral is the old Gothic or Muzarabic (mixti-Arabes?) ritual still celebrated in one of its chapels. The chapel was founded to preserve this ritual in its purity. The Muzarabes were a mixture of Goths and Arabs, who lived under the government of the Eastern conquerors of Spain, and were allowed — as so often the case under the chivalrous Moslems — to retain their Christian ceremonies. Mass, according to this rite, is very simple; there is no auricular confession; the creed is repeated when the elevation of the host takes place; the sacramental wafer is broken up into symbolic pieces representing the Incarnation, Epiphany, Nativity, Circumcision, Passion, Death, Resurrection, Ascension, and Heaven, and there are prayers and collects of great beauty and eloquence connected with the service. Originally only the Lord's prayer and the words uttered by Jesus at the Last Supper constituted what was called the Apostolic mass, developed afterward into the intricate and gorgeous organism of high and low mass. The mass is now often performed as a mere curiosity, for which a small fee (!) is expected, and though once permitted in many churches, is now con-

fined to this plain little chapel built by Cardinal
Ximénes. The last spark of a dying faith has
thus taken refuge in this out-of-the-way corner,
where it is tolerated like the swallows that build
in the sculptured cornices, and not absolutely
driven away, from pure inertia. The contrast between it and the splendid spaces devoted to the
other worship — the girdle of resplendent chapels
that runs around the cathedral and fills every inch
of it with all the wealth of art and imagination —
the multitude of waxen tapers, images and paintings — the forest that has gone to sleep there and
suddenly awakened into soaring pillars and arches
full of the delicious bloom of seven hundred and
fifty painted windows — the jubilant silences and
echoing avenues strewn with kneeling figures —
poor human flowers strewn and trampled on before the cross of the Redeemer: the contrast between this and that is just the contrast between
plain reason and sensualized imagination. There
can be no pure flame burning at the end of this
long taper of Catholicism; the light is murky,
the wick is enveloped in human grossness. At
the cathedral door the usual tableau of beseech-
ing and supplicating humanity; and for five hundred years it has been lying there, just in the
same posture; attudinizing hypocrisy, *tableaux
vivants* on whom the vermin is almost a mode
of locomotion, and who, like an ancient cheese,

would walk away in spite of themselves were they not ironed to the spot by human greed. On glancing up, a mighty rose-window, huge as one imagines the wheels of Ezekiel's fiery chariot to have been, meets the gaze; but the splendor of its coloring — enhanced by its counterpart on the opposite side and fitly emblemizing the transfigured blood of Christ — is unrevealed till one enters and looks up. Then the gaze wanders round through a jeweled chromosphere, a transformation of sunlight into parterres of flowers, a sublime picture and allegory in emblazoned glass, an unknown iridescence from all the violets, lilies, and roses that ever bloomed, flooding the pillared distances beneath and lifting the soul to sweet meditation. These windows alone are enough to redeem the whole uncomeliness of Toledo — Alcázar, Zocodover, and all. One sees in their beauteous light the bruised and bleeding souls of a whole episode of Christianity eloquently recalled to amber and purple life — the vanished gardens of Spain a-blaze in these painted fields again — the gold of Hispaniola, the spices and musk of the Philippines, the passionate colors of the Indies, the blue sheen of undiscovered seas, all throbbing again under this choired and vaulted city of the dead archbishops, the cathedral of Toledo. The pillars sing under the vivid glory; the *retablo* behind the high altar — one of the masterpieces of that infinitely peopled, multiform, and many-colored Gothic — becomes conscious to the touch with all the laden thought and suffering of its twenty-seven artists; the tombs of kings and cardinals lying here become full of life. The filigree work, fine-drawn as a spider's web, waves in the colored air, and the church is vivid with the congregated throng of its clergy. What a pity that the choir stands just in the middle of the cathedral, — a church in itself, seventy feet long and forty-five wide. This is generally the case in all the great Spanish churches; a thousand pities, for a Gothic cathedral, like an avenue of trees, must have an uninterrupted vista, else the effect is spoiled. This, too, is full of marvelous stalls, all carved and time-worn, with marble pavement, a huge, eagle-shaped lectern and two other lecterns in bronze and wood, mellow with age. Beautiful jasper pillars divide the stalls: the recesses in which they are placed are of alabaster; saints, prophets, and patriarchs perform a singular religious dance in half-relief round the cornice. German and Italian schools have vied with each other in encrusting this microscopic detail; while in front rise stands with mighty singing-books magnificently illuminated, with leaves as thick as the back of a knife. It would simply be impertinent to attempt the usual expedition around the chapels. It is a pilgrimage from one age and style of ornamentation to another. One may, however, well stop before the Puerta de los Leones or Gate of Lions, above which, like a glorious flower, shines a great rose window twenty feet in diameter.

We were fortunate enough to see part of the Virgin's wardrobe, or *tesoro*, which they were bringing out of her boudoir (one might have called it) for the approaching feast of the assumption. There was a single *manta* belonging to her in which seventy-eight thousand pearls, and countless rubies, diamonds, and emeralds are embroidered. The attendants carefully inspected the floor with a lighted candle when this gem-encrusted rag was taken out of its case. Queens, popes, archbishops, and kings have given to it lavishly of their ignorance and superfluity. The Virgin's crown, without the stones, is valued at twenty-five thousand dollars, and she has her mistress of the robes in the chaste and exemplary Isabella II. On occasion the Virgin doll blazes with jeweled millinery, and is followed (spiritually) by all the great dames in the kingdom, who deem it an especial distinction to take care of its wardrobe; and landed estates are administered in its name. A writer tells us that our Saviour is treated as a constitutional king, and called 'His Divine Majesty,' and the soldiers present arms when an image like this passes a barrack, the royal march playing all the while. Moreover, when rival processions meet, which is not seldom the case in this land of processions, a regular battle sometimes ensues, and they insult and pelt each other's images.

To show the extent to which this image worship is carried, I take up a journal at random and translate a few every-day paragraphs like the following: ' Saints of to-day. — San Casiano and San Ipolito, martyrs (did you ever hear of them before?). Worship: The general jubilee of the forty hours in the parish church of Santa Maria, where to-morrow there will be high mass, and in the evening prayers and *reserva*. The Novemdial of Our Lady of Atocha (a stick supposed to have been brought from Antioch, one of the most venerated images in Spain) continues being celebrated in her church, and the Transito church in San Millan; and Don So-and-so will be the orator of the evening, ending with the *reserva* litany, and *salve*. Visit of the Court of Mary. — Our Lady of Remedies in San Ginés, and Our Lady of Health in Santiago and San José.'

These are quite chance paragraphs, and are taken from a paper purchased at the common stand in the street below. And such are and have been the immemorial interruptions to becoming and doing something, which now, even in this nineteenth century, are in full blaze. If, instead of visiting Our Lady of Health and Remedies with supplication, the good señoras and señores would use abundant pure cold water without and within, abstain from the unwholesome messes they are served with at breakfast and dinner, use less bad tobacco, change their linen a little oftener, and not respire, expire, and perspire continual garlic, our Lady might be left to herself and welcome, and a great deal less crime and vice be prevalent through the length and breadth of the land.

As for Toledo, it is a perfect nest of similar observances. For a man of business — the Spaniards are mostly men of leisure, having and getting nothing to do — to live in a place where every other day there is a *festa*, when banks are closed, and the remorseless *concierge* tells you to come *mañana*, would be out of the question. The cicerone who accompanied me in my rambles was quite dismally sarcastic at the 'stumps' called a park, the total absence of amusements (except passing counterfeit money), the flinty pavements, ruin, and age of the place. One could heartily sympathize with the poor wretch doomed to execrable French and Toledo for the rest of his days. He took me to the great square Alcázar, which Carlo Quinto turned into a palace, — a structure of Moorish origin, with two or three spacious and beautiful *patios*, spotted here and there in this vivid sunlight with the blood-red trousers of Spanish soldiers, who have taken up their abode within, — as nearly everywhere else in the land, — while wild ringing of trumpets, calling to dinner, saluted our arrival. A short distance below stands the military school of Santa Cruz, formerly a hospital, a foundation of Cardinal Mendoza, whose tomb is in the cathedral. There are several rich *patios*, a grand staircase, and much marvelous plate-work, — a term which one will often meet in Spain, meaning an infinitude of delicately-molded detail, such as is seen on plate, Spanish *plata* (silver), *plataresco*. It was full of little sticks and puppets of Spanish soldiers *in nascendo*, who, to my eye, even when full grown, are the smallest soldiers in Europe, especially the officers; they have no figure, no distinction, no air. Here and there, men and women of gigantic size are to be seen, principally in the country, — but who can come to any size by living on pepper-pods and *puchero?*

There the pupil soldiers sat in groups on this fairy staircase, themselves more florid and individualized than the Moorish and Renaissance balustrade on which they leaned, — each one a little world of self-conceit and personal pomp; polite, too, when addressed, and far from devoid of excellent qualities. In another part of the town a bit of a chapel is shown, called the Christ of the

Light, where, quotha, the Cid's horse Bavieca dropped on his knees one day when he was passing by, in homage to a miraculous light, identically the same as that placed there by the Goths hundreds of years before. I can testify to its still being inhabited by Goths, — or Vandals who exact tribute of every peregrinating Peter that may come that way.

But, after the cathedral, go to the most charming cloister of San Juan de los Reyes, and meditate among its light and lovely arches, so sad in their utter loneliness and decay, so full of blue sky, and shining air, and neglected flowers, lingering there by the kindly sufferance of the custodian. The church and cloister are famous among the famous for their stone-work, where the marble is so wonderfully carven that it lacks only color to be living verdure, full of a Puck's dream of birds and leaves and animals and statuettes, twining about the columns, and intermingled in mazy confusion. From the well in the centre of the cloister garden Antonio drew a jar of crystal water, and drank a draught in memory of the Moorish kings, the lovers of untainted *agua*.

So, you see, Toledo has compensations after all!

XII.

> Madrid, **Princesse des Espagnes,**
> Il court par tes mille campagnes
> Bien **des yeux** bleus, bien des yeux noirs.
> La blanche ville aux sérénades,
> Il passe par tes promenades,
> Bien des petits pieds tous les soirs.
> DE MUSSET.

IT was a characteristic stroke of policy with the Spanish kings to remove the capital from places teeming with dynastic associations, like Seville or Valladolid, to a city of the centre, known only for the wide plains that surrounded it, its pure air, and its spacious possibilities in the future. Is it not Thucydides who, in the great Sicilian expedition, lays so much stress on the power of association, according as the cities he describes as taking part in that great event had Athenian or Peloponnesian memories behind them? At all events, it is quite likely that disaster would have ensued in Spain, had not Charles V.'s gout providentially let him find rest nowhere except in the pure air of the Guadárramas and the great Castilian plain. To this spot, as to a reservoir, flowed all the Spanish influences, — hostilities, friendships, kinships, common interests; here they all mixed, and lost the sharpness of their angles; and here, from the fusion of many heterogeneous elements, resulted a real capital, ugly enough withal, but free ground to all that stood upon it. A peep into the intricate annals of Spain in the Middle Ages will reveal half a score of jealous provinces, each striving for the mastery, each ready to take arms against the other, each eager enough to love God and serve the king, provided *its* God and *its* king were meant, and each filled with ancient rivalries, handed down from father to son, as the old Saxons handed down their swords and their jewels. 'Spain,' says a recent writer,[1] 'is a country of five Irelands, each discontented with the central authority, no matter what party wields it, and cordially hating and despising the other four.' The mere mention, therefore, of establishing the capital permanently anywhere, was like Roland's horn blown at Roncesvalles, — it made all Spanish Christendom dance and rush to the rescue. It was only now and then that the strong hand of some despotic prince took the rebellious provinces to task, and gave them, as it were, a good squeeze, that anything like the tranquillity of modern times prevailed in Spain. There is hardly a country of its extent so cut up by almost inaccessible mountains; hardly one where

[1] Campion, *On Foot in Spain*, 1878.

regnant peculiarity has developed in so many-sided a way, and national, or rather, provincial tendencies have so run along in the parallel lines that never meet. The brilliant Andalusian, the grave Castilian, the fiery Catalonian, the foolish Gallician, — these, and many more, are types as marked as types could well be, and each with its pig-tail of associations behind it which it would be sacrilege to touch. The Spanish provinces were a bed of live coals, which any chance wind might make a furious fire. The intense self-respect which distinguishes the Spaniard of the present day — his sensitiveness, chivalrousness in a certain sense, and *pundonor* — seems in those days to have possessed and pervaded the entire nation as a nation, and to have made it preternaturally susceptible to insult. Hence the constant challenges, combats, and wars that took place. Of course, the rise and predominance of any one of the many *reinos* into which the kingdom was divided excited very naturally the horror and detestation of the others, and made favoritism on the part of the reigning monarch a very critical thing indeed. Even in our own broad land, what a caldron public opinion becomes when there is the least hint that possibly the capital may be moved to this place or to that. The establishment, therefore, of a final and permanent resting-place for the King and Cortes, in their Bohemian wanderings from one place to another, was a matter of some delicacy. Madrid came to be the very Cordelia of cities, — overlooked, or hitherto trampled under foot by her ambitious sisters, but the only one eventually that received and entertained the king. The Moors, who made nearly everything they touched interesting, failed to imbue the desolate town with the least tincture of romance. Two or three pretty legends are all that are told of it in Moorish times. Just as the vandalism of the monks erased the precious works of the ancients to make glue of the parchment, or procure new writing surfaces, so nearly every trace of the Moorish occupation was carefully obliterated from Madrid. A new leaf was turned over, — and that absolutely blank. Hence the intensely prosaic character of everything connected with the modern town. There is not the least particle of poetry or imagination about the place. While nearly every other city in the peninsula is the centre of a legendary cycle, and is rich in clustered romance and folk-lore, Madrid is as tedious as a place can well be. It is said to be on a river; but unless one is fortunate enough to be present during the spring inundations, the river is as invisible as the classic stream that sank beneath the sea in its journey to the Fountain Arethusa: 'To long for a thing like rain in May,' is a Spanish proverb. However, to keep up the illusion, a large bridge spans a valley in the environs of the city, and here and there are pools of scummy water, at which your washerwoman, and many of her compatriots, assemble and wash the linen, in which you imagine yourself spotlessly arrayed during your sojourn in the Castilian city. As Madrid wounded no susceptibilities, it made an admirable place in which to establish the court; and ever since then it has gone on improving from year to year, as if trying to make the reconciliation still more complete. In certain moods, it is a real joy to get to such a place, — bright, busy, well paved, well lighted, clean, — especially after having been trespassing in so modern a fashion on such Ninevehs and Babylons as Toledo, Salamanca, and Alcalá. To be one of three or four hundred thousand people again, — to feel one's self a scrap of the delightful miscellaneousness of a great city, — accompanied by so much motion, cheerfulness, and companionship, — is, after the mortal hush of most of the Spanish cities, like a burst of pleasant music. 'Be mostly silent,' was, I think, a maxim of Epictetus; but *he* might well say that amongst the millions of Rome. A shop-window was company enough for Souvestre, who saw in it and its outspread merchandise vast possibilities of instruction and education. But when there is not even this: when 1555, or the year 1000, stands printed on every house and face you see, and there is not even the tiniest ripple of contemporary life afloat on the street, you become satiated with very emptiness, and even long (*sancta simplicitas!*) for a Spanish newspaper.

It is not necessary to take what Douglas Jerrold called 'a draught of a look,' to make one's mental picture of Madrid ineffaceable. You might dip it all in Styx, and still its individuality would be plain. I have it burning in me like a bunch of tapers: the beautiful green Prado, the sunlit, sloping streets, the huge palaces, the Romanesque churches, the market-places and colonnades, the Puerta del Sol radiant with electric lights at night, the squares, street-cars, and theatres, the crowds of well-dressed people, the magnificent fruit making great spots of splendor in the fruit shops, the sweep of the great saffron plains as they swoop down and seem to beleaguer the city, so suddenly do human habitations cease. Madrid breaks off as suddenly as an interrupted soliloquy. London melts into England and Paris into France, so insensibly, that it would be hard to tell where the city ends and the kingdom begins. (Am I stealing from Emerson?) Madrid, however, is a disk, as sharply defined as the moon on an autumn night. There is no delicate gradation of expansion; no half-city, half-country. You plunge as suddenly in or out of the place as in or out of a douche-bath. There is a very startling change of subject, from whichever side you approach it. All over Spain there has been 'gravitation to accentual centres;' the cities are heavy with life, while the lank extremities are famishing for it. There is no minute irrigating stream of plenteous vitality threading the country, and uniting its parts into a huge mesh system, as in Holland or Belgium. Spain has evidently far too much land, and far too few people. A single Spaniard can, perhaps, cover more geographical square miles than any other individual in Europe. Perhaps this communicates to his talk that largeness and indefiniteness which comes out so delightfully in the speculations of Sancho, or in the political talk of your neighbor in a railway journey.

I arrived at night, and was struck by the long rows of brilliantly illuminated streets that diverged from the stations, and seemed over-filled with people. The *calèche* in which I was dashed headlong over the cobble-stones down a long grove-embowered avenue, filled with lamps and foot-passengers. My only companion was a lady, who asked me to change seats with her, and seemed, as I thought, in a very anxious frame of mind about something. Her antics were quite unintelligible, until I perceived that she was endeavoring to cover something with her skirts, and then trying, with a refreshing innocency of countenance, to look absent-mindedly out of the front window: the object of all which was presently explained when the *calèche* stopped, and a customs-officer looked in.

'Anything contraband?'

To which I, in the guilelessness of several empty valises, boldly said for both of us, 'No!' as the lady seemed to have no luggage. When we started again, I found that I had been made the victim of a pretty misunderstanding. My companion, it seems, had a quantity of contraband stuff in a large bag, with which she was endeavoring to evade the rigid *octroi*, and this was the egg she was so uneasily sitting upon! She was profuse in her thanks, and presently an accomplice of hers got in, and returned the courtesy by offering me a cigarette. We soon got to the Puerta del Sol, — the great hotel centre of Madrid, — and I extricated myself from the rather oppressive affabilities of my companions.

In my rambles through Spain I have found the Spanish women, as a rule, singularly modest. Gibraltar — 'that cancer of Spain,' as Fernan Caballero calls it — must be excepted, where much immorality prevails. Morals are, no doubt, lax; but there is not that form of free and easy allocution so popular and prevalent in France:

'The glad, quick-eyed peasant girls, with great golden ear-rings and small silver combs,' so unctuously described by Lundgren,[1] the Swede, seem rather reserved than otherwise, at least to foreigners. Some tinkling Spanish lines on the subject run as follows: —

> 'De la raiz de la palma
> Hicieron las Isabeles.
> Delgaditas de cintura y de
> Corazon crueles.'

In Madrid I had no reason to change my opinion. I saw a great deal of grace and loveliness — not the peachy bloom of loveliness that we have idealized — the slender, spirituelle, Shaksperian women, with wit like a nettle and manners like a dove. To compensate for this there is nearly always an air of distinction about the Spanish women. (Will women ever pardon Goethe for making the serpent the *aunt* of the human race? At all events the rhythmic curves of the serpent flow through the figures of these women, and give them even a weird suggestiveness.) There are splendid eyes, pure complexions, classic profiles, but none of the brilliance and bloom of the north, nor the 'emerald eyes and hair of gold' celebrated by Cervantes in the Novelas Ejemplares. The snapping black eyes of the Frenchwoman, the large, languid stare of the

[1] *En Målares Anteckningar.* Stockholm, 1873.

Briton, are rarely met with in Madrid. The general suavity of manner has passed into the expression, and the result is great gentleness and luminousness of gaze, a rather fixed look, a lambent irradiation rather than the darting flicker of the Gaulois eye. There is more of the South, with its great, gentle passion, its summer sweetness, its large brightness and candor. A Frenchman's eye is like the green wine of Minho, a taste of which nearly takes you off your legs. Assault and battery can be committed by such an eye, and it sometimes has a flash which is a physical back-push.

Gautier is not wrong to lay so much stress on the mantilla and the fan, — the heavy artillery of the women of Spain in their wars with the men. Take away these, and how helpless become these sparkling señoritas! Return them, and every movement at once becomes eloquent. The thousand kisses of Catullus's Lesbia are no more potent weapons than this chain-armor of gossamer lace and these butterfly-wings of ivory and mother-of-pearl, all a-flutter in skillful fingers. It is no uncommon thing to see a Spanish woman on her knees deep in *aves* and *paternosters*, while her fan keeps up its swift automatic motion throughout the devotion. What execution is done at theatres and operas with this sorcerer's instrument would require new Iliads and Odysseys to tell. It is a very serious part of the Spanish woman's curriculum to learn all the secret riches of the fan, all the varied evolution and manipulation it is capable of.

A lovely midsummer night it was: the little balcony, entered by glass doors and hanging high above the street, looked down on the long triangular Puerta del Sol, where a fountain sparkled fairly under the moonbeams. A pleasant coolness floated in through the open windows from the distant Guadárramas, and the curtains flickered under the golden touch of a harvest moon. The balcony was just large enough for two chairs and was one of the most delightful perches imaginable from which to view the animated scene below. This view was like opening a large album of water-color sketches in vivid shades, having its contents suddenly endowed with locomotion.

There are men half of whose lives are spent in this square. If you stay long enough, their physiognomies become as familiar as your watch-chain; mustachioed apparitions with lemonade complexion, fiercely grappling with the inoffensive cigarette; needy hidalgos, who look a request for alms; mute Niobes, supplicating for you know not what, and Dying Gladiators that never give up till they have wrested your last coin from you. Not the least interesting are the monumental attitudes of many of these *habitués*, showing the years of careful culture they have passed through to become brevetted starers. Then there are embodied interjections: men who gesticulate like a Catharine-wheel; fantastic individualities that fight shadows and pirouette on their small feet in boots too tight for them; Captain Bobadils, recounting the thronging story of their exploits; and street-corner Mæcenases, tapping Art on the shoulder. To the 'Gate of the Sun' all men come as to a temple; it is the Sublime Porte of Madrid. The lower stories of nearly all the houses and hotels around the square make a garland of cafés from which music and light stream till far in the night. How many hundred-weight of mirrors, plate-glass, chandeliers, and marble tables are found in this magic circle; how much swallow-tailed humanity serves the crowding visitors; how many cisterns of red, white, and blue drinks; orange, strawberry, cherry, and lemon water; of *agraz* made of green grapes and poured out of bottles as long as umbrella handles; of beer-lemonade, or of the exquisite drink made of Valencian almonds roasted, ground, and iced: a calculation of all this, I say, would require a more expert arithmetician than I am. The cheese-ices, the whipped chocolate and coffee, the banana, apricot, and orange glacés, with the butter-ices made of butter and *unlaid* eggs taken from poulets, form no inconsiderable item of this evening entertainment. I noticed but few women in the cafés, and the men as often as not had their hats on. A waiter would now and then throw a crust out to some doleful in-looker from the streets, when the recipient of the charity would go off with a grateful 'Gracias!' To add to the medley of murmurs by day and by night, quails and crickets kept in tiny cages send forth their cheerful voices and serve to elicit all the overflowing tenderness for which the Spaniards and Italians have invented so many charming diminutives. How little does our stiff Anglo-Saxon tongue know of the caressing grace and melody of these terminations! And how different is the point of view that will name a child Tears or Miracles or Thanks or Dangers, from that which delights in Sally Ann or Simon! As different as the 'Apes of Tarshish' that still run over Gibraltar Rock are from one of the sturdy redcoats that protect them.

'Teresa and four ducats can do nothing, but God, Teresa, and four ducats can do anything:' a famous saying of one of the patron saints of Spain, that well illustrates two or three phases of Spanish character; its boundless faith, its hope, and its charity. The energy which made the good abbess venture on founding a great convent at Toledo with only four ducats, has utterly died out; or has it gone into the preternatural brilliance with which they make their boots shine? or passed into these midsummer flies which, in 1285, says the legend, stung to death forty thousand Frenchmen and twenty-four thousand horses, and in 1684 demolished an entire French army?[1]

Another writer has a pleasant chapter on the influence of tradition in Spanish life. In it he recounts many curious circumstances connected with Peninsula customs and habits. For example, he says that in the Budget of 1870 there was a chapter called the 'Charges of Justice.' This consisted of a collection of articles appropriating large sums of money for the payment of feudal taxes to the great aristocracy of the kingdom as a compensation for long extinct seignories. The Duke of Rivas got thirteen hundred dollars for carrying the mail to Victoria. The Duke of San Carlos draws ten thousand dollars for carrying the royal correspondence (!) to the Indies. Of course this service ceased to belong to these families some centuries ago, but the salary is still paid. The Duke of Almadovar is well paid for supplying the *baton* of office to the Alguazil of Cordova. The Duke of Csuna — one of the greatest grandees of the kingdom, a gentleman who has the right to wear seventeen hats in the

[1] Hare, *Wanderings in Spain*, p. 49.

presence of the Queen — receives fifty thousand dollars a year for imaginary feudal services.[1]

And this cheerful little comedy while Spain was tottering on the verge of bankruptcy.

An Englishman was once traveling in a train between Valencia and Tarragona with some Spanish women. One woman remarked to another how sweetly her baby was smiling in its sleep. 'Yes,' she said, 'it is laughing at the angels, which it only can see.' 'I have such a buzzing in my ears,' said an old woman to another. 'It is the sound of a leaf,' she answered, 'falling from the Tree of Life.' And so they will go on poetically, saying that the tarantula was once an impudent woman so fond of dancing that she even went on with it when the Divine Master passed by; hence she was turned into a spider with a guitar stamped on its back, and those it bit had to dance till they fainted: the daughter of Herodias, in Spanish legend, danced on the frozen waters of the Segre till she fell through and it cut off her head, which continued to dance by itself; again, if a certain little bell associated with divine worship, is heard to tinkle, even at a theatre in the midst of a performance, actors and audience fall on their knees till the Sacrament it announces has been carried past. Spanish custom speaks of the host as his Majesty. Thus,

[1] Hay, *Castilian Days*, p. 52.

when, after a prayer, the consecrated wafer is placed in the mouth of a dying person, a priest, after a few minutes, approaches with a napkin, and asks '*Ha pasado su Majestad?*' (Has his Majesty gone down?) As in England, in several ancient libraries, the books are chained to the cases, so in Spain a library is found now and then with its book-backs turned to the wall. Periwinkles are not periwinkles, but 'the tears of Jesus Christ.' The same conservatism of habit which, since Edward II.'s time, compels the Sheriff of London when he is sworn in, to count six horse-shoes and sixty-one nails in token of education, — counting at that time being a sign of culture, — in Spain used to impose a heavy fine on physicians who did not bring a priest to their patient on the second visit. Such was the uncertainty of medical practice in those days! European sovereigns are all 'cousins,' and in England, whenever there is a coronation it falls to the lot of one of the Dymokes of Scrivelsby, clad in full armor and mounted on a charger, to ride through Westminster Hall, and three times throw down an iron gauntlet, challenging to mortal combat anybody who will dispute the right of the new sovereign to reign. So in Spain on similar occasions, Hay reports a strange custom in connection with the Dukes of Medina Celi, who centuries ago laid claim to the succession. The duke living at the time protests at every new coronation, whereupon the court headsman immediately proceeds to the Medina Celi palace and threatens instant decapitation unless the duke signs a paper abdicating his rights to the throne of all the Spains.

Spanish history has been epitomized as seven centuries of fighting and three thousand battles. The provinces of Spain were never harmonious — father against son and son against mother, till the strangest sorts of hatred were engendered; and the uncertainties of to-day are largely connected with that vibratory theory of politics which from the very beginning has run through the minds of its inhabitants and converted the country into a sort of hereditary revolution. Here in Madrid, in the very teeth of the Puerta del Sol, the passer-by can stand and listen to passionate controversies, on which the fate of empires would seem to turn, but which last hardly longer than the breath that utters them. The last bandit, the last vine-blight, the last swarm of locusts in Murcia or Old Castile, the ever-shifting panorama of parties (of which there are a baker's dozen), the legs of the last dancer or the new theatre-combinations, will on occasion be quite as passionately discussed.

Every traveler will be struck with the gay colors of the houses, — yellow, green, gray, pink, white, mauve. They are singularly fresh and new-looking. Under such a sky colors jut forth with extreme sharpness, and are preserved to a degree quite unknown in northern countries. Here long golden or rose-colored façades covered with a multitude of moldings and balconies, with a quaint tower peeping over from behind, and a range of ancient dormers blinking at you like hooded owls, form most interesting interruptions to the straight lines one is accustomed to view in most new European capitals. Such color-freshness communicates a cheerfulness to Madrid as far removed as possible from the dingy drizzle that oozes down from the Parisian eaves the year round. None of these Spanish houses are very elegantly furnished except those belonging to the highest nobility. The most charming Spanish house I was ever in was the one described at Aranjuez; and even that confined itself wholly to the æsthetic side. In a land of no chimneys and no fires there cannot be much interior comfort. That greatest of luxuries, a true fireside, is unknown.

To enjoy Spain some knowledge of the language is of course absolutely necessary. Fluent speaking acquaintance with colloquial Spanish is by no means easy of attainment, for there are many terms quite indispensable in every-day intercourse which are not found in literature. The literary Spanish is a highly finished and elaborated dialect, and while in five or six of the great provinces — the two Castiles, Estremadura, Andalusia, and Aragon — what is known as 'Spanish' is very generally spoken and often admirably spoken, even by peasants, the traveler who goes to Spain with a memory full of Cervantes, Quevedo, Mendoza, and Leon will find himself sadly unintelligible at the very first railway station. It is a peculiarly insidious language to Italians; for while the languages are just enough alike for the two nations to understand each other tolerably, there are innumerable differences of detail, termination, application of words, and syntax. The rough Arabic-Gothic *j* is a standing trial to every individual, of whatever nationality, that attempts a conversation in Spanish. Toledo, Valladolid, Burgos, and Madrid are all well-known for the purity of their Spanish, like Coimbra among the Portuguese and Blois and Orléans in France. One must confess that the Castilian suffers in a comparison with the Tuscan, though the Spanish insist that the Italian is a 'lady-language,' too dainty for men. A curious fact in the language is the number of meanings borne by each word — meanings, so to speak, riding in front, behind, and pillion-wise, all on the same horse. The far-fetched associations, too, which have filled so thoroughly figurative a language, are often very difficult to catch, and the constant sharp-shooting of abbreviated proverbs is as hard to make out as the 'rubrica,' a royal flourish which the Spanish kings write in lieu of a name on public documents. It was a saying of Charles V. that Spanish was a language to speak with God. Perhaps the good king's apparition would be frightened out of its wits if it could listen to the present slang of Madrid.

Whoever goes to Spain, says an Italian writer, will learn to pronounce with reverence the name of *beans* (garbanzos). Whatever abhorrence the Pythagoreans, following a sort of fastidiousness which prevents the Portuguese from uttering the word for *dog*, may have had for this vegetable in ancient times, has turned into as special a predilection among the non-Pythagorean Spaniards. One would like to have the dish pointed out — flesh, fish, or fowl — into which this leguminous omnipresence does not enter. People may talk of the Spaniards living on honey, snails, mushrooms, and eggs; but to these *beans* must be added in all the majesty of sovereignty and with all the rights of primogeniture.

As for *puchero*, — imagine a whirlwind in a larder, with the result boiled in a huge pot, — and you will have some idea of this national dish. It is perhaps going too far to say that one would be looked upon as a scandalous drunkard who emptied a bottle of wine at a meal in this country; but the Spaniards, wine-drinkers though they be, are abstemious and are apt to stare at the foreigner who drinks much. The ordinary table-wine is too much like acidulated blood for my taste, — a thick, heavy, spurious *Val de Peñas*, strong enough to make the roots of your hair tingle. The Spaniards, who are themselves an animated fermentation, rarely drink to excess. 'Mais c'est une vieille et plaisante question, si l'ame du sage seroit pour se rendre à la force du vin,' says old Montaigne.

The *Palace* shows in what a grand way the Catholic kings could expatiate when they had a chance. Some idea in general may be given of one part of it by mentioning that there is a school attached to educate the children of the servants. It is a truly magnificent pile, of vast extent, the most characteristic part of which is the roof, where roost a perfect covey of superannuated partridges in the shape of pensioners and invalids. They no doubt look down on the world from their perch with true Castilian hauteur — a perch to which, like Lamb's friend, they have retired on one joke and forty pounds a year. The building is not much over a hundred years old, but in that time the most astonishing accumulations have been made; among the curiosities are pink and cream-colored horses; coaches and state-carriages of every description, a single one of which cost seventy-five thousand dollars; state-liveries; clocks without odd or end; and the most splendid collection of arms in Europe; while arches, columns, balconies, courts, and salons without name or number, disport themselves in and over its huge dimensions. The whole of this stupendous structure was occupied in the spacious times of good Queen Isabel. In the reign of King Amadeus most of it remained empty, to the infinite disgust of the Spaniards, who love a splendid extravagance and dearly cherish the good old Spanish vices. Amadeus took two or three little rooms and left the rest to be peopled by crimson-spotted flunkeys or their echoes. One of the king's predilections was for Virginia tobacco. He was an insatiate reader of everything that had to do with himself or his policy. His subjects despised him because he was a simple gentleman and preferred an unattended saunter through the streets of his capital or a drive in the Buen Retiro to all the majesty of the throne of Ferdinand. They hated his queen because there was an evil rumor that she knew Greek, Arabic, astronomy, and mathematics, which a Spanish queen had no business knowing; and there was an added bitterness because she would not attend the bull-fight. One morning they packed their trunks and went home to Italy, fortunate enough to get off unassassinated; and that was Alfonso's red-letter day. Don Amadeus, the First and Last, was no more.

'Charles V.,' reason the Spaniards, 'killed a bull with his own hands in the grand plaza of Valladolid; Pizarro, the conqueror of Peru, was a famous bull-fighter; Don Sebastian of Portugal, and Philip IV. of Spain fought in the arena; therefore why shan't *we* go to bull-fights and fight if we have a chance?' So, 'we have tried to assassinate that king, therefore why not try to assassinate this one?' Perhaps King Amadeus escaped because he was so ugly.

Shall I confess that I was not fortunate enough to see one of the great national sports in Madrid — a cock-fight? Palgrave, in his paper on the Philippine Islands, says it is unsettled whether the Malays got this sport from their Spanish conquerors, or whether the Spaniards imported it from the Philippines. The diabolism of it — apart from Sunday being the favorite day for the performance — is so purely horrible that it need not be dwelt upon, nor how the Malay (the Spaniard too, doubtless), when his house catches fire, is said to run for his game-cock before he does for his wife. The wretched creatures are made to tear each other to pieces by means of long steel gaffs, while an ecstatic crowd gloats around, and betting goes prosperously on.

The Cock and the Bull form a large part of the Spanish story.

In a quaint little canzonet on the Nativity of Christ the shepherds go out saying, 'Adieu, Sir Ox; adieu, Sir Mule, may God be with you!' which illustrates a sort of tenderness the Spanish have for these animals.

Another quaint illustrative feature of popular habit or habitual modes of thought may be gathered from the following couplet forming an inscription for a bridge in one of the remotest provinces: —

'Detente aqui, caminante;
Adora la religion,
Ama la Constitucion,
Y luego pasa adelante.
(O passer-by, detain thee here:
Religion first adore;
The Constitution next revere,
Then pass on as before!)'

There is no word more frequently on the lips of Spaniards, or more popular — for names of streets and squares — than *Constitution*. The familiarity has evidently bred contempt, for genuine constitutional government seems entirely unknown.

One makes strange street acquaintance in a saunter through Madrid. First of all are the gorgeous nurses who have plucked the rainbow from the sky and cut it into gowns for themselves. The sole relic of costume to which we are accustomed is the penitentiary stripe; therefore the more surprise at these Hebe-butterflies flitting about the sidewalks with great children in their arms, looking like gigantic hollyhocks. They come from the North, and, together with their infant charges, are the great patronesses of caramel sugar-sticks (*azucarillos*) and the confections called 'angel's hair.'

It has been well said that Madrid is the thirstiest city on the globe. Hence another picturesque element in street life, — the *aguadores* and *aguadoras*, individuals that hawk the former and the latter rain about the thoroughfares, hoping that somebody will buy. A not very agreeable invitation to the dance is the sight of these individuals administering comfort to their very dirty selves out of the glasses intended for Your Worship. As a Frenchman wittily remarked, day and night the cry of *fire! fire!* (matches) is answered by the cry of *water! water!* in this fire-and-water ridden town. Then the rattan-sellers at the street-corners, the shrill wail of the women crying newspapers, the blind fiddlers and gutter-pickers promenading the Alcalá street, and the veterans of this, that, and the other war, stretched out on the pavement, covered with scars and medals, and invoking your compassion; these lend no little enlivenment to a morning walk. Perhaps, as in Portugal, a huge, antique-looking chariot, drawn by oxen, may come along, having its axles rubbed with lemon-juice that they may screech the louder and scare off the ghosts at night. There are many beautiful shops too, in which, according to the old Catalan custom of using geese for watch dogs, the clerks seem placed to frighten off visitors. The bookshops are exceptionally full and frequent, and Irving, Ticknor, and Prescott occupy prominent places, while there is laudable store of European literature. The contemporary writers, Hartzenbusch the dramatist, Breton de los Herreras, the comedy writer, Zorrilla the poet, Gayangos the Orientalist, Guerra the archæologist, Amado de los Rios the critic; the romance writers Becquer, Fernandez y Gonzalez, and Trueba; the revolutionary poet, Quinta; Espronceda, called the Spanish Byron; Gallego, Della Rosa, de Rivas, and many others, are abundantly represented. There is a very active literary movement going on in Spain at the present moment, and a great deal of sound culture exists in the circle that is settled in Madrid. Castelar is of course the hero of the hour, both in literature and politics, — a man of wonderful eloquence, financier, historian, critic, traveler, political economist, poet, and statesman; but unfortunately possessed of such rhapsodic tendencies that he forgets the critical faculty altogether and has become a voluptuary in rhetoric. To read his Recuerdos de Italia, is like finding one's self again among the more lyrical passages of Volney, Obermann, or Chateaubriand.

Madrid is a great place for pictures: besides the National Museum, — one of the finest and largest collections in the world, — there are nine or ten private galleries, belonging to wealthy bankers and noblemen. Fourteen or fifteen libraries are scattered through the town, none of them, perhaps, so complete as the Ticknor Library at Harvard, which is acknowledged to be the best collection of works relating to Spanish literature in existence. Therefore, just as the American has to go to the British Museum to study American history, so the Spaniard, much as he hates a journey, will have to come to this country for information concerning his. The National Museum is unrivaled in Dutch and Flemish pictures, and in single masterpieces of Italians and Spaniards. Velazquez, Goya, Murillo, and Zurbarán, can be seen in perfection in Madrid alone. The most exquisite Van Dycks and Titians hang on the walls. 'To understand how it is Spain possesses such a gallery, we must recall her as she was, — mistress well-nigh of the world. Italy, Naples, the Netherlands, England, were all at one period under Spanish rule or influence, whilst she had at her command the wealth of the New World. Charles V. was a munificent patron of art; his son, Philip II., inherited his artistic tastes, and added greatly to the treasures collected by the emperor; whilst Philip IV., whose portraits are so numerous in this gallery, contributed still more largely to the royal collection. He commissioned Velazquez to buy works of the great masters in Italy, and ordered the Spanish Ambassador in London to purchase a great part of the fine collection of our Charles I., forty-four of whose pictures are now in this gallery. The gift of a picture was a sure way to royal favor; and in the days of Spanish ascendency, monarchs and subjects gladly proffered their gems of art to the Spanish king. Such is the history of this royal collection.'[1]

Among the 2,000 pictures, there are 43 Titians, 10 Raphaels, 34 Tintorettos, 25 Veroneses, 64 Rubenses, 60 Tenierses, 65 Velazquezes, 46 Murillos, and 38 Riberas. Such a gallery is indeed 'a thing ensky'd and sainted.' The money value of a collection like this is incalculable; what must be the artistic and æsthetic value? Spain might almost pay her national debt with it. Even if one picked out the plums and left the rest, enough would remain to compare favorably with many a European gallery. We may esteem ourselves fortunate in this country if we can even purchase engravings and photographs of its mas-

[1] Tollemache, *Spanish Towns and Spanish Pictures*, p. 47.

terpieces. The long hall is beautifully lighted, and contains a rotunda, lateral galleries, and a basement and up-stairs. The amazingly complicated lock which shuts in this great collection is not the least of its curiosities. It looks almost as if a steam-engine were necessary to turn the key. The white-haired door-keeper is one of the most gracious specimens of his kind that I have ever met. He actually spoke not Ollendorff, but French, and smiled radiantly at each individual visitor as he entered. A catalogue — not without defects, as seen in the criticism on it in a recent Revista Contemporanea — has been lately issued. Many of the pictures are hung entirely too high, and cannot be seen to advantage. For its size and importance, there is no museum so unexplored as this. Many suppressed convents and public collections have contributed to it. 'Radiance in archangels and grace in Madonnas,' to quote Ruskin's phrase, may there be seen in abundance; and so far as likenesses of the Spanish kings are concerned, one cannot reproach this gallery, as Carlyle did the galleries of Berlin. 'The Berlin galleries, which are made up, like other galleries, of goat-footed Pan, Europa's Bull, Romulus's She-wolf, and the Correggiosity of Correggio, contain, for instance, no portrait of Friedrich the Great.' Here they hang in unimaginable abundance, eight or ten a-piece now and then, — Charleses, Philips, Ferdinands, Medicis, Baltasars. I never remember to have been in a European museum which did not contain a Marie de Medici, and here she is, huge as ruff and farthingale can make her, — a sea of fat in point lace. Rubens, with his transcendent simper and naked Flemings, is in force: a painter who certainly succeeded better with satyrs than with nymphs and graces, for he was a man of gross nature, and could paint tipsiness and impurity to perfection. I never saw one illumined-looking female face by him: and yet who could paint children more exquisitely? 'The splendid Fleming,' says Motley, 'rushed in and plucked up drowning art by the locks, when it was sinking in the trashy sea of such creatures as the Luca Giordanos and Pietro Cortonas.' A Pompejan lamp is not a whit more suggestive than many a Danäe or Venus of Titian and Rubens. And, as Longfellow says, who would have one of these hanging in his hall?

The museum forms a stately pile on one side of the Prado, probably the finest drive in Europe. There is not the radiance of verdure possessed by the Champs Elysées, nor the freshnesss and luxuriance of the English parks; but in length, extent, and situation, the Prado excels them all. Here and there along it are spots which are fashionable or not, according to the caprice of the hour. The *Buen Retiro*, a charming park, lies beyond. The city abounds in theatres, bull-rings, circuses, *zarzuelas*, cock-pits, and clubs. Barring the keen air, Madrid must be a fascinating residence in winter, especially in carnival time. A wide, handsome, sunny, airy place, abounding in squares and promenades, every part of the Peninsula is accessible from it, and it is possible to reach the French capital in a few hours, and with a single change of cars. Tram-ways penetrate the city in many directions, and meet in the Puerta del Sol, the centre of a star of streets which radiate thence. Though they collect fares rather frequently, the amounts are small, and the mules that are used make the trams spin along at a signal pace. The city is well provided with cabs and fiacres, and the offices of the railways all have a series of omnibuses, which convey the passenger to and from the station for a mere song. This custom is general through Spain and Portugal. The ticket-offices are all grouped about the Puerta del Sol, without which life and soul of it Madrid would be eviscerated indeed. The stations are literally besieged with *calèches*, insidiously named after the various hotels which they serve. Woe to you if you get into one of them without previous stipulation. At the station, every one has to take his turn in purchasing his ticket, superintended by a policeman, and every coin is duly rung and tested by the railway official on the marble slab provided for that purpose. Gold and silver — even copper — are freely rejected by this Rhadamanthus, who is as careful and inflexible as a man should be, out of whose pockets Mephistopheles' 'herrliche Löwenthaler' have to come, in case false money has been handed in. Caution in money matters is a shining virtue in this country, where national bank bills are scarcely taken outside the city of Madrid. Inn keepers and store-keepers are full of tricks, and gladly pass their useless coins on unsuspecting foreigners. Letters of credit are the easiest to get along with: Spanish bankers are proverbially polite; and though you run constant danger, owing to the great number of church holidays, of getting out of money, and having to wait inconveniently, you always get what you want in the end. An excellent habit it is to travel with a church calendar and holy-feast book in one's pocket. The intricate numbering of Spanish houses, and the obscure dens occupied by many Spanish business firms, render it quite difficult sometimes to find an address.

'Portugal is a safe country; there are no brigands; the only thieves keep inns, and the only formidable beasts live in them.' I wish I could say the same of Spain. As to safety, two or three attacks on trains took place about the time of my journey. Spaniards, I was told, have a whimsical repugnance to traveling first-class in the same railway carriage with a foreigner; as soon as a foreigner gets in, they get out, and herd together in suffocating closeness, rather than run possible risks from alien fingers. Many a long ride to and from stations, at unheard of midnight hours, have I had to take, to keep the inconvenient appointments of the trains; a fact which renders travel unnecessarily fatiguing and hazardous. As to inns, and those that keep them, the less said the soonest mended. Spanish apartments are like the earth that brought forth 'the living creature after his kind, cattle, and creeping thing.' If the most conciliating cheapness can be any palliation for this state of things, then the cloak may be thrown over the multitudinous sins of boarding-houses and resting-places in the land of the Cid. The traveler in this land is always the traveler militant, ever on the defensive, ever 'glowering round the corner,' to use an odd Netherlandish phrase. If the patriotic Spaniards would rebel against this tyranny, and do with the inn-keepers as Latouche says the Lisbon people do with the ever-increasing dogs of that good town: 'A net is drawn, on a dark night, across a leading street, and the dogs of a whole neighborhood driven to the spot; as they become entangled in its meshes, a man kills them with a blow on the head, and throws their bodies into a cart;' if the patriotic Spaniards, I say, would establish their nets in the Puerta del Sol and its purlieus, for example, and proceed as the practical Portuguese do, I am sure the golden age would not be far off in Spain.

One of the many manias which possessed the Spanish kings was a mania for clocks. Clocks big and clocks little, musical and non-musical clocks, mantel clocks and centre-table clocks, clocks in season and out of season, garnished their palaces and echoed through their apartments. And yet no Spanish king ever knew the time of day or night. Their morning was other people's bed-time, and their night was usually the world's morning. Hence the long list of groaning ambassadors who, knowing the Spanish punctilio, confused it with punctuality, and spent hours of their precious lives in antechambers awaiting audience of their Catholic majesties. And nobody ever had an engagement with these devout sovereigns who did not come to the conclusion that the Spanish clocks, like their august possessors, were the slowest, stupidest, and most backward of their kind. The bewildered Bourbons promenading among their clocks and yet oblivious to either the value or the flight of time, are good illustrations of the state of things in Spain. Everything is behind time and behind the times. Spanish dinners are later than anybody else's; Spanish newspapers are stale with yesterday's news; the very passion of the people for late hours, late and long morning naps, late church hours and light disregard of early industry, shows that a special Providence has appointed certain nations to bring up the comfortable rear of civilization — Nations of the Evening — while their brethren are all a-flush with the future and the light of the morning far ahead.

And what a charming specimen of the Nations of the Morning I found in James Russell Lowell, the poet, critic, scholar, and statesman, who now waits on Don Alfonso for us at the Court of Madrid. He seemed almost an anachronism in the ancient Castilian city; the busy, brilliant Yankee, full of our intensest Anglo-Saxon life, a man of many resources and many thoughts, no doubt, too, in those infinite leisures of Spanish life, thinking out one of the beautiful studies and criticisms which he has so lavishly given us in My Study Windows. Madrid is so plain and sunny in the cloudless Castilian air that — by way of exception to most Spanish cities — there is not the least trouble in finding an address, no matter how remote from the Puerta del Sol. The wayfaring Spaniard, too, is very polite, and, after informing you at great length of all the streets and turnings you are to traverse, bids your grace 'go with God,' with a phrase that has come down from ancient times. In one of the many bright streets that run into the Prado — the Champs Elysées of Madrid — I found the United States' coat of arms blazoned over a door which I was not wrong in taking for that of the American Embassy. A cheerful, lightsome house, with marble hall and steps, stained glass, subdued tones of wall and wainscot, and a charming and unaccountable absence of 'business,' tobacco, shreds of paper, spittoons, and other paraphernalia appertaining to the usual American office. One could see that here, at least, in all this broad Spanish peninsula, was culture. Here, too, one felt certain, could be found English books and transatlantic periodicals, — a redolence and aroma of that great outer life in which Spain takes so little part. A kind reception soon opened the way to a pleasant conversation, to which Mr. Lowell's humor and imagination lent no little charm. For a moment the visitor imagined he had made a mistake and found himself in the presence of the English minister, so thoroughly English is Mr. Lowell's appearance and accent. Is it usual for Bostonians to trill their *r*'s and broaden their *a*'s *quite* so much as the author of the Biglow Papers does? But we will not accuse so sincere and distinguished a man of affectation. Half a life-time spent at Harvard in drilling French consonants and Italian vowels into beginners has, no doubt, left its impress, and transformed, if not transfigured, Mr. Lowell's pronunciation. He is a fine Spanish scholar, and his Harvard lectures on Cervantes, no less than on Dante, are well-known. He takes the greatest interest in the quaint life around him, and is a studious observer of Spanish politics. The Spaniards, said he, have reached a condition of anarchy politically to which our rotation-in-office system is rapidly bringing us. Government succeeds government with unpleasant haste, and one round of office-seekers after another is eating up the country, reminding one of the proverb about the climate of the north of Spain, — 'ten months hibernal and two months infernal.'

The conversation turned on the curious customs and observances of peninsular life, the grave courtesy of the people, their Oriental extravagance of expression, their habit of dating their letters from *your* house (which Mr. Lowell says is dying out), and the serious inconvenience of admiring anything belonging to your host. Apropos of the latter, Mr. Lowell told a story of an American admiral which may bear repeating. The admiral had just arrived with the fleet at one of the Mediterranean ports, and a hospitable Spaniard, learning of his arrival, sent him an invitation to dinner, which was accepted with Jonathanian readiness. Dinner over, the party adjourned to the drawing-room, where Admiral Jonathan, after the fashion of his country, began to admire first one thing and then another, especially one object of great beauty and costliness, thinking all the while merely to compliment his host on his taste. 'It is at the disposition of your grace,' replied the courteous host. Stares, polite excuses, refusals, apologies, proved vain; the object was packed up and sent to the admiral's ship, who, happy in the possession of a rare work of art, took no thought for the morrow when — the Spaniard sent for it! This empty phrase — 'at the disposition of your grace' — is all that survives of a once princely custom. One of the Spanish kings gave Charles I. the jewel of his picture-gallery because he had carelessly admired it. The habit of presenting people with any object they admired was once universal, and still survives — as General Grant can tell us — among the Mussulmans of Constantinople. Things are sent home to you, but you are expected to return them or send something of equal value. The most cordial invitations are given to dinner which all the codes of all the Castilians forbid you to accept. They are invitations to those Barmacide feasts in which the Spanish imagination delights — culinary castles in the air.

The acceptance of such an invitation would provoke a scene both ludicrous and distressing. The Spaniard means to be polite, and in his flowing, flowery way, he is; but be sure you have your stock of reserves and reticences and engagements on hand. There is no dinner at the Spanish home; the hostess has but one gown, and that she sleeps in; and all the market-money evaporates through the end of the host's innumerable cigarettes.

Mr. Lowell has a high opinion of Don Alfonso and says he is far from being a specimen of royal cram. He was particularly struck with the originality and independence of his views on the masterpieces of Spanish literature, which he had evidently read and studied with care. The young king is popular — a popularity which he owes largely to his poor young queen, who so lately passed away. No matter how infamous their deeds, Spanish kings and queens are nearly always idolized by their subjects. Personal popularity has been their one solace — clocks excepted — and Alfonso, who is hardly twenty, comes in for his share.

Mr. Lowell spoke with great indignation of the contemptible uses to which American ministers to foreign countries are put by their peregrinating countrymen; and added that our representative at a certain great continental court was literally no more than a *valet de place*. His business was to tell people when the museums were open, what theatres to go to, who were the swell milliners and tailors, and when they could be presented at court. This is a fact. One half the time of these august beings is spent running about with old women, showing 'governor' this or 'general' that the 'sights;' purchasing opera-tickets, peradventure, or hunting up names and addresses at the various bankers'. The other half is spent in drawing the salary.

In an easy and pleasant manner a half hour slipped quickly away. Mr. Lowell talks admirably, but one can hardly recognize in this hearty, healthy, exuberant man, the poet of exquisite nerves and fancies, the lover of Chaucer and Dryden, the imaginative and eloquent writer who has told us with so much grace so many things old and new. His spiritualities and subtleties he casts like a fine spray over that larger self which is seen in his writings, while he reserves for more common uses the rich and strong flavors of a unique personality. Touch him anywhere, and there is an anecdote; life for him is a recollection, a witticism, a line of poetry, an epigram, a camel's hair brush with which to paint conversation with multifarious incident. His intimate friends must, one conjectures, enjoy a rare treat in intercourse with so choice a spirit. He cannot fail to inhale the fine poetry of Andalusian and Castilian life, and one day we shall have it returned in some work of peculiar grace. It is a comfort to have ourselves represented by such a man of pure genius and quiet literary force, after all the Cushings and Sickleses of the latter days. It keeps fresh the traditions of Washington Irving, Taylor, and Bancroft, and infuses an element of poetry into the arid air of diplomatic intercourse, an element which cannot fail to refine ; besides, it shows that literature is still a power and wins its recognition even at Washington.

XIII.

And they produce a host of books, written by Musæus and Orpheus, children, as they say, of the Moon and the Muses, which form their ritual. — PLATO, *Rep.* ii. 365.

THERE is a certain eloquence in figures, when applied to Spain.[1] Without going quite so far as the Greek epigram, that says, 'All things are known to him that holdeth Number,' — a formula which a well-known mathematical journal has adopted as its *Lasciate esperanza*, — there is still a great deal of truth in the saying. Whether the Spaniards are special arithmeticians or not, it would be hard to say; but there is hardly a nation against which numbers count so tellingly. Every year the official annuary makes a pitiable revelation; every year there are the confessions of some statistical St. Augustine. The length and breadth of the land are annually harrowed by the remorseless Guia Oficial de España, or the Anuario Estadistico, publications which enter into all sorts of miscellaneous details, and read like the reports of a lazaretto. All the hemp of the Philippine Islands would, according to

[1] The figures in this chapter are approximate.

many Spaniards themselves, hardly suffice to hang the rogues that prey on the revenues, fill the government offices, and cry ' *Viva el rey*' with boundless enthusiasm every time a new Alfonso or a new Amadeus lands at Barcelona; and, it might be added, all the sugar of Cuba is hardly sufficient to sweeten the annual pill of ruinous taxes, government monopolies, huge civil lists, pence for the grandees and pounds for the princesses. In the last hundred years the population has hardly doubled; the nine millions of 1768 are about the eighteen millions of 1878. Within this period there are years in which the population absolutely fell off, or, if there was increase at all, so slow and laborious an increase that it made no impression on the statisticians, and remained unregistered in their contributions to economical science. As far back as 1842, the population was only three times that of the State of New York now. Ninety Spaniards per English square mile were all the most ardent census-takers could muster in 1860. This is a meagre showing indeed for a kingdom with nearly 180,000 square miles of continental land. Our population was in 1870 nearly ten times what it was in 1790, or as many times as four millions (1790) will go into thirty-eight millions (1870). Our census has been taken but nine times, while it would be difficult to say how many times the

Catholic kings have tormented themselves and their subjects with the Israelitish hankering after numbers, and the vain hope of immense increase within abnormally short periods. Madrid has the population of Brooklyn, and is much the largest city; while in 1874 there were but four cities (Madrid, Barcelona, Valencia, and Seville) that had over a hundred thousand inhabitants. Such famous cities as Malaga, Valladolid (the 'rich' of Spanish legend), Murcia, Saragossa, Granada, and Cádiz have to be left entirely out of these chosen four. It would hardly be fair to compare the slow growth of these old historic cities with the marvelous growth that gave us in 1870 fourteen cities with 100,000 inhabitants and over, and that showed Michigan in 1820 to have about 9,000 people, and over a million in 1870. Province by province, as far as they go, the eleven ancient 'kingdoms' composing the aggregate of Spain will compare very favorably with as many of our States in population, not in area; where they have eleven, with a handful of islands, we had thirty-seven in 1870, not to mention the ten territories, any one of which, perhaps, might pocket the whole peninsula. Andalusia (17,000 square miles, about the size of Switzerland) has the population of Virginia before West Virginia was filched; Old Castile (41,000 square miles, larger than all Portugal, and twice the size of the Neth-

erlands) is not quite so populous as New York;
the provinces of Granada, Valencia, and Galicia
would compare favorably in population with Indiana, Kentucky, Missouri, and Massachusetts,
each of them somewhat exceeding a million. Up
to 1820 Virginia had always taken the lead in
population among the States; so Old Castile, the
special battle-ground of the Cid, and the province celebrated in his early romantic story for a
thousand mythical and legendary incidents, seems
long to have had the ascendency in mere multitude, if not in positive force. The nearly eight
millions of our increase between 1860 and 1870
would represent half the señores and señoras that
disport themselves in the Spanish cities, and think
' *La España es todo;* ' and if one added to these
the incidental eight millions of foreigners that
have landed on our shores during the last fifty
years, almost the entire population of the puissant realm of Alfonso would be approached.

Again, take the matter of salaries and civil
lists. Alfonso's individual civil list amounts to
nearly a million and a half of dollars; the four
infantas get $160,000 among them; $200,000 or
so go to the royal refugees, who spend their leisure and their money in building palaces in Paris.
Two millions go to the relatives of the king, the
last of the sixteen kings who, since the foundation of the united Spanish monarchy, in 1512,

have, with an interval or two of republics (1868, 1869, 1873, 1874), been on the throne of Spain. How niggardly look our vice-president's ten thousand dollars, and the chief executive's fifty thousand; while compare the White House with the Hapsburg and Bourbon palaces! The House of Bonaparte and the House of Savoy did not stay long enough to make their mark on the architecture of the country.

The five kings of the House of Hapsburg began with Charles I. (with three Philips sandwiched between) and ended with Charles II., in 1665. The eight Bourbons stand by themselves, or might be put side by side with the eight Bourbons who from the time of Henry IV. to the time of Louis Philippe, leaving twenty years for First Republic and Empire, sat on the throne of France. But altogether the most important periods in French and Spanish history were those periods when their legitimate kings were visiting foreign watering-places.

The reformed or transformed Spanish constitution of 1876 (a year after the date of Alfonso's accession) is quite the most recent experiment in constitutions by articles and clauses. The threescore years and ten of the patriarch are exceeded by the nearly four-score rules of the constitutional monarchy, the constitution for which is, so far as the glitter of phraseology and the glow of generalization are concerned, quite a papier-maché constitution. The King is the Executive, and the legislative power rests in King and Cortes. Our Senate and House of Representatives are paralleled by their Senate and 'Congress;' but we have no such classification of senators which, since the Constituent Assembly of 1876, has applied Darwinism to politics, and 'selected' the higher body of Spanish representatives. Our purely elective principle is unknown to Spain, for Spain has senators by their own right, life-senators, like Irish peers, and elective senators. Hereditary grandees, with an income of $12,000; the king's sons; admirals of the navy; captains-general of provinces (corresponding remotely to our governors of states); the nine archbishops; the patriarch of the Indies; and the presidents of the council of state, supreme court, and court of accounts of the realm, are senators in their own right. As usual with European constitutions modeled more or less after the English, the right of dissolution and convocation of Parliament dwells in the king. Elective senators hold for five years; half the whole number constituting this branch of the upper house has to be renewed within the same periodical limit, and the whole when Parliament has been dissolved. Groups of 50,000 souls send each one deputy, named in certain electoral juntas, to the 'congress,' or popular body of the Parliament. The crown nominates the 100 life-senators, paralleled to some extent by the 75 life-senators out of the 300 in the French assembly; certain bodies called state corporations and those who pay the largest contributions are entitled to elect the 130 elective senators; while the rest are those fixed and motionless bodies which we see in the English House of Lords, and depend for their places on what is called 'their own right.'

Many travelers note the contrast between the admirable self-government of the provinces, districts, and communes, and the general corruption, incompetency, and feverishness of the central circle at Madrid. The Spanish *fueros*, or local charters, are amongst the most ancient in Europe, and show the early period at which local self-government and municipal autonomy were fostered and developed in Spain. These local administrations are singularly jealous of the imperial Walhalla at Madrid, — a collection of deceased functionaries, already rendered harmless by the death of their political influence, and engaged for the most part in waging warfare with shadows. The system of these local administrations is very excellently arranged: first, a community of at least sixty persons elects an *ayuntamiento*, or board of aldermen, numbering from four to eight-and-twenty, over whom a mayor or *alcalde* presides, assisted by his deputies. This board is elected every two years, and has complete control over communal and municipal taxation and the department of local justice. It elects the mayor annually, whose executive functions we have an edifying example of in Cervantes' La Jitanilla. Then communal life finds another reservoir into which to flow, and that is the provincial parliaments, an important factor in administrative and representative life in Spain. The various *ayuntamientos* elect the members of these country legislatures, which meet every year, and are vested with great powers and privileges, guarantied by the imperial parliament. Everything relating to the government and administration of the provinces, with their inner circles of communes, is in general in the hands of these parliaments and *ayuntamientos*. The Madrid luminaries shine equally on the just and on the unjust, and exercise a sort of transcendental jurisdiction and supervision over the general and permanent interests of the state. The new constitution has interfered as little as possible with the staid and equable functions of these old-fashioned representative bodies, in which Spain finds her chief strength. Their existence from ancient times has made the Spaniards the intense politicians they are, and many a name which has shed lustre over the national history began to twinkle in the provincial assemblies.

In naval affairs our one admiral, one vice-admiral, and eleven rear-admirals are offset in Spain by one captain-general of the fleet and twenty admirals. The ships are manned by conscription, chiefly from districts along the coast, and are numerous and powerful for a country so deeply in debt. Our army, commanded by its general, lieutenant-general, three major-generals, and half a dozen brigadiers, is ludicrously small when compared with the large forces officered by the five captain-generals, sixty lieutenant-generals, one hundred and thirty-one major-generals, and two hundred and thirty-eight brigadiers of the Spanish army. The officials of the Spanish army form an army in themselves, not to mention the titular dignitaries, effulgent in lace and gold, who dazzle the popular imagination and keep up the silken memories of the past. But then there is a force of one hundred and eighty thousand men, rank and file, to officer, which accounts somewhat for the abnormal growth of titles. Four years' service in the permanent army is required of every Spaniard over twenty; then comes the active reserve, composed of those young men who, omitting the four years of active service, are beyond the years determined by law for the permanent organization; the second, or sedentary, reserve is composed of those who have served effectively for four years, unless they desire to adopt the soldier's profession permanently, when they are allowed to do so within certain limits. At twenty-eight a Spaniard, after serving eight years in the active or the reserve force, is free from military service, as the Germans are, barring the *Landwehr* and *Landsturm* service, required in emergencies. Habits of idleness are undoubtedly generated by this turn-about fashion of military organization. Idling in barracks, service in dissipated Mediterranean towns, contact as observers merely with the great spectacular pageant of large cities, and easy day-dreaming along the Sierras with the ostensible object of crushing out brigandage infallibly lead to moral and physical degeneracy; and *quantum mutatus ab illis* comes to one's thoughts on comparing the gigantic armor of the Armeria at Madrid with the pigmies that guard it outside.

Perhaps there is no country so solidly Roman Catholic as Spain. The whole country adheres to this religion in a lump, save a leaven of some three-score thousands of other faiths, like the six hundred thousand Protestants of France. Perhaps the Pyrenees have more to do with it than is generally acknowledged, for it was but recently that the great transit-roads now in operation were drilled through these mighty barriers, and a little light from without illumined the Stygian murkiness of the country. And perhaps the concentrated type of Spanish Catholicism is due to this isolation. At all events, prelates innumerable infest the country. While populous England has but two archbishops and twenty-eight bishops, thinly populated Spain has Dante's mystic number of nine archbishops, with nearly five times that number of bishops. Cathedral and college priests and dignitaries swarm. The monks in the country not quite a hundred years ago would people a town of sixty thousand inhabitants, the nuns another of thirty thousand, and the inquisitors, big and little, a village of twenty-five hundred. In all, the number would equal the present entire population of Louisville. The swarming confessionals, the uneasy consciences, the self-tormenting religious life of the country, called this myriad brood into existence, and put it down statistically on the registers of the kingdom precisely as we find it for the year 1787, when quite different things were doing in this country. The 'high-priest of this ghostly metaphysics' is the Archbishop of Toledo, who at times thunders transcendently from his great cathedral, and attracts an attention almost equal to the Holy Father himself. The established church is of course maintained by the state, which binds itself through the constitution to keep up the worship and the ministers of the Roman Catholic religion, and entirely lacks the liberality with which the French constitution provides for the maintenance of Catholics, Jews, and Protestants alike. Protestant worship, if not done absolutely by stealth, like religious worship in the times of the Catacombs, is entirely private, and cannot be publicly announced. Forty years ago conventual establishments were suppressed, it is to be hoped forever, and their property reverted to the nation. 'The mediæval notion of the church as a political estate, with pomps, honors, and powers,' has thus vanished, and all the vast housings and hospitalities of mediæval ecclesiasticism have now been comfortably converted into untransferable public debt certificates bearing interest at the rate of three per cent. The churches and parsonages as the guardians of the remaining spiritualities of the kingdom are exempted from this conversion.

Most intimately connected with the church is the astonishing condition of things in educational matters. 'It is not good for man to learn,' has been the precept of the Spanish educators; and with such diffidence and delicacy have educational methods been pressed, and with such modesty and bashfulness received, that the kingdom is still in extremest ignorance. One of the many immoralities which women were not to practice was learning to read and write ; and with such rigor and felicitous success was this prohibition inculcated, that in 1860 there were only about seven hundred thousand women out of nearly seven and a half millions in the whole kingdom able to read and write. The ignorance of the men was not quite so monstrous ; yet thirty years ago only two millions out of the total population could even read, and in some provinces fourteen out of fifteen were totally ignorant. Here, then, is a veritable paradise for Lindley Murray, Webster's spelling book, and the Clarendon press! In 1860 science had one hundred and forty-one devotees in the higher institutions of the country, medicine about a thousand, law nearly four thousand, and theology about three hundred ; admirable showing in a population of nearly thrice six millions! The 'science' is annually exhibited in the miraculous doings of the priests, the law in the interminable controversies of the courts, and the medicine in carrying round a gold-headed cane as insignia of the Æsculapian art.

While in fifty years our railway system has grown from twenty-three miles in 1830 to over eighty thousand miles in 1878, the State of Illinois alone had a system in 1875 nearly double that of all Spain in 1877 (three thousand six hundred miles). Lobbyism is certainly in the ascendant in Spain, for nearly all the railways are what Anglo-Indian politicians call 'guarantied,' and receive subventions from the government. Private individuals and companies own them exclusively, and nearly every town of any importance is connected with one or the other of them. They have some two thousand post-offices to our two-score thousand; while the four-score million letters which passed through theirs in 1876 stand in rather singular juxtaposition with the seven hundred millions passing through ours the year after. Twenty thousand miles will quite cover the length of their telegraph-wires, while six times that number will hardly cover the length of wires in the United States. The foreign and governmental dispatches embrace nearly half the messages sent by telegraph in Spain; private telegraphing seems a luxury, and is comparatively little resorted to.

The country is crushed by an overwhelming public debt,— nearly three billions of dollars two years ago. It broods over the land like a thunder-cloud, ready to burst at any moment and scatter ruin far and near. Deficit after deficit is the sad tale of the Spanish budget year after year. Two hundred and fifty thousand dollars a day as the cost of a civil war indefinitely prolonged soon brought the debt to the enormous figures it now occupies in the national ledgers; everything seems verging to an abysm of repudiation. Spain can only borrow at frightful rates of interest, and with imminent peril of doubling the debt in a short period. The ten million dollars' worth of wine which she sends England annually is but a drop in this immeasurable bucket. Her entire amount of imports and exports would not much exceed the trade balance of exports alone in our favor for the year 1878. Where, then, is money to come from with which to extinguish these obligations? England, France, and the United States all have enormous resources; but Spain? One can appreciate and sympathize with the despair of the Spanish minister of finance when he pathetically approaches this subject. There is plenty of taxation, direct and indirect, but there seems to be an impassable gulf between revenue and expenditure never yet bridged over by any Spanish cunning. The unctuous Isabel could scatter a quarter of a million dollars in a single visit to Andalusia; and that will suggest precisely where much of the money has gone, — cultivating popularity is a good old Spanish vice, and cultivating fields is not. Expenditure bears the proportion to revenue of 32 to 27.

Still, there is yet hope for poor old empty Spain, with two such glorious wings as the Philippines in the East and Cuba in the West to keep her buoyant. And then the Canary Islands have a perennial song for the ancient mother.

The Philippines are twice as populous as Switzerland, and have an area much greater than England and Wales. Cuba is a good deal larger than Ireland; and Porto Rico is one fourth the size of Belgium. The special wealth of Porto Rico seems to be in slaves, which in 1875 were not far below the number in the most flourishing period of ancient Attic slavery. While Portugal has abolished slavery throughout her possessions, Spain still clings to it. As, for mere revenue, one would rather be Duchess of Lancaster or Duke of Cornwall than Queen of England or Prince of Wales, so the Cuban planter, in mere opulence and voluptuousness, is generally far before the much-envied Spanish grandee. A peep into a grandee's house is occasionally a rather dismal spectacle: all his ancestors hang in the Madrid picture-galleries, all his furniture is in the art museums, all his lackeys are in the army, and he himself is tottering on the verge of bankruptcy. Everything wears a second-hand look. Many of them can say in the words of their national hero, in his bitter reply to Don Alfonso: —

> 'Y de lo que hube ganado
> Vos fice señor y dueño,
> Non me lo confiscáredes
> Vos, ni vuesos consejeros,
> Que mal podredes tollerme
> La facienda que non tengo!'
>
> *El Cid*, cviii.

A great change has taken place in Spain since Bryant's visit in 1857,[1] when there were but one hundred and forty miles of railway in the kingdom, with projected lines to Lisbon, Bordeaux, Barcelona, and Cádiz. All these lines and many others have been built, and one may now go from Paris to Lisbon with but two changes of trains, — one at Irun, and the other in Madrid. Decent railway stations, however, really do not exist in the peninsula. In those happy times of twenty years ago the queen would go out at six o'clock in the evening to take her morning walk; and as for dining before ten o'clock in the evening, or retiring before three at night, it was quite impossible. Piety and dissoluteness went harmoniously together: —

> 'Nam, fatebimur verum,
> Dulces fuistis;'

and Isabel consoled herself by appointing this or that archbishop her private confessor. We have no reason to think that there was any such admirable plainness of speech between them as Gil Blas used to his friend the Barber on the occasion of his reading the sonnet. The scandal of this memorable reign has left an abiding impression.

'Whatever Aristotle and all the philosophers may say, there is nothing equal to tobacco,' was

[1] *Letters of a Traveller.*

a saying of **Molière's**; but will it be believed that good cigars are easier to get in New York or London than in Spain? All the odds and ends of chopped Christendom go to make up the *cigarritos* which form so essential a part of national existence in the peninsula, and various are the diseases chronicled by the doctors as engendered by the indulgence. If 'milking other people's minds was a characteristic of Goethe,' filching from other industries is a characteristic of the tobacco industry here. Twenty-five dollars a hundred is no very exceptional price for a good cigar; while the vanilla, opium, or other scenting or stimulating mixtures in which they are steeped give rise to innumerable grades of prices.

From the Pyrenees on the Spanish side, and from the hills of Galicia and Asturias in the northwest, numbers of crystalline streams flow down abounding in salmon, while at any Mediterranean town excellent sea-fish are found. Fish should certainly be procurable in great quantities where Lent is so rigorously observed, and the whole population fasts once a week. Everybody knows what great delicacies the red and white legged partridges of Spain are; while the Mediterranean marshes in the east and southeast are, in season, full of ducks. Woodcock, snipe, hares, sandpipers, deer, and wolves are abundant in certain localities. The remoter

Sierras are said to contain plenty of roebucks, chamois, and wild goats; but I will not vouch for the astounding number of ducks (8,000 to 10,000) said sometimes to be brought down by five or six guns in one month round Gibraltar.

The dances, the lotteries, the bull-fights, the costumes, the festivals, have all given rise to many a locution difficult to understand without some special knowledge of the provinces, the home circle, and society such as we find it a-saunter through Spain from May to November. Everything is permeated with the spirit of the old gallantry; even the ladies' garters are covered with embroidered inuendoes and souvenirs of a frolic imagination. A good deal of landed proprietorship is said to have grown out of prizes in the lotteries, — a universal fever encouraged by the state, insatiable of the earnings of the poor, and two or three times a month putting the entire kingdom on the rack of expectation. There is considerable revenue to the state accruing from the drawings, but the misery to the unlucky blank-holders is not to be described.

A Spanish hidalgo who can arrange his winter cloak in the orthodox seventeen different ways may call himself finished in the art of personal decoration; but one should hardly take advantage of his proverbial politeness by doing what Dumas, in his *Paris à Cadiz*, I think, said *he* did : by simply admiring what his *caballero* friends had on from time to time, he was presented with the individual pieces of a rich and complete costume ! The streets, full of such cloaked and sombreroed figures, certainly have an interesting mediæval aspect ; while the satin, silk, or black lace mantilla, worn shopping or going to mass by the women, gives a piquancy to the street unknown in other European cities. I saw but few white lace veils, which are reserved for grand occasions, — such occasions as Desaugiers wittily describes in his Inconveniences of being Rich. No Tanagra figurines, exquisite as are these lately discovered specimens of Greek *genre* art, can flirt a fan more daintily than a Spanish girl, from the fan which is a delicate landscape, a miniature comedy, or a painted love-song in itself, to the fans arabesqued with steel on radii of sandal-wood or ivory. The cry of the wandering fan-seller soon becomes one of the familiarities of the Spanish open-air experience. He generally carries his fans along with knives and matches. Every month, nay, almost every week, has its *verbenas*, *veladas*, *festas*, or fairs, each with its pilgrimage, its holy vigil, its procession of confraternities, its blessing of mules and donkeys, its turkey-killing, its sending of bonbons or bouquets on birthdays, or its apotheosis of pastry-cook shops into illuminated bazaars of Christmas cakes. It is a matter of difficulty *not* to be born on a saint's day.

'The toilsome way and long, long league to trace' is somewhat alleviated by the trains of muleteers and their mules, which Bedouinize through the remoter parts of Spain, and permit a traveler to join them for safety and society. The ancient high-roads are admirably kept up, but one soon, with Bryant, begins to long for Dr. Piper or Walter Scott, or some other lover of trees, to reclothe this amber denudation, and reconvert the nation from the silly notion that trees harbor birds that destroy the crops, forsooth. It is part of the humor of the past that travelers in Spain, before starting, used to call in a priest for absolution, a doctor for the final dose of medicine, and a notary to make their wills. Traveling is now tolerably safe, especially in the company of the muleteers, who are frequently jolly fellows, and, though entirely guiltless of reading or writing, are full of wit, sense, and helpfulness. They do not, like the Arabs, swear by the 'wind,' the 'wood,' or 'the honor of the Arabs,' but by the saints and martyrs, and with astounding copiousness and ingenuity. Oaths are nearly always ungrammatical, and those of the Spanish muleteers are peculiarly so. Being in their company for a few days is like being in the company of Congreve's, Farquhar's, or Wycherly's comedies once more. These trains move as lazily as the currents of the five or six canals, which draw their long-drawn length through the land, and vivify certain kiln-like parts of it. Inland navigation, however, languishes, in spite of the large rivers which, with their hundreds of tributaries, flow through the country, sometimes, like the Tagus, for a distance of six hundred miles. And in a region where there are more fossil ferns than living ones, and more petrified than actual vegetation, no very highly developed agricultural system can be found; and where land which has borne a crop of wheat is left fallow instead of being cultivated with clover and grasses, trees are supposed to produce malaria, and other national idiosyncrasies come into play, no very great receptivity of ideas prevails, nor can any very revolutionary changes take place in the hereditary 'works and days.' There would certainly be embarrassment nowadays in finding the two evergreen oaks to which, in the ballad of Doña Sol and Doña Elvira, the two countesses were tied by their sovereign lords. In the closing rapture of the Antigone, the chorus of ancient Thebans cry out: 'Wisdom is far the best: age bringeth wisdom;' a maxim of antiquity by no means applicable to this country.

Geologically, one can fancy few countries more instructive than Spain. The mountains are rich in varied formations, in fossils, in cretaceous and carboniferous deposits, while streaks of quicksilver, lead, copper, and iron show a mineral wealth far from fully developed as yet. Four or five immense mountain ranges cross the country in every direction, leaving a central table-land half the size of Italy, and filled with mineral springs of every description. It is a very striking sight, in the neighborhood of Cádiz, to see the whole low-hung horizon filled with pyramids of glittering salt of great height, produced by the spontaneous evaporation of the climate, and piled up thus from an unknown antiquity, awaiting export. The sea is simply allowed to flow into numerous shallow oblong water-beds, and in a short time a sheet of crystals is left behind. Some years ago it did not rain for nine years in the province of Alicante; one can therefore imagine what an electric engine the sun is among the salt marshes of Andalusia; 'the sun, that great natural farmer of Spain, supplies every want, clothes, feeds, and makes a perpetual summer and harvest.'

The nearest approach to a picture of a Spanish plow, it is said, will be found among the Egyptian monumental pictures, while in the book of Deuteronomy the curious may discover the description of the olives and vines, as now cultivated. There is nobody to follow Scott's aphorism, and 'plant the acorn that may send its future ribs of oak to future victories like 'Trafalgar.'

The prosperity of France is, perhaps, largely due to the five millions of six-acre farms into which the greater part of the country is divided; minute and thorough culture is the result by no means to be found in the remaining fifty thousand estates of six hundred acres each. The majority of the real estate in Spain is similarly divided into small farms of six or seven acres, and fifty to sixty bushels of corn an acre is no unusual yield in the corn-bread provinces of the north and northwest. From sixty to one hundred dollars an acre in vine or fruit land of good quality is probably as much revenue as average Andalusian soil will bring in. One thousand gallons of wine an acre are said to be no very extraordinary yield in some parts of Andalusia, while labor is cheap at thirty or thirty-five cents a day. One of the delights of summer are the heaps of grapes found on every table at every meal, frequently set off by olives of gigantic size. Olives luxuriate in limestone regions; from one to ten bushels are yielded by each tree in good seasons, while the only mathematics the Spanish seem to know are the straight lines in which they plant them. An acre of such trees will produce over three hundred pounds of olive oil, consumed in amounts of nearly five gallons per head annually.

The value of the orange plantations of Catalonia, Malaga, Alicante, Valencia, and Murcia is rather hard to get at; thirty or thirty-five dollars a tree is, I believe, a very usual valuation, and a cluster of twenty trees will yield a revenue of some six hundred dollars. Five thousand dollars is considered a good price for two acres and a half of oranges, though I am not sure that the figures are correct. Three thousand dollars an acre is no uncommon price for the irrigated land of Valencia, —

> 'Hácia Valencia camina,
> Tierra rica, hermosa, y llana.'

The whole atmosphere of Malaga is perfumed at certain seasons with the raisin-drying, when the muscatels are hung in the sun, and the produce of the graperies is getting ready for the plum-cakes of following Christmases. The grapes are freely given away, and there is a good-natured stare if you offer to pay. The quais are covered with the small, square boxes, awaiting shipment to England and France, and thousands of hundred-weight voyage to distant countries every year. Huge claret-colored oval figs are found upon the breakfast-tables at Barcelona and Cádiz; the landscapes of the South are frequently brightened by wavy almond-trees full of fruit, and the pomegranate, date-palm, and lime are abundant. Begging, therefore, must be one of the conventionalities of the country, for there is certainly enough to eat.

Spain, in such a series of panoramic slides, might be made to yield results most interesting to the agriculturist, statistician, and political economist. At one time the most splendid empire in Europe, her reduction to the necessitous and agitated status of the present would afford a study of peculiar value. She is a group of nationalities, as marked and distinct individually as the Irishman and the Englishman. The inter-action and inter-dependence of these, with the gradual elaboration and evolution of national character, as we find it to-day in all its precision, will, let us hope, some day find an historian worthy of the theme.

XIV.

> As from an infinitely distant land
> Come airs, and floating echoes.
> MATTHEW ARNOLD.

MADRID is not specially rich in suburbs or environs, but it makes up for them by two towns of great interest which, though not, strictly speaking, either suburbs or environs, may conveniently be classed under one or the other head. The Arabs have left their trace in the name of the one; and in the other lingers a ray of pagan antiquity which serves to connect the Roman dominion livingly with the present. I refer to Alcalá (the Castle) and Aranjuez (? Ara Jovis) — the one green and gracious with all the trees and memories planted by Spanish kings from the second Philip down to the present time — a series of heroic avenues and silver waters; the other unique in its one benign possession not gathered by external accretion, but born in itself, as if for itself — gray old Alcalá, — and itself alone, in all the civilized world.

Here is a picture: it is summer — summer just touched with the light of twenty years ago;

behind, the great belt of Appalachian pines, sombre and soothing, stretching their great gentle arms over the green South; in front the Gulf of Mexico, melodiously large and light in the summer sun, a thousand-fold Medusa-masque, not turning to stone, but with a perennial smile on it, and such beauty as is only known in the far South; the white sands go to meet it, and there is a delicious ripple where they come in contact; there are wharves and white sails and idle fishermen seining or mending their nets, and gulls that sparkle on the June air strangely as they lift their white breasts to the sun; a great yard opens its ample arms and incloses a lovely bit of summer in the shape of lawns, orchards, and parterres, among all which stands an old house, a house of happy childhoods, many refinements, active-minded children, — some with a streak of poetry and mystery across their natures, like the bars on an old escutcheon; others hunters, or wanderers, or fishermen, quick to go, and fearless to shoot. The place is all breadth and beauty, with a wide air, a wide view, a wide winsome sea, ever poetizing this houseful of children and stilling them into meditation, they know not about what. The wide, long, precious galleries; the lazy-flapping awnings to keep out the sun, the figs, and scents, and orchards, and great glowing hydrangeas burning blue in the sun; the weird pines and strange sand-bars at evening when the tide goes out — what are all these to one of these little fellows who has found in this villa by the sea a case full of old books, and among them the Adventures of the Ingenious Hidalgo Don Quixote de la Mancha? How the whole summer transforms itself into laughter for him, and the genius of that happy summer becomes the genius of Cervantes!

A traveler in Spain who does not perform the pilgrimage to Alcalá is worse than the Mahometan on whom his code enjoins the pilgrimage to Mecca, and who dies without having fixed his eyes on the Holy City. True, the journey may entail dirt, fatigue, bad air in close railway-carriages, and some hours of fasting in the birth-place of Cervantes itself; but what is this to the man who can touch his soul with its associations but once in a life-time? In the prologue to his gracious book it is the *desocupado lector* — the idle reader — that he addresses, and who has ever been so busy as to grudge idling an hour away over the story of Cervantes?

It was one gray afternoon of hottest summer that I left Madrid and took the Saragossa train to spend a few hours at Alcalá, about an hour's ride in the slow Spanish train; a blanched afternoon; not a gray afternoon in the sense cloudy, for the Spanish light is so powerful that a veil of clouds becomes simply a mass of translucent pearl-color, and the light from yellow turns to white; a faint, filtered, pearly afternoon when Madrid seemed to justify its reputation for exquisitely thin, pure air, and the Guadárramas towards the Escorial shone sharp and clear on the northern horizon. No railway, perhaps, ever approached or left a town in a picturesque way; and Madrid forms no exception. There is a singularly sharp line drawn between it and the surrounding country. There is no long lingering suburb-like approach — one moment you are in Madrid, the next you have glided lazily out into the landscape that the Spaniards poetically call *patria* — only by a figure of speech surely, for a more done and overdone country, worked to the quick and exhausted to the core ages ago, it would be hard to imagine. Travelers never tire of their abuse of this heartless-looking country; but there is a fascination in its gray, gaunt tints, its general haggardness, and the emaciation of the landscape-forms which, without being analyzed by the Spaniards themselves, attaches them to their country deeply. It is like the hollow cheeks and gaunt form of Don Quixote himself, for if not taken in over-doses, travel in Spain weaves a subtle spell over the traveler which is as strong as it is inexplicable.

Four or five leagues are traversed before any vestiges of human or animal life are seen, except here and there a squalid posada, an inn, or a hamlet, such as Cervantes himself has immortalized by making it the birthplace of his hero. He was imprisoned in Estremadura by certain wretches whose dues he had been empowered to collect; he was seized and thrown into the village 'calaboose;' whereupon, in revenge, in its very prison, he began the story of Don Quixote, and, like another Bunyan, danced the village figures — Cunning, Romanticism, Credulity — for the delectation of the world, up and down the magic-lantern canvas of a fantastic allegory. And for three hundred years the world has stood before the wonderful puppet-play with smiles and tears.

Perhaps now and then may be seen in the distance the *ganado* of some reputed cattle-raiser, — the herd of bulls destined for the bull-rings of Seville or Madrid, attended by men on horseback, with long poles — huge jovine and bovine creatures, anything but suggestive of the graceful legend of Europa; or flocks of brown sheep hardly distinguishable from the pasture-grounds where they are huddled together; or the same long-horned goats that peep out from between the covers of Cervantes' romance, and recall the celestial speculations of the good Don. The whole landscape is intensely uninteresting. To one, however, 'hoodwinked with fancy,' the hardness of its tone is compensated by the wealth of events that have made of it one of the great battle-grounds of Spanish history.

Presently, to the right, a low line of hills is descried; then a little verdure; then a group of stately elms following a stream —'*las riberas del famoso Henáres,*' themselves of Cervantes' Galatea; then a bridge; then a striking aggregation of church-pinnacles and quaint spires; and then the train draws up at Alcalá. Not exactly at Alcalá either, for like many Spanish railways this one has the habit of ignoring towns and dropping its passengers at a station, some distance from the town. A general scattering takes place: some follow the dusty road lined with trees; others take to the fields and enter the town by various streets which debouch into a paddock where, following immemorial custom, the grain has been trodden out by animals. We see it is a town of ecclesiastics by the priests that alight from the train and make a bee-line for their haunts in the gray, ancient rookeries before us. Alcalá was once a famous religious centre, and disputed the supremacy with Toledo itself — the prince and pinnacle of Spanish hierarchies. Not to yield to Toledo was as bad as not to admit the divine right of kings in Charles's and James's time. Toledo was the heart of a huge ecclesiastical system; its archbishop was a sort of pope; and its enginery embraced every appliance from a cathedral to a thumb-screw, to win the faithful and compel obedience.

In Alcalá one sees relics of a similar state of things: a huge system gone to wreck; a pope unfrocked; a silence the more intense after its vivid student life of the sixteenth century; and a series of noble buildings moldering gradually to pieces under the neglect, the changed faith, or the poverty of the present. 'A man is a rascal as soon as he is sick,' said Dr. Johnson; so it seems with intricate religious establishments which, as soon as they become 'establishments,' give signs of inherent decay and drop to pieces. And the ruin which they involve is material even more than spiritual. Here in Alcalá, I think one can count nearly a score of immense convents, their owners now dispossessed and the buildings turned into barracks. Has the abrasion of Time rubbed the 'church' off and left the 'militant' behind?

> 'E tamben as memorias gloriosas
> D'aquelles reis, que foram dilatando
> A Fé, o imperio,'

cries Camoens in the beginning of his immortal poem. 'The glorious memories of those kings' have proved insufficient to their memorials. Alcalá, the brilliant university-town of Cardinal Ximénes' creation, the birth-place of Katharine of Aragon (there is something noble in the great K of that name) and the Emperor Ferdinand, the home of Crazy Jane, the fashionable resort of the clergy, for three hundred years the intellectual centre of Spain; how little remains of all this in this statuesque stony-faced town with its overgrown palaces and dwarfed individualities, its penury and its purple, its white glory in the brave Castilian annals, and its utter strangeness and meanness to-day. You wander along its arcaded streets and wonder in which of them Cervantes was born; you stop before huge churches and wonder in which of them he was baptized. The place is silent save for a few crawling old women, an auctioneer bidding bravely in the gathering dusk to a crowd of females, and the men sitting in the squares inhaling the twilight, as it were, or staring at the weird carvings on Ximénes' university. With its splendid past you unconsciously contrast its squalid present. There is one straight long street; a cathedral; and a pretty square with marble benches, rows of trees, a fountain, and a booth of some wandering players, such as Molière or Cervantes himself wrote farces for in their 'journeys.' There is a strange richness on the old town just now, too, for the mist is pricked by the thousand-arrowed sun, and long floods of flickering orange light are pouring over it and poetizing it. Cervantes' whole story passes before one phantasmagorically in the twilight — an odd procession of haps and mishaps, of luck and ill-luck ; the student, the soldier, the captive, the saint ; one-armed, in prison and then out, politely ignored by Lope de Vega, the man of twenty-one million verses, then courted by kings' sons ; now at Madrid, now at Salamanca, and now at Valladolid ; always and ever in need of money and never having it; his story has a divine cheerfulness in it, despite its pathetic vicissitudes ; one is drawn strangely and tenderly to the man ; and the city of his childhood, taking on some of the glamour of his own inexhaustible spirit, arrays itself in a beauty not at all its own, and is put away by its visitor as one of the choicest bits to remember.

In a funny little church near the plaza this funniest of babies was baptized ; the birth-entry has been discovered ; it is signed by parson and sexton, and the never-ending dispute among the Spanish towns for the honor of being his natal place is put to rest. One can look at Leslie's quaint and lovely pictures now in peace, and let one's mind fly from them straight to old Alcalá that mothered this wondrous child and sent him abroad as the Only-begotten of Smiles. In good Saint Mary's church-book, it reads thus : 'On Sunday, 9th Oct. of the year of our Lord 1547, was baptized Miguel, son of Rodrigo de Cervantes, and of his wife Doña Leoner. Juan Pardo was godfather, and he was baptized by the Bachiller Serrano, curate of Our Lady. The witnesses being the sacristan, Baltasar Vazquez, and I that baptized him.'

Hundreds baptized there before and since; but never another child of immortality has strayed into the old church.

His biographer quaintly records that Camoens' hair was 'verging toward saffron-color.' Cervantes' had the same tinge; and it was doubtless to this Gothic strain that he owed his ambient humor, that scintillating lightning of the eyes that is laughter illuminated. This rich humor did not seem to bubble up in him till he had visited Andalusia, and fed it with the varied experience of that romantic country. How full of splendid movement is that time! It seems a perpetual pageant and procession; moving courts, marching armies, wandering lordlings and their retinues, a Canterbury jingle of pilgrimages, a happy spirit of poetry and romance. with the boundless story of the New World in people's ears, and the brightness of its new hope eloquently spreading over the incredulous nations. Verily, a rare moment for some daring combination. And Cervantes was the result! And to think, too, how near he came to being an *émigré* to America! What would poor Don Quixote have done in our wildernesses?

Walking down the Carretera de San Geronimo in Madrid one morning, I came on a little square bright with pleasant summer verdure — one of the oases of Madrid; in the centre was a fine granite pedestal, and on top of that a statue of Cervantes arrayed in antique Castilian cloak and short-sword — the picture of morning freshness and pride. The attitude is one of great simplicity and nobleness such as he so lovingly brings himself before us in, in his charming prefaces. He stands before a large building over which is written LYCEO CERVANTES in large letters. He has thus become the symbol of intellectual advance in Spain, and stands on his sunny pedestal as if well conscious of it. It is a fine thought thus to bring a great writer constantly before the plastic minds of boys and girls, and make them feel his potency perhaps long before they have become practically acquainted with his works. In Alcalá the sleepy burghers have awakened sufficiently to call a street after him; and on a wall somewhere in the town is a placard announcing the fact of his birth — surely for old Alcalá the most important event that ever occurred under the shadow of its church-steeples. One is free to say that probably the world at large would care little for Spain if Cervantes had not been born there. There is something very lovely in the serene, sweet-tempered way in which he took his misfortunes, and, with the rest of that Bohemian age, wandered from town to town in search of a living. As the youngest child, he was the devoted favorite of his mother and sisters, as we see by the latter good ladies' giving their whole earthly possessions to ransom him from captivity when he was a prisoner in Algiers.

Unfortunately for Alcalá, the university was removed to Madrid a few years ago, and has left behind it nothing but its lordly shell in the Colegio de San Ildefonso. Like many Spanish things it requires distance; then it looms up superbly, and has a rich and grand air. Near at hand San Ildefonso's is not devoid of clumsiness, but there is a grandeur in its solitude, its galleries, its empty *patios*, and carven halls that saves it from contempt. The busy zoöphytes that filled this empty shell — eleven thousand of them in number at one time — have gone, and the nineteen colleges that composed it have dwindled into nothingness. Alcalá, they say, was once crowded with merry assemblies — no end of 'Spanish Students' and 'Golden Legends' were found here. Their rags, their songs, their guitars, their impecuniosity, their light-heartedness, have passed into a proverb, and point the wit of an ancient rhyme. There is much in their traditional life that recalls the happy shiftlessness of the German universities of to-day — of Heidelberg (or Idleberg it might be called), for instance, where top-boots, and *schlägers*, and beer, and dogs, and ogling constitute the curriculum.

Near by San Ildefonso's is a Moorish-Gothic chapel, which is the shrine of a great scholar. Here all the Arabic, Hebrew, and fanaticism that once illustrated Cardinal Ximénes lie enshrined beneath a bit of dog Latin. You seldom see a more exquisite creation of art than this medallion-hung, griffin-sculptured, robed and foliated tomb, on which a white ghost of sheeted marble lies outstretched in the shape of the effigied cardinal himself. It was uncanny in that dark old church, with its domed dusk, its aged Spanish women, its vesper hush, its deep and spiritual silence: the ages seemed to meet there in a multitudinous *conversazione;* it was a polyglot stillness amid which reigned this exquisite lump of transfigured stone with its white waving hand, its imperious white feet, its stony snowy glance. There was a bier laid with funereal cloth at the door, awaiting the last sad offices to be performed over some departed burgher: a bell tolled solemnly in some upper space of the mysteriously peopled twilight; there was a yellow pallor of dying light along the clerestory windows: the whole place had a scent of age and perishableness. One could readily imagine the worm-like ornaments of the pillars detaching themselves and floating in long, dragon-like undulations through the weird nave; or the heavy angels of the high altar withdrawing on phantom pinions, or overshadowing vengefully the whited geniuses of the tomb. A living creature *creeps* in such a place; historic reminiscence becomes a life-chilling ooze; one's spinal column turns into a column of mercury that falls to the freezing point, and there is a flight of warm and winsome sensations. Why should men carve a memory of ice and crystallize it in marble and drop it in the painted air of an old cathedral like this, and leave it to chill the generations as they gaze, for example, on the tomb of a Ximénes?

A quick, warm walk to the little church where Cervantes was baptized, at the other end of the town, brings back the blood, and recalls one from shadowy speculations to the quaint tableau of October 9, 1547. I do not think a hair on the head of a single member of the ancient community has changed since that date. The houses bulge over the street, blink out of their slit-like windows, go on all-fours, and turn up their dormer eyelids in a contempt as infinite now as then. Spanish soldiers make love in the old immemorial fashion, now as then. Their blue and scarlet apparitions go in and out the great doorways where the old monks housed in bygone times; and the flitting silhouettes of Spanish señoritas move to and fro behind the blinds watching them, at the old game of Romeo and Juliet. A few cafés and confectioneries here and there serve to suggest that a drop of modern life has somehow or other trickled into the antic place, where one all the time expects, like Milton, to listen to A Solemn Musicke. It is a place of ancient gases and ancient lasses, as one can see on peeping into the *gasioza*-shops with their ministering Hebes. You cannot imagine a merry eye being born in Alcalá, or a glittering pen cut out of its goose-quills. Cervantes, therefore, must have been, — so far as his early youth was concerned — a lump of pure genius, for there was nothing in his birthplace itself to give the stir, and strangeness, and sweetness, which we find in those early years, any more than one could guess the Alhambra interior from its outside. His mellowest work, too, came in his old age — an age that ended at sixty-nine, the same year and day that Shakspere died — then he put his hand down into his deep and rich memory and brought forth the rare bit of the second part of Don Quixote. There was a strong analogy between the life of Cervantes and his older contemporary Camoens: only, while one devoted his epic genius to the singing of chivalry — the fates of the illustrious Gama and the 'Gente Portugueza,' — the other devoted himself to 'smiling it away.' There was a common element of wandering Bohemianism in both, a common passion, a common resource. The sad spectacle of Camoens' servant begging bread from door to door for his needy master is only equaled by the penury and misery of the latter days of Cervantes or Spenser. There was noble blood in both, and the same noble devotion to flowers, women, the sea, and the mother of God. There must have been great elements of beauty and strength in an age which could produce two such contemporaries, with only the narrow strip of Estremadura between. The most intense hatred of the Moors breathes through the Os Lusiadas; the same would not be hard to find in the comedies of Cervantes. The 'epic of patriotism,' as Bouterwek calls the poem of Camoens, is worthy to be put beside the matchless romance.

The country round Alcalá looks as if it could not produce a daisy, and yet the *boninas innumerosas* of the spring-time there give evidence of a secret fertility, late and long-mellowing, perhaps, but on occasion more than rivaling the luxuriousness of other localities. So Cervantes may have taken unseen sap from its life and soil, to reappear in its own good time. There is after all the tender beauty of the olden time on the old place — a secret persuasiveness and suggestiveness that calls us to linger in it and put it away with other ancient cities that are full of a sweet remembrance, — far out of sight but seldom out of mind. I felt more than a common interest in its casino, its shabby people hurrying to vespers, its Villa Cervantes, where an old house lifts its curious Spanish grace out of a shine of flowers, and where the trees were so green and so old; and for the fruit-stalls under the arcades, where heaps of delicious Castilian pears turned up their fruity gold to the gaze. The place had an air of aged Spanish lace about it — lace that has yellowed and petrified and now hangs in rare remnants here and there among the carved gables of the university, in token of a vanished opulence. One can in such a place, with the conjury of fancy, more readily call up a vision of such figures as Dante, Camoens, Leonardo, but above all, of Cervantes, to whom might be applied without violence the noble epithet which Lucan applied to Pompey:

CIVIS OBÎT.

XV.

> Now know I well how that fond phantasy,
>   Which made my soul the worshiper and thrall
>   Of earthly art, is vain; how criminal
> Is that which all men seek unwillingly.
> MICHAEL ANGELO.

IT is a rather singular pilgrimage to make, — a visit to the convent, palace, museum, and burial-place of the greatest and most sombre bigot of modern times; but Philip's Escorial is so true an exponent of his mind and character that no one should, of course, omit it. Many things may be ignored in Spain, but not this gigantic mass of individualized granite, redolent as it is of the dreams, penances, and ecstasies of a great monarch. Photographically considered, the Escorial is most interesting. The dark lights and shadows of the *camera* idealize the harsh tones and proportions of the building, as they are put forth with almost savage accent under this crying sunshine. A picture taken from above, on the mountain-side adjacent, permits you to look down upon a perfect maze of corridors, and cross corridors, courts, towers, domes, and gardens, with here and there the luminous flash of water, and the green presence of most curiously trimmed and tortured gardens of box. Viewed in this way, the whole forms an admirable picture. The guides sing the dullness and grayness of the place in heroic measure, so that on arriving at the station, all surrounded by bright beds of lovely flowers, one is agreeably disappointed to find anticipations of a stupid day not realized. Madrid is the centre of an ugly desert. An hour after leaving it, the country begins to break up into clumps and clusters of fantastic bowlders; the frame of mountains comes nearer, and presently the engine plunges into a tunnel, and then out among huge masses of splintered rock, the forerunners of the Guadárrama range, to the edge of which this mighty palace clings. Viewed with this background of superb mountains, with the thin air all a-quiver with heat and light, the plains beneath spreading their illimitable mummy color at your feet, the Escorial is like the fly on the chariot wheel, — a mere speck. Detached from its surroundings, and made the sole object of contemplation, the stupendous plan on which its architects constructed it fills the mind with wonder. It is then seen to have eight towers 200 feet high, and to be more than 150 yards long and 120 wide, while it covers 500,000 feet of ground: a pretty hermitage for a sour and ascetic king! It is a small Constantinople in itself. In all this vast mass of linear measure, uxorious Philip occupied a space not much bigger than that the old English chronicler mentions as occupied by the grave of William the Conqueror, — a cell unimaginably plain, whence he could witness the celebration of mass, attend to his voluminous breviaries and devotions, and exercise a spider-like superintendence over all the threads of his labyrinthine abode. What a picture: the great king hidden in this bee-cell, and sending his lynx glance thence all over the kingdom: a tableau of kneeling majesty, watching politician, self-abnegating voluptuary, grand inquisitor, and petty tormentor of four wives! What could proceed out of such a heart but a frozen torrent of granite dedicated to San Lorenzo's gridiron? Whether or not the monastery was built by Philip in consequence of a vow made at the battle of San Quentin (which he did not witness), and in compensation for a church of San Lorenzo, destroyed by him on that day (which he did not destroy), it certainly began to rise shortly after that memorable engagement, and in twenty-one years stood there on the mountain-side an accomplished fact. One would like to calculate the number of masons and artisans who died of *ennui* gazing on its stuccoed sides and freezing rigidities, before it was finally finished, and handed over (metaphorically) into

Philip's hands. The Escorial is his living heart: cold, massive, grim, full of a sort of bleak ornamentation, with one brilliant nook for a library, and a thousand obscure corners, where the rats and mice and flunkeys congregated, to eat him out of house and home, and then shove him ignominiously into his bronze coffin in the Pantheon beneath the high altar. The whole thing is an anachronism in this sunny clime. It reminds one of huge and homely London done in granite: the granite is the frozen mist and grayness of the great town; the corridors are streets, and through the whole is the dull throb of Philip's heart, like a sluggish Thames, meandering subterraneously. Great architects worked on it, but Philip himself modeled and molded them and their plans to suit himself, impressing his tyrannic seal on everything, and calling into dismal existence this palatial bore. Yesterday there were little driblets of court life sprinkling its impassive *patios*. King Alfonso and his court were there, and the chapel is shown with mysterious awe where the young king comes every day to hear mass before the altar where his poor young wife lies in state. How many faces are pressed against this iron *grille*, and how many eyes are strained in toward the ever-burning lamp, to get some weak glimpse and memorial of the dead young queen, so early gone, so pure and girlish in her gentle life. And then one thinks back from this heap of tender dust lying here, buried but yesterday, and called to the throne of Spain but a few months ago, to the icy crypt beneath, where the ghostly Philip himself lies, surrounded by his descendants, kings to the right, queens and mothers of kings to the left, all caged and labeled in this dungeon, like so many stuffed animals. What a contrast!

Well is this burial-place called a *Pantheon*, for it is full of pagans.

Charles V. lies above his son; and one defunct tyrant succeeds another till their ashes form a lye intolerable to the memory, in which all tenderness and remorse for them are dissolved away. After Charles's death had determined the position of the capital, and Philip ascended the throne, and Madrid was proclaimed the sole court, the son remembered his father's wish for a special mausoleum for himself and his descendants, and characteristically selected this secluded pine-clad spot in which to rear it. The seat is pointed out on the bleak hill-side, where he used to sit and watch the progress of the work, — a one-and-twenty years' vigil, — gathering within its Greco-Roman plan and vast proportions all that he knew of grandeur, massiveness, and simplicity. The first designer (Toledo) died — no doubt of *ennui* — during its erection, and the building was handed over to the great Herrera, who is said to have made several felicitous alterations, and to have relieved the hungry baldness of the original design by sundry innovations. A caserne, a penitentiary, a tobacco manufactory, all come into one's mind on the first glance at its immense and uninteresting façade. You can walk ninety-six miles up and down its passages, gazing at half a mile of fresco-painting, ascending eighty-nine staircases, looking through twenty-five hundred windows and passing twelve hundred doors, worshiping at forty altars, pacing fifteen cloisters, and admiring sixteen courts, not counting fountains, gardens, apartments, library, and church. A garden full of stunted trees, having scant vegetation, makes an effort to impress the spectator, but one turns almost with acrimony away from the wretched failure, and wonders at and detests Philip for eternizing his gloom in this gaunt spot. The water in the tanks is green with age, dust encases the trees and highways, all day long the sun blazes on the monumental ash-heap (*scoriæ*, hence the name) and tries to bejewel its angles with some poetry of tender light; in vain. Its ugliness cries to Heaven and makes an eternal appeal against the human cunning which has tormented it into existence. You enter the church and find it really an effective piece of severe and unornamented work, with four grand piers supporting the roof, a dome, a glorious screen made of precious marbles and gilt bronze, many altars, and a ceiling thronged with multitudinous arms, legs, anatomies, and physiologies of dancing saints and prophets, all by Luca Make-Haste Giordano. You behold the weary maestro involved in the complexities and entanglements of his own work and laboring day and night to get out of it, as out of a nightmare; hence the completion of the three thousand feet of frescoing in seven months.

Five minutes suffice to run the eye over this field of the cloth of gold and to wonder from what witch's caldron it all emerged. Chapels, altars, pulpits, organs, high chapel, sacristy, reliquary, and oratories fill up its three hundred and twenty by two hundred and thirty feet, with all the glories of the Renaissance. The combined effect is one of stately serenity, stillness, and solitude. No hymn or gorgeous ceremony could, however, warm up this ecclesiastical Labrador; the worshiper is oppressed with it, even more than with some of Sir Christopher Wren's three-and-fifty 'masterpieces.' The reliquary is a museum of saintly anatomy; seven thousand four hundred and twenty-one relics, bodies, heads, arms, and legs of martyrs, enrich this grotesque collection, besides the roasted reminiscences of San Lorenzo himself, a bar of his gridiron, his thigh and foot, etc., etc.; a shuddering restaurant fit to refresh the souls of devotees alone with spiritual food. Oh, one sighs, could it all be shoveled out and the whole place be sprinkled with fresh air and sunshine! Nearly every picture worth looking at has been removed to the gallery of Madrid, and what remain bear the fatal scroll: *restaurado.* The choir is above, opposite the high altar of the church, and on the way thither one stops to admire the colossal choral books, each leaf of which was once the skin of a whole calf. The choir stalls are of plain ebony and cedar, and in a dusky corner is shown the seat whither Philip used to steal and sit as he listened to mass, and here it was that he was kneeling when the news of the battle of Lepanto reached his ear, which he received unmoved, and then tranquilly resumed his interrupted orisons. The gem of the choir is the white marble Christ carved by Benvenuto Cellini, and bearing the master's autograph. It is in a narrow passage behind the prior's stall, but the space is all illuminated with its beauteous presence.

Any one who wants to see kings in rows and queens in tiers will descend into the jasper twilight of the Pantheon, and there kings like cucumbers are piled one on top of the other in urns, and queens lie on the other side, as strictly separated from their lords in death as many of them were by taste and habit in life. Twenty-six of these ghastly cases contribute to the pagan gloom of this Blue Beard's closet, but how many pages have they each contributed to history. It is indeed a sepulchral encyclopædia and epitome of Spanish history, with only a gap or two since the time of Charles Quint.

What a relief finally to emerge out of all this into the long and beautiful library, with its books bound in black or dark purple leather, with their edges turned outward! This is the single cheerful speck in that iron heart: a brilliant passion for collecting books, manuscripts and works of art. The collection was once much vâster and more valuable than it is now; but there is still a strange interest in looking at the fine breviaries of Philip and his father, running over the golden letters of the Codice Aureo, and examining through the great flakes of plate glass the splendid Persian, Arabic, and early Christian MSS. Here as everywhere else Philip's portrait looks down sombrely at you from the wall, and you already see in its wan features the elements of excruciating torment which the king suffered three months before his death. The palace occupies another huge slice of the building, and is full of tapestries, frescoes, halls, and staircases of more or less merit.

XVI.

Below, far lands are seen tremblingly.
SHELLEY.

CINTRA is a vision of summer pleasantness. But a jaded head and tired ankles cannot do it justice. From Toledo to Cintra is a considerable leap, but some days in Madrid, already described, intervened and bridged over the chasm Then Lisbon came in for a share of attention: finally Cintra, with its link of charm and association in the poetry of Lord Byron. No eye, resting for several hours on the south side of the arid Serra de Cintra, can conceive the fresh and living beauty of this north side, clothed in one compact mass of luxurious verdure. I had to rise at five in the morning, make my way through the unintelligible Portuguese of the sleepy Lisbon porter, walk to the Praça de Ouro (Place of Gold) and secure my place in the untidy little diligence which runs twice a day between Lisbon and the summer capital. The road led up and down for a succession of miles, through the mountainous streets along which Lisbon is built; then suburbs, villas of the nobility, farms and vineyards, many of them marvelously picturesque, one trellis and tangle of vegetation. A very singular feature of the landscape are the villas covered all over outside with the most vivid *azulejo* tiles, white, green, red, lilac, blue, variegated, arranged in disks, stars, geometric designs, landscapes, figures, animals; — or again, simply doors and windows framed in delicate glazed traceries of multiform pattern, looking very pure and pleasing in the transparent air. It must be said, however, that the Portuguese abuse this Moorish style of ornamentation. Their churches are paved and lined with tiles — which gives a strangely cold and grotesque look to the interior. Great walls covered with tiled pictures, such as one sees in the bottom of an old blue china dish; impossible fountains and gardens in lilac and ochre, glazed forests and glassy seas, icy landscapes in chill pea-green, *azulejo* trellis-work and arabesques that cast their frozen shadows on the inlaid pavement give one æsthetic catarrh and set one to sneezing. Such frosty ornamentation is unfit for church interiors where the corners shine with oil-paintings, beautiful painted glass throws its irradiations as out of a thousand open petals through the dusky ogives, and mysterious sweetness and gloom are the key-note to a true feeling. But in a summer villa hanging amid the terraces and heights in hot August sunshine with a garden full of heavy perfumes enfolding the villa-wings in summer glory, with filigree pavilions, marble fountains full of the sparkle of goldfish, a winding labyrinth of leaves and trees — what could be prettier than the tiles! I confess I was delighted with their coolness and purity of coloring and suggestion. The shops and houses in Lisbon are covered with them — sometimes a whole façade, sometimes an entry-way or show-window or staircase, and the coolness thrown back by them is a delightful refreshment. The vicinity of the capital presents the same general aspect as Spain, except of course the magnificent azure serpent of the Tagus, which twines in and out the land like a luminous cord to some immense curtain. The Tagus as if in a sort of contempt continues small so long as it lingers in Spain, but when it touches Portuguese soil expands gloriously till at Lisbon ten thousand ships can anchor safely, and an unrivaled panorama of hill and field spreads on each side.

We met little on the road to Cintra save windmills and asses without number, and carriages going or coming, with tourists to or from town. The wealthier classes of Lisbon make Cintra their midsummer sojourn. It is only fourteen miles from the capital, near the mouth of the Tagus. It is rather strange that no railway is in operation to connect the capital with it. One was attempted and abandoned a few years ago, and people are content either with these antiquated diligences, or with paying the exorbitant charges of the Lisbon cab drivers (twenty-five shillings going and returning). Many miles are traversed through almost a desert, nothing save wind-mills flapping on the brown hill-sides, and here and there an aqueduct throwing its arches over a valley. At length the diligence climbs into keener air; the ascent is continuous; a glimpse of the distant Tagus-mouth is obtained, and then the sun-baked hills jealously intervene, and one is whisked on in choking dust for another hour. Suddenly a delightful arcade of trees is entered, long and shady and charming as a church aisle; deep walls on each side festooned with ivy and green with moss; waving branches above and around; an ancient arched gateway; a long Portuguese village, with horses and carriages standing in the shade, another reach of ashen fields and scorched acclivities crowned with wind-mills stretching their skeleton sails in the windless air, as vividly azure as the tunics of Perugino's angels; then another and another delicious arcade of trees, with glimpses over into vast gardens full of lemons, myrtle, and fuchsia, as if one were winding through a great green, tubular bridge hanging in the blue air: then

Cintra is reached, 'the most blessed spot in the habitable world,' exclaimed the phlegmatic Southey. There can be little doubt of it. It lies in my mind with two or three other views — like a sunrise from Vesuvius and an evening on Gibraltar: a sunny, leafy place, where the trickle of delightful water is always in one's ear and there are views such as nowhere else under heaven, not even from the Alhambra. The terrace of the hotel, beneath which lies the town, — house-tops, church-steeple, and all, — commands such a view as Vasco da Gama must have gazed upon when he stood between the two seas and exclaimed 'O Mar!' (the Sea!) The terrace is overhung by horse-chestnuts, and the hotel is built on both sides of it with an iron gate in the centre. The whole mountain (from eighteen hundred to three thousand feet in height) is a mass of stairs, terraces, garden walls, and villas (one of which was built by Vathek Beckford), and is wrought into all these as minutely as a piece of ivory. What a contrast between this tropical wealth and that blazing Sind beyond the mountain! Opposite our terrace rises the gloriously picturesque mass of the Portuguese Alhambra, — the palace, prison, chapel, and garden of Cintra, built and inhabited by the Moorish sultans, the favorite summer resort of Christian kings, rebuilt by Dom João I., and finished by Dom

Manuel. Its external aspect is far more striking and characteristic than that of the Alhambra. It covers an entire hill by itself and in its curious blending of Arabic and Christian styles — its groups of graceful *ajimez* windows with the horse-shoe arch and pillar between, contrasting here and there with a groined ceiling or a pointed ogive — gives a quaint interest to the pile which is not found in the Alhambra. It is literally a pile, clustered richly on its hill-top, one side of which is deep in impenetrable green, and the other looks out on a long, paved court-yard with a series of conventual looking buildings to one side. The court is entered by a huge, arched gateway guarded by a soldier, and the palace by a staircase to one side rather hard to find. The interior is almost entirely plain and uninteresting. The brick floors are covered with creaking planks; a few rooms have Moorish *azulejos* in many colors half-way up the walls; here and there quaint and antic doors representing serpents, fruits, and flowers intertwined; a fine marble mantel sculptured by Michael Angelo; numerous rooms filled with modern furniture covered to keep out dust and moths, and a hideous chapel with roof of inlaid wood in lead-color and maroon, intermingled with bunches of gilt grapes and stars, are found. The most interesting parts of the palace are the kitchen, the Hall of Swans the Hall of Magpies, and the Hall of Scutcheons, — above all the perfect garden that lies in great masses of bloom terraced along one side of the hill; the whole place, palace, gardens and all, is perforated, so to speak, with a most curious system of water-works. In one room, glazed, wall and floor, with tiles that almost have the brightness of precious stones, is a beautiful Moorish fountain and basin; while you are gazing in delight at it, the vicious little thing spirts a minute jet all over the apartment, and you retire discomfited. Again the slow-witted cicerone brings you into a large court-yard containing another fountain made of most graceful, twisted columns, surmounted by a jumble of imps and angels; then there is a great square of illumined sky; then a suite of *ajimez* windows; the whole spot a pool of golden sunlight and poetry, with such beatitude in the air that you would never leave if you could help it. Then a trickle is heard; you glance to one side, and lo! a huge china *boudoir*, brave with pictured blue and white tiles, wherein a mimic rain-storm has begun, ceiling, floor, sides, angles, all seem to rain fine jets of water, and the marble floor is soon a pavement of water sparkles.

Such are some of the legacies of the Moors. And there is a large tank built for the swans, sent to a Portuguese queen, which were at one time a great curiosity. One of the most curious apartments has a ceiling entirely inlaid with figures of snow-white swans, with reversed golden crowns around their necks. In another you glance up and see an aviary of magpies, each magpie holding a scroll in its beak with the legend *Por Bem* (In good part) written on it — the reply given by Dom João I. to his queen, Philippa of England, on being discovered in the act of kissing one of the maids of honor, whereupon the present curious painted roof was ordered as a sort of satire on the royal cordiality. The Hall of Scutcheons is also called the Hall of Stags, and contains a ceiling covered with the coats of arms of seventy-four Portuguese noble families, two spaces being empty on account of the treason of the houses of Tavora and Aveiro to José I.

The entrance to the queen's apartments contains a rich window full of painted glass; after which follow her bed-chamber, dressing-room, and parlor, with no end of presses, wardrobes, silk-padded fauteuils, divans, étagères, piles of mattresses, cases of old china, and common tables, chairs, whitewash, and yellow-papered walls. The whole building is thus a mixture: one moment you fancy yourself in one of Baedeker's hotels *not* marked with a star; you stare at numbered rooms, wooden floors, rickety beds and lounges, winding passages, and ill-lighted entry-ways; then you draw up before an interesting historical relic like the prison of Dom Affonso, or the huge kitchen with its enormous steeple-like flues which give so bizarre an appearance to one side of the palace-crowned hill. These flues are at first a puzzle; they look like church spires or the vats of a porcelain manufactory, and stand together in close neighborhood with the Moorish windows and pavilions, in a manner entirely nondescript. One would not have them away for the world, however, such piquancy and peculiarity do they give to the mass of brick, marble, and stone to which they are attached. The jewel of the whole aggregation — for aggregation it is — is the marvel of a garden which clings to one side of it, and has been dug out and terraced with boundless pains and taste. No pen is equal to the views from its arbors and summer-houses. Through an empty window-frame, beneath which on each side is a marble seat, to one side a basin full of glittering water and gold-fish, overarched by a wicker-work of vines translucent from below as the sun strikes them, the Atlantic is seen, serene as another Heaven; to the left the zigzag mountains of Cintra crowned by the Hieronymite convent and the Moorish castle; beneath gardens, villas, a vast undulating plain laid out like a map, so remote that only its masses of white houses can be descried as they are congregated into hamlets and villages; above, the Palace of Cintra reached by the eye as it climbs through a vision of splendid dahlias, plumbago, geraniums, crimson Virginia creeper, honeysuckle, and every sweet-scented flower and glossy leaf, truly a delightful scene. Then the keen point to the air after the heated theatre air of the plains below, is alone compensation for the diligence journey, the dust, and the dreariness of the road.

The Palace of Cintra, however, is far from being all; it is perhaps the least in this exquisite mountain nook. Wandering entirely by chance along a road which I noticed other people following, and which ascended gradually and wound gently upward, I came on another terrace with parapet, stone seats, and water bursting from the mountain-side into a mighty basin. Here a rest; then on and on up, past one country-house after another; a church or two, seats, parapets, water-tanks, and deserted houses, into a green and meandering road full of warm spice-smells and piney slopes. Huge granite bowlders covered with ivy, lichen, fern, and moss soon overhung the deep road, and beneath them seats had been formed in various places and shadowy recesses to rest in. Then arrival at the gates of a palace, to which the road led, where a guide in Phrygian cap (such as you see in Canova's sculpture and all over Catalonia), took some others and myself in charge, and became the knight that heralded to us all the glories and legends and antiquities of the spot; how this and that spot was celebrated, and for what; how Dom Fernando, after the suppression of the Hieronymite convent on this granite hill, converted it into a Moorish-Gothic castle and adorned it wondrously with towers and battlements, delicate Moorish arches and traceries, terraces, pictures; how the spot was full of the spirit and the memories of Vasco de Gama, whose colossal statue with spear and shield was pointed out on a lofty rock, near which his long absent vessels were descried returning from their great voyage; how there were painted windows figuring Vasco on his knees, the Virgin above him, and his faithful ships by his side, — all this and much more beguiled the way up the hill, till we actually reached the *Pena Palace* and its most voluptuous of earthly situations.

The hill appears conical, and is everywhere transformed into a garden, winding spirally up, with such a circle and wire-work of walks, through pink and purple avenues of hydrangeas as only a king can charm into being with his Spanish gold. If the view from the Palace of Cintra is lovely, this is transcendent; the whole of Portugal seems to be at your feet, framed on one side by the Atlantic, which at this moment was a perfectly serene and silken volume of illuminated water, most magically still. The Tagus, with a crescent of beach just beyond, was absolutely distinct, and a large steamer was just entering it, looking, from where we were, like a toy ship drawn by a loadstone in a basin of water. Lisbon lay lay along it for four or five miles; Cintra, town and palace, was far beneath; Mafra, the Escorial of Portugal, was visible, and a net-work of interlacing high-roads and habitations, all lying beneath us, like bits of marvelous still-life. The view changed every moment as we wandered from parapet to parapet of the palace, round tower after tower, in and out the intricacies of the Gothic battlements. From these serene pinnacles the world was a lovely dream: it was all so thoroughly and charmingly idealized: it seemed impossible to descend again and grapple with the every-day world.

> 'Lo! Cintra's glorious Eden intervenes,
>   In variegated maze of mount and glen;
>   Ah me, what hand can pencil guide, or pen,
>   To follow half on which the eye dilates.'

But descend we must; and a ramble through the convent-palace, to visit the fine carved windows and doors, the alabaster screen of the chapel with its transparent delicacy and filminess of execution, — carved into a beauty resembling a mass of white japonicas with light behind, — proved not uninteresting.

Then the chatty old Carthaginian took us through the gardens, where geraniums, camellias, and Brazilian colias grew in thickets (a rare rose here and there), and where often the shadows lay so deep that the sunshine, which trickled through, was whitened into moonlight, till one looked up into the illumined green ceiling above and caught the leaves palpitating like the throat of the summer chameleon, all green-gold with the subtle light. Truly, Meander itself could not surpass these walks in their winding desires. Everywhere water (in the Land of No-Water!), in pipes, tiles, troughs, or gathered into sunlit reservoirs, or flowing from under arbors thatched with pine-straw, or beneath a Moorish dome, such as one sees in Mahometan cemeteries: water, water down the loveliest cascades of ferns and moss and cresses, stealing in silvery embarrassment away from human sight into spaces, where nymphs and fairies dance before the nimble imagination, and there is hardly ever a flicker of scaring sunshine. And in the heart of the Pena garden is its heart of hearts, where there is flame and odor from summer to summer, a perpetual shrine of Vesta and Proserpine: the flower-maze and conservatories. It was quite delightful to come out into all this fragrance and floral illumination, glowing as

it did, like a lamp, with every conceivable color.
Here it looked as if all the imprisoned beauty of
the soil had played a radiant trick on its jailer,
and suddenly broken bounds, the Undine of
flower-sprites. With longing eyes we hung over
the richness of this spot. Our lady companion
picked a white Lamarque and secreted it in her
pocket, while her husband engaged the guide in
conversation. We all drank now and again of
the natural ice-water flowing from the rocks.
There was not the least sense of exhaustion; we
were in such pure air, so high up. At the gates,
a few coppers (of enormous weight: get a carpet-
bag instead of a purse, for Portuguese money!)
satisfied the guide, who was far from being aware
what intense pleasure he had given us all, and
then I took the road on down the hill, after a
courteous invitation from my Portuguese companions to partake of their lunch.

Such are but two of the bright pages of Cintra.
Walks to see the sun rise and set, moonlit strolls
along the deep roads, with high stone walls on
the sides, debouching on terraces, each commanding far-stretching landscapes; visits to the
old palace, near which Marshal Junot and the
Duke of Wellington signed the convention of
1808, which prevented the French invasion; the
quinta of the poet-navigator, Dom João de Castro, where there is a chapel containing the heart

of the great sailor; the cork convent, with its twenty cells, lined with cork to keep out moisture; Mafra and its palace, its mausoleums, its marbles, belfry, clocks, and bells; its 5,000 doors, 866 rooms, and space on the roof for 10,000 soldiers; an oblong of heroic proportions, designed in imitation of the Escorial: enough for a summer at Cintra alone!

XVII.

> As filhas do Mondego a morte escura
> Longo tempo chorando memoraram;
> E, por memoria eterna, em fonte pura
> As lagrimas choradas transformaron:
> O nome lhe pozeram, que inda dura,
> Dos Amores de Ignez, que alli passaram.
> Vêde que fresca fonte rega os flores,
> Que lagrimas são a agua, e o nome amores.[1]
> <div style="text-align:right">CAMOENS, <i>Os Lusiadas</i>, Canto iii.</div>

A NIGHT train from Lisbon brought me to Coimbra. It was too dark to see more than the brimming Tagus, which we followed for many miles under the rays of the waning moon, now hanging like a golden half-lemon over the water. The night was so fresh that I almost forgot I was in Portugal. Indeed, Lisbon is famed for its inequalities of temperature. Nothing could be pleasanter than the weather during my stay. The

---

[1] Mondego's daughters mourned her fate obscure,
  And as they mourned did cherish it long time:
In ever-living sign a fountain pure
  Urned of their tears transformed: the cunning rime
The nymphs wrought for it while the ages dure
  Was 'Inez' Love,' that passed amid that clime:
Lo, many a flower sprent with dew above, —
  'T is dew of tears: the fountain's name is Love.

extreme heat of Spain is unknown, and from every slope and hill-side up which a street ran came refreshing draughts, recalling the early summer. If the summer temperature is always what I have experienced, I should decidedly pronounce for Portugal in the dog-days. The Atlantic is so near, and the mountains so high, that every breeze is laden with coolness. The early drive from Cintra to Lisbon almost rendered an overcoat necessary. But fortunately we had the wind (and alas! the beautiful palace too) at our backs.

Coimbra is the Oxford of Portugal. There is an ancient university here, composed of eighteen or twenty colleges, and attracting from one thousand to twelve hundred students annually. Originally Lisbon was the site of the university, but it was removed hither by Dom João III., and here it has stuck ever since — a miracle of plainness and ugliness on its plateau, high up above the town. It is redeemed, however, by the arches of a splendid old aqueduct which throw their graceful spans in among the university trees and give an air of high antiquity to the modern looking buildings. To one side is a handsome terrace, which looks down upon a pretty botanical garden, full of walks, tanks, and hot-houses. In one tank a water-lily spread its huge leaves and one lustrous starry blossom, gold in the centre, with lilac apices, lay on its mirrored disk. As usual, immense clusters of dahlias and heliotrope, feathery palms and waving bananas, Brazilian pines and monkey-trees. It is a beautiful scene: the noble arches of the aqueduct high over head, then the terrace, then the colored carpet-like masses of the botanic garden, then the olive-bordered Mondego far beneath, most richly edged and framed in with cane, corn, hedges, and Lombardy poplars, while on the opposite heights a line of vast conventual buildings runs along, surmounted by bell-towers and crosses. The students, without hats and in long black robes, walked and talked about in the quadrangles, or paced up and down with serious and meditative mien. Groups of professors, in the usual everyday-dress, stood about and chatted. 'The university system at Coimbra is professorial, as in Germany and Scotland; not tutorial, as at our two great universities. There is a small literary fact connected with one of its professors in the sixteenth century, which may interest our men of letters at home. The celebrated George Buchanan was for some years a professor at Coimbra. There is every probability of his having been the friend and instructor — for he was twenty-two years his elder — of the great Portuguese poet Ferreira, the precursor of Camoens, who polished, refined, and classicized the Portuguese language, almost to the same extent that Pope and Dryden did our own tongue. That the essentially classical Ferreira should have availed himself of the instructions of a man like Buchanan — the most brilliant scholar of his century, and the best writer of Latin prose since the age of Tacitus and Virgil — is so probable as to be akin to certainty.'[1]

The hill is wound round and round by roads, each ascending above the other (like the successive coils of an old French coiffure), until the summit is attained, which opens into a quaint square, fronted on one side by a large Romanesque church, and on the other by a large brick building, painted red and surmounted by a figure of the Virgin, all glittering in rays and glories. From below, from the pretty promenade on the river bank, the compact and serried mass of buildings, rising one above the other, has a very striking aspect. On my way up I dropped in at the *Sé Velha*, or old cathedral (there are two), supposed to have been built on the site of a mosque. It has a fine entrance, richly carved screen, and seats covered with blue *azulejo* tiles which make the blood run cold. It is another vision of the bottom of an old china dish, magnified to the size of the wall of a church, but none the less common-looking for all that. Another church has some carved choir-stalls, tombs of early Portuguese kings, cloisters in the

[1] Latouche's *Portugal*.

flamboyant style, and a sanctuary full of relics of Dom Henriques and Dom Affonso. What most captivated my eye was the crowd of peasants about the streets in gala-costume. Very striking and picture-like were the groups of women in their black or dark-blue short-gowns, vividly embroidered bodices, elegant old-fashioned ear-rings and lockets, and astonishing black sombreros. There they sat or stood in sombre clusters eating or minding their wares, some of them dispensing with the huge sombrero and having the head covered with a spanking silk handkerchief. The antique Moorish jewelry they wear — moon-shaped gold ear-rings of immense size and weight, solid or filigree — is an heirloom from the Moors. It is in admirable contrast with the fine dark olive faces, lustrous eyes and hair, and dark petticoats. Their hats are exactly like the men's except that black velvet bands and bows are substituted for the tufts generally worn by the men. Booths are spread along the river side and ceremonious bartering has been going on all the morning. Below, in the wide vale formed by the nearly empty river, stand strange Portuguese boats laden with firewood and pine boughs; flags flutter over improvised shops and booths, and knots of women wash and sing as they stand beside the limpid streams flowing here and there through the wide river-bed. Dozens and dozens of them go down the stairs to the river side with water-jugs precisely like those taken from Pompeii — big-bellied, slender-stemmed, such as the Greek girls bear to the fountains, — and when they are filled from the river, poise them most gracefully on their heads and wend their way homeward, without more forethought. How like Caryatides some of them look with these antique jars statuesquely balanced over the jetty hair, and wide, lustrous eyes looking out curiously from beneath. The students need not study Michaelis' plates, for here are Greek scenes enough. And then at Lisbon the antique chariots, with wooden wheels turning the whole axle, drawn by gigantic steers and guided by Gallegos in Phrygian cap and with the ancient goad, — what recollections they recall of pictures in classical dictionaries and passages in Virgil or Theocritus! All the environs of Coimbra are richly wooded, which is a rare treat in this peninsula. The old place was once the capital, and the Cid had something to do in the pre-historic times with wresting it from the armed infidel; then it rose to new celebrity in the Peninsula war, during which Massena's forces were routed in the vicinity by the Iron Duke (that second Cid, whom one meets as everlastingly as the effigies of Ferdinand and Isabella in Andalusia).

Here, of all places, is the spot to learn Portuguese in its purity, — to master the intricacies of the syntax, the declined infinitive, the Latin-like pluperfect indicative, and gerund, the sixteen diphthongs and six nasals, with sounds as difficult as Russian, or that exist, perhaps, in Chinese alone. Here, under this professorial inquisition, is the spot most carefully to guard against the two thousand Brazilian upstarts that have insinuated themselves into Portuguese diction since the discovery of Brazil. Here is the spot to learn the *taboo* put upon many Portuguese words which it is not good taste for ears polite to hear, or tongues to utter, such as *swine*, and others; as a pendant to which our euphemistic American *limbs, casket*, etc., may be mentioned: a practice which prohibits the king from being called by his name in certain countries, and in others, the wives from pronouncing the first letter in the names of their husbands. Here, too, you may learn to address your tailor or your shoemaker as 'his illustrious lordship,' and hear the newsboys calling each other 'Your honor;' or you may observe the rich steak of Jewish blood running through the nation, or listen on summer or winter nights to a thousand superstitions of were-wolves, white women, or phantom horsemen.

A great interest centres round Coimbra from the tender and romantic story of Inez de Castro. Over the river is the haunted looking Villa of Tears (*Quinta das Lagrimas*), where she was treacherously murdered by her husband's father in his very presence. She had been secretly married to the Infante Dom Pedro, when Dom Affonso IV., his father, caused her to be seized and put to death. Many a famous poem and legend have gathered their amber about this great tragedy of love and death, and embalmed it in verse. The chateau lies near the river bank, with a great orange-garden in front, and an olive grove behind. It is without chimneys, and is painted a vivid yellow, and there are spacious pleasure-grounds to one side, with a spring, overshadowed by some grand cedars, called the Fountain of Love. On one of the trees is the inscription in Portuguese: '*Eu dei sombra á Inez formosa*' (I gave shade to lovely Inez). The most famous account of the story is the episode in the third canto of the Lusiads of Camoens, — the great poet, of whom a fellow poet wrote: —

> 'Nem o humilde logar onde reposiam
> As cinzas de Camões, conhece o Luso.'

'Not even the humble spot where rest the ashes of Camoens is known to the Portuguese.'

The story goes that Dom Pedro rose against his father, ascended the throne, and put the murderers to death; and fair Inez, after lying seven years in the grave, was disinterred, and crowned Queen of Portugal, while all swore fealty to her. Her body lay in the cloister of Santa Anna, near by, — now in sad and strange decay. There is a mournful sweetness in the summer air about the old palace; sleepy shepherds pasture their black and white sheep under the lindens; the Mondego has a gentle and regretful murmur as it hurries by the blood-stained spot; the rich field of waving Indian-corn in front is full of whispers and harmonies, breathed strangely on the yellow air; grapes hang over the wall, and press their jeweled wine out on it as a memorial libation to the savage story, and the cedars that overhang the Fountain of Love are sweet and low as marriage-flutes on the widowed wind. What grace and genius and grandeur there are in this troubled story!

XVIII.

'T is time to sail, — the swallow's note is heard,
  Who, chattering down the soft west wind is come,
  The fields are all a-flower, the waves are dumb,
Which erst the winnowing blast of winter stirred.
Loose cable, friend, and bid your anchor rise.

ANTHOLOGY

THIS is my last day in Portugal, and a very proper place to spend it. There are few sites more attractive than the mountains (they are hardly hills) along which Oporto extends, with the bright Douro far beneath, and the thickly wooded opposite heights rising covered with vineyards, convents, and manufactories. Oporto is the second city of the realm in importance and population, and is the capital of the densely peopled wine-province of Minho. The O in its name is the Portuguese definite article; hence the name of the place is, simply, The Port, like Le Havre. It is a common thing in Portuguese to have the article accompanying the name of a place, *A Bahia* (The Bay), *O Cairo* (The Victorious), and others. Oporto has plenty of life with its 120,000 busy people, its docks, quays, ships, and wine stores. The sea is but five miles off, hence the delightful temperature. Yesterday and this morning it absolutely *rained*. One can hardly, without having summered in Spain, conceive the refreshment in the word. The dust is laid, and the neighboring fields and elevations have a glorious green. For heights and depths, ups and downs, compare Oporto with Edinburgh or Toledo. And yet, in spite of it all, an admirable system of street-cars exists, which penetrates the city in many directions, while as many as five mules are sometimes employed in pulling the trams. These railways traverse the principal streets, and extend to the pleasant suburbs. The houses rise in tiers amphitheatre-like, and along the river side there are two most beautiful promenades, one high above the other. From the upper one a singularly charming prospect opens up the Douro, which is spanned by the thread of a railway bridge, with one superb arch beneath; beyond which, soft green meadows, waving cornfields, and wooded heights are set, as in a most lovely curve, intersected half-way by the green sheet of the river. The other is the famous *Rua dos Inglezes*, or English Promenade, which extends from the foot of the *Street of Flowers* out to the baths of Cadouco and Foz, through long avenue of elms. There are few more charming promenades, and at the end the royal Atlantic beats white and thunderous against an ancient fortress, and the rocky sea-side resorts just mentioned. There is a line of villages here forming the Brighton of Oporto, only far more bright and winning than the dingy English watering-place. The beach is covered with bathing-suits put out to dry, booths, bath-houses, and bathers. The smell of the salt sea is sweeter than any perfume, and the divine wealth of curling, surfy water that rolls in at one's feet, so endlessly varied in color, form, and mass, is an infinite delight to a lover of sea sights and sounds. The country all around Oporto is covered with pines and Indian-corn; and the river is lined, for a hundred miles up, with villas, vineyards, and port-wine storehouses. The drawing seems all done by immense, dull-eyed, long-horned steers, often driven by little girls and boys, and held together by a most curiously carved Moorish yoke. The same wooden wheels and chariot-like shape, as at Lisbon, are seen in the vehicles they draw.

One of the curiosities of Oporto is the Street of Flowers, lined on one side by small goldsmiths' shops, in which is seen a rare display of fanciful Moorish jewelry, — great filigree hearts, stars, medallions, links, ear-rings, bishops' rings set in opal, amethyst, or chrysolite, sixteenth century repoussé work in silver, and the marigold gleam of Brazilian topazes; others quaint and massy, some inlaid with scenes from Holy Writ, many of astonishing size. They are identical with those worn by the peasant women of Coimbra, and are of a workmanship peculiar to this part of Portugal. The gold of which they are made is well known for its purity, and the workers are men in whose families the profession has been for generations, just as the Jews of Amsterdam have monopolized diamond cutting, and the men who keep up the repairs of St. Peter's are said to form an hereditary guild. What a contrast between the sombre-gowned, dark-faced peasant woman, with short vivid black hair and eyes, and weighty sombrero, and her jewel-laden ears and neck, — not to mention the basket of stale fish she carries on her head! There is nothing in the least to remind one of Tizian's masterpiece, and yet this too is a picture worthy of the great Venetian. There is something gipsy-like in the intensely dark faces of these women, with their coarse Indian hair, wrinkles, and melodious voices. The street cries of Lisbon are often strangely sweet; and from what poor little stunted women — literally compressed into a sort of human parallelogram by the perpetual carrying — these cries issue! The vast deal of carrying and street crying done in Spain and Portugal by men, women, and children is a constant surprise Probably it arises from more than the mere necessity of living, from the indolence of purchasers who — such is the effect of climate — might not consent to live at all were their food not brought to them. At any rate Oporto, Lisbon, and the Spanish cities are filled from daylight till dark with these two-legged perambulating markets lifting up their voices in constant warning to the sweet nothing-to-do-ers. There are of course markets everywhere in the great cities, — and places of intense animation they are too, — but whatever is left over from them seems to be cried about the streets to the delectation of all concerned. Add to this the needy knife-grinders, brass-and-copper kettle menders, and hawkers of maps and lottery-tickets, and a Spanish or a Portuguese town becomes anything but a 'golden tumult.' As for the jaunty cab-drivers of Oporto and other cities, they are perfectly unscrupulous, and belong to the worst of their kind. Their watch-word is extortion. Sometimes (as in a case which occurred while I was in Lisbon) they follow their demands by threats and blows. The traveler can always avoid them, however, by inquiring his way to the central ticket-office in the city, where there is always an excellent line of omnibuses in communication with the train, and at prices which are extremely moderate. The purchase of a first-class ticket entitles one to a seat in the omnibus, and to a certain amount of luggage, and the price of the omnibus ticket is seldom more than ten cents. The cabman will extort his dollar with the greatest impudence; and further woes may be expected if the over-anxious traveler step into cabby's parlor without first making a bargain. It is, however, the same all the world over.

Characteristically, of the eighty thousand or so pipes of wine annually made in the province of which Oporto is the capital, not a drop is found on the *table d'hôte*, John Bull absorbing nearly if not quite nine tenths of it. Cintra, Oporto, and Gibraltar are the only places in the peninsula where I have not found wine lavishly served at breakfast and dinner. The English tradespeople are magnificent creatures: they must have all or none, and interference is an insult to 'free trade.' The slopes, walls, and terraces of Oporto are draped in the richest vines. The country is near enough the Alpish region of Galicia and Asturias to be blessed with showers, and ample verdure is the result. A curious anachronism in all this intensely southern region is the wooden-bottomed slippers, with uppers of leather, worn by the lower classes. You hear a perpetual clatter from them, up and down the steep, flagged pavements and streets of the city. They are without back pieces, and the foot is simply slipped into them Turkish fashion; the result being a very awkward gait, recalling street scenes in Belgium.

One does not notice essential differences between Portuguese and Spanish, except that the former are stiller and darker people, rather slow-witted, superstitious, commercial and courteous, who in spite of their prolonged intercourse with England know no English, and not much beyond their saints' calendars. It is a significant circumstance that Shakspere is being translated into Portuguese and Chinese simultaneously. The book-stalls are lined with French and Spanish books; guide-books to the country, unless written in Portuguese, I found it almost impossible to get; and I had really some difficulty in Lisbon in finding a Portuguese grammar. The coquettish mantilla, which gives so much grace to Spanish women, disappears entirely as soon as the line is crossed: ugly Paris hats and bonnets succeed; and in the number of advertisements of ships sailing to Brazil, etc., one sees at once how the Portuguese who travel have come to be more cosmopolitan in character and dress than their prejudiced neighbors who do not. The decided improvement in the hotel fare is also a sure sign of superior civilization, and the abhorrence in which the Portuguese hold a genuine *toros de muerte* bull-fight is another. The language is very soft and pleasant and resembles French of the Limousin type, being perhaps less stately but more melodious than the Spanish. Portuguese grammar presents some very interesting peculiarities and many close resemblances to the mother Latin, so that a piece of fourth century Latin and a paragraph of Portuguese placed side by side are quite startlingly alike. A singularly interesting feature, of the utmost value philologically, is the resolution of the future and conditional present into their constituent elements when a pronoun is used as object. The same thing occurred frequently in old Spanish. It is known that the Romance future and conditional come from composite Latin forms, the infinitive present being prefixed respectively to the present and imperfect of the Latin verb *habere* (to have), to form future and conditional; *aimer-ai = amare habeo*. In Portuguese *I shall write*, etc., is *escreverei*, but if a pronoun — the reflexive of the third person for example — be found as object, this may follow the first element *escrever* (which is an infinitive); to which it is then added, joined by a hyphen, and followed by the rest of the form; the only divergence being that in these terminations from *habeo* the original *h* of the Latin verb reappears, escrever-se-*h*a (it will write itself, be written); confirmation enough — if the case needed one — of the etymology of the Romance future and conditional. The strong nasalization of the original Latin is another peculiarity, the substitution of *m* for *n* (*um* for *un*), of *r* for *l* in Spanish and Arabic words (praça for p*l*aza), are other marked tendencies. The predominance of nasals in both brings the spoken language quite near the French in sound. Spaniards and Portuguese of the educated classes can understand one another, though the differences in words for familiar things are considerable. Here the four centuries of Arabic have had considerable play and left deep traces in the Portuguese. A Portuguese lady assured me with much gravity that the languages were altogether different, but her philological knowledge did not extend beyond an occasional rather piercing curtain lecture to her lord and master, who would forget himself and address the Spanish railway officials in his native tongue. The Brazilians have further softened the Portuguese, just as the Hispano-Americans have done the Castilian. The Brazilians even claim to speak better Portuguese than the Portuguese themselves.

Portugal is full of negroes. You see plenty of 'Aunties' and 'Uncles'; and an American is fully possessed with the notion, from his own associations, that they must all speak English, till he addresses one, and gets a stare of real Ethiopian wonder in return. In Spain they are very rare, except in seaports like Cádiz. The Spanish of the provinces and the country apply 'Aunt' and 'Uncle' to almost any man or woman beyond middle age, just as the custom is in the

South, with the negroes. The Sicilians do the same.

In spite of the excellent food in the principal cities, Portugal is very backward in hotel accommodation. In the busy, thriving town of Oporto, for example, the best hotel is a den kept by an Englishwoman, built half a century or more ago, and wretchedly furnished. The same is the case in Lisbon and Cintra. At Coimbra, the hotel was purely and simply disgusting; we had to pass the kitchen, which was radiant with brass and copper kettles, to reach the dining-room, but through a series of tortuosities equal to the ornamentation of the old black-letter. When you got a view, it was of something horrible, except that from the rickety balcony adjoining my cell the eye could feast on the pretty Mondego, the bright fair with its tableau-like groups; and beyond, a garden of glossy-leaved orange-trees, now out of fruit and bloom. The head-waiter was an exact image of an antique bust of Socrates. Arriving at such a place after a long and devious walk through dimly-illuminated streets, at four o'clock in the morning, and with a peculiarly wild-looking porter to carry my luggage, one can imagine my feelings at seeing the house, the Socratic vision appearing at an upper window, demanding who was *there;* and above all, the aspect and experiences of the Hieronymite cell itself;

all this in contrast with the solid silver knives and forks, of antique design, with which we were furnished at breakfast and dinner. Taking these four large cities as typical, accommodation in Portugal is at the lowest.

XIX.

'Go on, go on, it is alike the Paradise of Nature and of Art,' — and they took courage and went on, and found it, as so many thousands of travelers have done since, the most perfectly beautiful place in the world. — HARE.

LA GRANJA is a true *château en Espagne*, a castle in the air nearly four thousand feet above the sea, an airy Versailles, hanging on the mountain-side in all the beauty and pride of a Spanish grandee, abandoned to solitude and decay.

There is something most interesting in the glimpse of Versailles-like towers and spires which one gets when finally emerging from the mountain-side, and looking down on the plateau on which the palace is situated. It is a panorama of green trees, bright verdure, darkly-clothed mountain-slopes, runnels of gliding and glittering water, a boundless expanse of lilac and yellow *llano* beneath, and far-sweeping avenues of poplars and elms, forth from all which peep the weather-cocks and steeples, belfries and pavilions of a Louis XVI. château, slate-roofed, slit with innumerable windows, with grilled doors, graveled walks and sparkling fountains. How the air is laden with petunia and heliotrope and Madame de Genlis, all in one!

The approach to La Granja is by long-winding avenues of pines, — thick-tufted, pale-leaved, yellow-bodied fellows, covered with lichens, and bathed knee-deep in brilliant bracken. It is a delightful drive down the Guadárrama mountains, with galloping mules, cracking postilions, and swearing *zagal*. The air is full of minute particles of frost, which sting the cheeks deliciously, and bring charming souvenirs of winter drives to their warm, tingling surfaces. The train is taken as far as Villalba, and then diligences are in waiting to convey passengers — to the clouds. I confess, the prospect of such a journey was most agreeable. The heat had become intolerable in Madrid. But visions of gurgling rills, many-voiced fountains, blankets at night, murmuring pines, and majestic sierras flickered and floated in the warm Madrileño atmosphere, and made the call to make a trial imperative. A curious thing about the matter is why the stupid Madrid people do not profit by these lovely piney glens and fastnesses, and, like the French, transform them into enchanting nooks for summer idling. But they prefer to welter in the heat and stench of their fussy Frenchy city!

La Granja would make a capital sojourning place for weary aristocracy and worn-out middle-class. What a tonic there is in its bracing air! There is an Alpine freshness and sweetness in it, and the palace garden is alive with flowers. A few strays of the diplomatic corps, — a wandering marquis, or misplaced attaché, — are all that is met or seen of fashionable life in the place. The brick tiles, with which the houses of the town are covered, are as lonesome-looking as if they never harbored guests beneath their red cylinders. Grass grows in the streets; the booths are nearly all closed; the hotels empty; the very post-office, where one reads *Correos* in big letters, seems deserted and forlorn. The diligence comes rattling down the empty high-road, and only a few old women in yellow petticoats and crimson head handkerchief are there to receive it. A vast iron gate is entered, on each side of which is the usual monumental but not mute beggar, and the diligence draws up before the post door. As one enters the gate, a glimpse of the palace-façade is caught in the distance running round three sides, with towers and chapel in the centre, hospitably throwing its arms about some fine beds of flowers. The place was once a farm or *grange* (whence the name), but was purchased by Philip V. and changed, to the tune of millions, into what is called in Spain a *real sitio*, or royal demesne. It was here Queen Christina, just deceased, was compelled by some soldiers to sign her abdication: and here, also, her daughter and successor, both as queen and abdicator, Isabel the Second, was fond of coming and bathing in one of the fountains, while various sentinels stood guard, to prevent the curious from seeing how a queen bathed. This and that kingly nobody lies buried, forgotten, in this remote nook of the peninsula, having suffered that generous oblivion which posterity too readily accords to crowned insignificance. This castle in the air, which so many of them loved and labored on, is their enduring monument, — a sunny, silent place, full of sylvan tranquillities and poesies, going to decay, as it would seem, like some hapless St. Cloud, yet, in its very decay, lovelier far than the splendid original. The wide gates of the park are thrown open to the public, and one enters the spacious promenades almost alone, save for the troop of romances and intrigues, that dart out of every nook and corner, and people one's imagination busily as the spacious avenues open and wheel in every direction. It is this very genius of pensive history which makes such an old spot so charming. Flowers and vases and fountains one can have any day, and for far less money; but seldom so sweet a troop of light-footed associations and poetic reveries. The old palace is an eloquent picture in the rich August air. Caryatids, Corinthian pillars, urns, and balconies, all seem bending beneath their weight of ghostly souvenirs. In the gardens the whole pagan mythology has been disemboweled, and changed into pumps! Olympus has become a Château d'Eau; the muses, graces, and goddesses are dancing streams of water, cascades, *jets d'eau*. Wherever you look, splendid heaps of bronze and marble, apparently afloat on the melted silver of this Guadárrama mountain water, form themselves into vistas, and beckon fantastically through the green arcades. Urns of fruit in bronze, with climbing monkeys for handles, stand in rows on the balustraded terrace, and look down into the water. Beautiful white marble vases, sculptured with geniuses, dragons, coats of arms, foliage, and masks, glitter up and down the graveled beds, and alternate with floating and pirouetting mythological figures and winged grotesques, walks and drives, mazes and labyrinths, wondrous masses of clipped box, formed into bells, domes, and squares, spots radiant with chrysanthemums of every color, — that favorite of the Benchers of the Temple, — flights of marble steps designed for falling water; long parallellograms of brilliant water formed into falls and cascades, emerald-green with reflected light from the overhanging trees; marble seats, quaintly carved, and cold as ice under the bosky elms; trellised hedges of endless variety; circles and half-circles hollowed out of the umbrage, as it were, and furnished each with its glittering basin, griffins, sea-monsters, and tritons, — such are a few items in this fascinating garden in the air. The principal wing of the palace looks out on a cascade, down which the waters foam over variegated marbles, and the twisted and fantastic torsos of spouting and writhing animals. Before the palace is quite reached, the cascade ceases, and breaks, as if by magic, into a delightful flower-bed, which continues the silvery torrent in its own tumult of impetuous bloom. At each side dusky avenues extend, in which black-robed priests may be seen pacing the green graveled darkness, and meditating some soul-saving homily for the Sunday, —

> 'Ah, yet doth beauty like a dial hand,
> Steal from his figure, and no pace perceived!'

A step further, and there is a workman chipping the draperies of a marble statue; others are tossing great beams of water over the trees and plants from huge hoses. Bees and yellow-jackets betray the presence of honey. Above, over the cascade, the invisible greens, and blues of the Guadárrama pines form a middle distance, while far above them tower the pinks and lilacs, the crags, and faint fantastic peaks of the Sierra, eight thousand five hundred feet above the sea: a solemn and singularly beautiful background for all this nimble water, earth, and air.

Days might be spent wandering over the château and grounds of La Granja. Green trees and grass are not so frequent in Spain that they can be passed by with indifference. And then the pranks and felicities of tiny mountain torrents with no other object in life than to throw themselves in your way, and be spanned forthwith by most graceful bridges! At long intervals the *Guardia Civil* are encountered, with their bright yellow straps, rifles, linen-covered caps, and dark blue uniforms, watching the road and keeping it free from brigands.

La Granja is a stopping-place on the road to one of the most interesting cities in Spain, — Segovia. It is a wonder that Segovia is not better known, the picture and image of what an old Castilian town used to be; walled, battlemented, and buttressed, to the delight of all artists, as it is. You descend gradually into the plain from La Granja until suddenly the city rises before you on its hill, towers, flamboyant cathedral, and all, for all the world like an ancient engraving of long-vanished times and places. Nothing could be more effective than the grouping: first the cathedral with its many pinnacles, and spire three hundred and thirty feet high, surmounting a high hill; then clustering spires and towers from other churches a stage lower; then glimpses of mediæval houses and narrow streets huddled thickly about the centres of spiritual life; then an ancient amphitheatre almost complete, and last and most wonderful of all, the valley leapt by the grand aqueduct of Trajan, with arches in some places a hundred feet high, while through a gigantic network of arches are seen green groves, churches, city walls, and warm blue sky. You cannot conceive the grandeur of this aqueduct, certainly the most perfect in the world. It is built of gray and black granite, without cement, is many miles long, and near the convent of San Gabriel forms a bridge of three hundred and twenty arches. When Segovia was sacked by the Moors, they destroyed thirty-five arches, which were restored in 1483 by order of Isabella. But it is said the new arches can even now be distinguished from the old by the inferiority of the workmanship, though a very able architect was employed to rebuild them. The water comes from the Rio Frio, and is capital. There is a double row of arches at Segovia, one superimposed upon the other; and the whole has a look of immense age. The road enters the town under them, and very striking is the effect looking up and back at the towering structure. The diligence literally flew over the steep streets, seriously endangering the necks of both passengers and promenaders, and finally drew up in a square the strangest and oddest imaginable. Hogarth or Cruikshank alone could do it justice, for there is something positively humorous in its aged and outlandish houses, arcades, and the grand indifference with which the cathedral turns its back on the whole. There is not a hotel in the place, and for the first time since my arrival in Spain I am housed in a *casa de huespedes*, or Spanish boarding-house. Houses with furnished or unfurnished lodgings for rent hang out a paper at the corner or in the middle of the balcony, according as the apartments are or are not furnished. A *casa de huespedes* is far cheaper than a hotel, and for learning Spanish customs, traditions, habits, and ways of thought, of course far superior. Useful acquaintances are formed, introductions are obtained, and the rather intricate machinery of social life explained, to one's ease. The *casa de huespedes* (La Burgalesa) in which I am ensconced at present squints at two churches and stares on the square. A bare-faced clock opposite tells the time at most unconscionable hours; and beneath it, as in nearly every Spanish city, is written *Plaza de la Constitucion;* which would all be very well if the thing existed. Beneath us, in the same house, is a casino and a dentist's establishment, and beneath these, a restaurant and café; so that we are well up among the swallows and church-steeples, too high even for the beggars to descry us with their ophthalmoscopes. Walking by chance through one of the streets, I saw an arched gate-way — Segovia still has massive mediæval gates with ponderous wooden doors — which led down through the Calle de la Luna (Street of the Moon), into a charming walk beside the town walls. There was an extensive view down into the valley; the walk was dotted with priests and artillery students, here in great force attending the artillery school; and the green trees and wide open space were in sharp contrast with the dense, close structure of the town, the buildings, houses, cloisters, and tall steeples, observable everywhere within the walls.

The cathedral is inimitable, — pure Gothic, lustrous with painted glass and pillars that shoot up to a great height before they radiate over the groined ceiling. The central nave rises ninety-nine feet, precious marbles and splendid gilt *rejas* abound, and there is a lightness, purity, and grace about the interior which I have seldom seen in these great, massive Spanish cathedrals. There is no whitewash, and all is as it was ages ago. Perhaps there is not in all England such a cathedral, and Segovia is a place of perhaps fifteen or twenty thousand inhabitants! Such miracles could faith do. What would not one give to have such a cathedral — such a fountain of memories, munificences, prayers, and hopes —

translated to our land to fix and solemnize our fickle people. Out in front of it are venerable grave-stones with armorial designs, crossed keys, and inscriptions in Latin and Spanish engraved on the flat slabs. It is a common thoroughfare, and thus the living walk over the heads of the dead. It is finer than Tarragona cathedral, and lighter and lovelier every way. A carved gallery runs around under the painted windows, and over the altar of the Capilla de la Piedad is a famous masterpiece of Juan de Juni, representing the Descent from the Cross, much admired and greatly reverenced. Other old churches make you stop to admire their noble towers, richly carved gateways, galleries with groups of pillars like an exchange, and traces of Moorish work. And then you halt again before the city gates, the mint, the curious and magnificent pile of the Alcázar, the deep-flowing Eresma, the time-mellowed Casa de Segovia, — all forming a vast open air studio for an artist, filled already with bits that cannot be surpassed. And it is six hours' hard riding by diligence to reach this picture-land! Would a railway diminish or increase its charms? Suppose you were in a reverie, looking on the Alcázar and thinking how in the olden time a court lady (doubtless in a reverie too) let the Infante Don Pedro slip out of her arms into the Eresma below and had her head cut off for the slip, — all quaintly memorialized on a slab in the chapel of the Alcázar, where the royal baby is represented holding a sword: suppose, I say, you were in such a reverie communing with the thousand memoried Past: would not the scream of the railway engine be rather discordant? And then the other legend which is connected with the old pile about the naturalized Dutch Spaniard, Duke of Rippero, a favorite of Philip V.: how he lost favor with the king, was imprisoned here in the Alcázar, escaped, became a Protestant, then a Mussulman, then a Pasha and general-in-chief to the Emperor of Morocco, and then died a pauper in a hovel of Tangier, — how would such a legend look by the lurid glare of the engine lantern? Or could you ever read Gil Blas again, who was confined in one of its prisons? No doubt much of the poetry, and many of the pictures of the place, would steal away, and a prosaic, hollow-hearted old town, full of grasping hotel-keepers, French bonnes, chocolate, and pale ale would be the result.

XX.

> ' Now give us lands where olives grow,'
>   Cried the North to the South,
> ' Where the sun with a golden mouth can blow
>   Blue bubbles of grapes down a vineyard row!'
>   Cried the North to the South.
>   E. B. Browning.

THE ride from Madrid to Salamanca is through the same stony desert with which a traveler in Spain soon becomes so familiar. At the Escorial the Guadárrama begins to throw out grand granite crags, and the country loses to some extent the repulsive yellowness and barrenness which signalize the neighborhood of the capital. The only place of interest passed between Madrid and Salamanca is Avila, a small, ancient town containing a few churches of interest and especially the tomb of Don Juan, the only son of Ferdinand and Isabella, who is buried in a church outside the town. At Medina del Campo trains are changed, and at five in the morning the train for Salamanca taken. Six hours of miserable waiting in the station, surrounded by filthy peasants of every province, with continual hubbub, singing and drinking, were an ill preparation for the glories of Salamanca. It is one of the rare instances in which I have had to wait for a train in Spain. Never punctual, the trains nearly always connect more or less directly with each other; there are few branch lines — *empalmes* in Spanish; — the railroads adhere to the general direction of the ancient turnpikes and show the correct instinct which guided the Spanish forefathers in selecting the most practicable routes. These pikes are magnificent highways and run from one end of the kingdom to the other. They are all macadamized and furnished with granite league and mile posts, showing the distances and directions. *Posadas* (reposing places) and *ventas* dot the roadside as it winds over the mountains, and trains of sumpter-mules and *arrieros* give a little animation to the otherwise dismally solitary scene. The Romans had already established excellent highways, one of which led to Rome by way of Seville, Leon, and the South of France. The Goths and Moors established others, which were multiplied by the Catholic kings, and are now consummated by a system of railways fast covering the entire kingdom. Spain does not abound in small towns; hence these roads run from city to city and link the more populous neighborhoods together at a very great expense. There seems to be no country life; there are no grove-embowered châteaux; it is a pilgrimage from one large town to another, without intervening links. From the length of the roads and the slowness of the speed, traveling, especially in summer, is a great hardship; one suffers greatly from thirst, hunger, and weariness, in spite of the *aguadoras* or water-women, who infest the stations with their jugs of oily water, and the *fondas* where an infinity of scraps is served for breakfast and dinner. First-class traveling is alone tolerable, and were it not for the dust, the spacious compartments, holding from eight to ten persons and designed for passengers of this description, would be very comfortable. Owing to the lack of comforts on the road, Spaniards travel with the oddest medley of hand-luggage, always including bottles of water, melons, fruit, wine, lunch-baskets, and a multitude of valises. The carpet-bags and trunks are curiously old-fashioned and such as people elsewhere would be ashamed to use. The people are hospitable, and always offer one whatever they may be eating among themselves. Smoke, smoke, smoke, everywhere, without parley and without objection; there are no compartments reserved for non-smokers. The trains are all dilatory, and the so-called express to Medina as much so as almost any.

At eight we arrived at — a plain. I looked about for Salamanca, and it was some time before I discovered in the distance a cluster of towers, hardly distinguishable, in their yellowish coloring, from the level around. Spanish railways have a stupid habit of stopping at some distance from the towns they pass, which necessitates a very inconvenient transfer to a series of filthy omnibuses, which, with their clamorous porters, clutch up the bewildered traveler and convey him at a gallop to the town. This is the case at Pampeluna, Saragossa, Alicante, Granada, Valladolid, Burgos, and Salamanca. Perhaps the expectation is that the town will develop and grow out towards the stations — which, in the case of Salamanca, has certainly not been the case. The air was singularly fresh and pure, and the drive pleasant, despite the excessively rough driving. The omnibus drove round the fine plaza, and finally drew up — nowhere particularly, leaving its occupants to go whither they would, in my case to the *Fonda de la Rosa*, which stood written in large letters at the back of the omnibus. I looked round in vain for the Fonda; it was nowhere to be seen; but with the aid of a porter I threaded my way through the arcades of the square into a long narrow alley, then through a sort of stable-yard up to my apartment in the hotel. The place was infamously dirty; insects swarmed; my windows looked picturesquely on a court-yard, where three black pigs were grunting and discoursing over heaps of garbage, occasionally varying their entertainment by coming upstairs and threatening to invade my sanctuary. A chambermaid, in astonishingly short petticoats, pumps, braided hair, high Spanish comb, and brilliant colors, tripped in fantastically, inquired about my wants, and then disappeared, to be followed by a sort of stable-boy with a cup of tea and no milk. I pitied the Bachelor of Salamanca of the good old times, when even these things — insects and all — would have been luxuries; and went stoically to work to arrange my toilette.

This is the principal inn of the place, whence the diligences depart, and where railway tickets are sold.

Salamanca itself, however, amply makes up for the shortcomings of its inns. The glimpse of beautiful towers and clustering churches, illuminated by the soft rays of the rising sun, which I got at the station, realized itself in a series of most interesting architectural monuments. Salamanca was the seat of a famous university, which came even before Bologna and Oxford, and ranked next after Paris; at a time, too, when university architecture was ecclesiastical, and the Gothic in the ascendant. Hence the large number of houses, convents, and churches which, in their elaborately decorated façades and doors, recall the bygone glories of the place, and bring before us the ten thousand students that thronged these streets, the mighty prelates, abbots, and scholars that lived and reigned here; the great navigators that visited it and argued with its learned professors; and the busy life, half conventual, half scholastic, that filled every crevice of its monastic and literary establishments. There is a magnificent plaza, surrounded by nearly a hundred pillars, in the centre of the town. A series of marble medallions, containing portraits of great citizens, all with their names duly turned into Latin, runs around the plaza, which has now become a charming garden, with a fountain in the centre, though bull-fights used to take place in it, and twenty thousand spectators looked down from the roofs and balconies on the scene. Under the arcades, all the trades in Christendom nest in miniature; the shops are delightfully old-fashioned, with such backwardness and benightedness in their very aspect as would provoke the irony of a Parisian *boutiquier*. One is delighted to see advertisements of circulating libraries put up here and there, whereby the ancient reputation of the place as a great literary centre is kept alive, and the illusion of the intellectual preserved, amid what looks very like withering squalor. The good people of Salamanca promenade up and down these arcades in the cool of the evening, and nothing is wanting save the rich costumes of the fifteenth century to make the place look exactly as it did when Columbus held his famous dispute with the doctors of the university. The arcades were not in existence then, but you see many a time-stained house which was; and a very little imagination is needed to recall the pictorial groups, the transcendent discoveries, and the world-wide interests of those times.

A few steps from the plaza bring you to the church and convent of the Jesuits, now an institution for the education of Irish priests, founded originally by Philip II. The interior of the church is like that of nearly every other Jesuit church, — a mass of gilt, whitewash, sign-painters' crucifixions, and revolting images, — a Bartholomew's Fair of idiotic sculpture and wooden statuary. One hastens from it as from an architectural debauch, and suddenly a wonderful portal stands before one, looking for all the world like a piece of rich old yellow Venetian point, petrified, and thrown over the wall, — the façade of the university. It is a glorious piece of platework, not chiseled silver, but dainty and detailed and multitudinous in its fancies, as the work of a December frost on the pane. Opposite stands the meditative figure of Fra Luis de Leon, the poet, standing in bronze on a white marble pedestal. To the right run the elegant cloisters surmounted by an exquisite cornice representing birds, animals, and all the dim religious light of monkish fancy carved in the open daylight. It is quite a wonder of fantastic skill.

Farther on, after threading one narrow street after another, the fine old Gothic cathedral spreads its nearly two hundred feet of length and breadth before you, with one of the finest portals in the world, — simply a masterpiece of minute carving, in which the mellow-tinted stone is as sensitive as water, and has taken a myriad of impressions from the bounteous hand and brain of the workman. Within all is serene, lofty Gothic: pillars like organ-reeds, which break on the roof into sheaves of curves and pillarets light as air ; colors in the glass which rival the richest silk, groined recesses, with portraits projecting from circular gold frames, gilded organs and canopies, a choir full of rarely elaborate stalls, wherein the canons were sitting as we entered, and chanting mass, while veiled Oriental-looking women knelt and worshiped at pictured altars. Adjoining is the old cathedral said to have been built by the Cid's confessor, Fra Geronimo. The ascent of the tower is well worth making, provided — as is nearly always the case in Catholic countries — the sexton is not ringing the bells, as the view over the town and suburbs is admirable. The river Tormes, celebrated in song and story, is seen lazily twining about the town and running in under the old Roman bridge, watering the *huertas* of the city, and making them one vivid spot of verdure in the encircling dun. Beneath is the Arzobispo with its delicate portico, the work of Archbishop Fonseca; the courts and cloisters of the university; the spires and belfries of the parish churches; the Gobierno, and the barracks; a heaped, tumultuous *coup d'œil* such as Asmodeus might take pleasure in, all eery and idealized from this great height, and bathed in such Olympian light as only Greeks and Spaniards know. Off in another obscure nook of the town is the convent of Santo Domingo, glorying in just such another portal as is seen in the university and cathedral, — the dream of some poet and genius, who laid his head upon the stone and dreamt this dream of angels for our delight. The cloister adjacent is the town museum. What do we not owe to the sculptor-poets who have bequeathed us these marble pages so magically illuminated by their gentle geniuses? One after another we turn them over: not one is like another or ever will be, any more than two human minds can be alike; each one has the imprint of its own author, different from any other; they are as variously rich as a page of Tasso or Tennyson, and their authors, after dreaming and poetizing these lovely visions into existence, have gone to sleep again and left them to us as a gentle benefaction! Breathe tenderly on them, Rain and Sunlight and summer Air; these precious pages are humanity's and ours: inalienable possessions, not to be given or granted away by any law under heaven, but bequeathed to us by the hand and spirit of Unknown Genius.

Salamanca has an old donjon keep, with a tower and buttresses which form a perfect picture, the Torre del Clavel; then an old house called Casa de las Conchas, which is covered all over the outside with large carven shells. The streets and street corners abound in characteristics of just the sort to transfer to a gallery, and one is constantly reminded that Spain must be visited, not for its *present*, but for its *past*, when it opens its antique volumes generously and displays such treasures as no other country has to offer. Remembering this, a light and easy bridge is thrown over the otherwise impassable gulf of its dirt, its indolence, its love of tradition, and its indifference to improvement. It is the land of pomp, punctilio, and all the *p*'s in the primer. Nobody advances, — except the women; progress of a weak, imitative kind begins to percolate in through the Pyrenees; but the general tone of the life is monotonous continuity, sameness, and stagnancy. Enchanted stillness reigns as if the land lay under the tree Yggdrasill. The men smoke cigarettes from morning till night, and the women, — well, they fan. Who reads? I have often asked myself this question since I have been in Spain. I did not see a bookstore in Segovia or Salamanca. At Madrid they are numerous, but so is the foreign population. The shop windows, where there are books at all, are full of obscene publications; a few illustrated papers are sold in Madrid, but I do not remember seeing a single magazine or literary paper pure and simple. The people are passionately fond of oratory, and have always excelled in it. Was not Quintilian a Spaniard? But alas, where are the wit of Martial, the poetry of Lucan, the philosophy of Seneca? Four of the Roman emperors, Hadrian, Trajan, Theodosius, and Honorius, were Spaniards, but not one of them was perhaps of specially great intellectual force. The doctors of Salamanca were celebrated for their erudition, but what has become of it? The university is now a fifth-rate college, and learning languishes. It is, however, an encouraging sign to see through the towns *Gratuita Instruccion Publica*, *Instruccion Nacional*, and other cheering evidences of awakened intellectuality set up over large buildings, designed for the education of the people. Shops where saints' legends and lives of the Virgin are sold are not so numerous as might be feared in Catholic Spain, always renowned for this special wealth. Image-worship, however, flourishes to a fearful extent, and divine honors are paid martyrs and martyresses as copiously as of yore. A curious relic of superstition is the practice Spanish women have of making the sign of the cross before the starting of a train. Another is the passion for naming children, not after the Virgin herself, but after some one of her numerous appellations, *Dolores* (pangs), *Mercedes* (thanks), *Nueves* (snows), and so on, which signifies that the children are under the protection of that special form of the multiform, Protean, and multitudinous Mary. The late queen was, therefore, Doña Maria *Mercedes* de Borbon; Mary Thank-you Bourbon; how suggestive of Dr.-If-Jesus-Christ-had-not-died-for-thee-thou-hadst-been-damned-Barebones, euphoniously called Dr. Damned Barebones, for short!

Valladolid should not be connected in the same paragraphs with Salamanca. It is a squalid old Castilian city, once the capital of Spain, till the lugubrious Philip mortified its flesh by removing the capital to Madrid. It has this same look of intense mortification to-day, as if it had never recovered from its humiliation, but lay in ashes and filth ever since. After the grace of Andalusia, the cheerfulness of Madrid and the fertility of Valencia, Valladolid's gaunt and sinewy thinness makes an unpleasant impression. Be it the wretched inn (del Siglo), the nasty *mesa redonda*, or the midnight arrival in a strange place, the city contrasted unfavorably with others. A long walk up and down its streets hardly removed the impression, in spite of the intense picturesqueness of the great square, and the pleasant shady promenades along the Douro, here as full of water as at Oporto, where it empties (would it were Valladolid !) into the sea. The psychology of impressions of travel is a curious thing. A train ten minutes behind time can de-apotheosize an ideal and take all the poetic atmosphere, that has been waiting for you for a thousand years, out of a place, leaving nothing but its utter shell behind. The evil glitter of summer on interminable yellow downs brings the imagination to a point of exhaustion, whence nothing can recover it. The slime of a yellow river may coat the fancy with its mucus till there is no distinguishing between beauty and the beast. Even Hesiod and the Egyptian calendar-makers knew that times and seasons exert a talismanic potency; even a glass of water in the furnaces of the Spanish hills may give back to one a recovered sense of life, and make the vistas and gardens of the soul light up and flash afar with eloquent activity.

Valladolid perhaps was seen in an unfortunate hour, when evil planets were in the ascendant and inauspicious influences abroad, for it failed to bring the fountains of interest into play. A languid glance is cast at the house where Philip II. came into the world; another at the palace which saw the marriage of Ferdinand and Isabella; the house where Columbus breathed his last is conscientiously searched out and the house once occupied by Cervantes, too; but your tangled feet soon refuse to wade through this thick golden sunshine and tattered city; a homeward instinct seizes them, and before you know it, you are at the hotel breathing the odors of the approaching *olla* and wondering whether the slatterns, male and female, will ever get themselves ready for dinner. The very flies weary waiting for them, and depart out of the dining-room window like winged mendicants bound for some more hospitable refectory. It would be a great gain if the Spaniards could take to heart the following maxims of Brillat Savarin: 'The destiny of nations depends on the way in which they nourish themselves.' 'Tell me what you eat, and I will tell you what you are.' 'The discovery of a new dish does more for the happiness of the human race than the discovery of a new constellation.' Add to which Emerson's saying that the 'kitchen-clock is more convenient than sidereal time;' and apply to the Spanish cooks the rule which Lowell says used to be applied to children, that 'they were annually whipped at the boundaries of the parish, on general principles;'—put, I say, these maxims and practices in operation and more good would be done to Spain than perhaps by the Code Napoléon.

The cathedral is a granite scarecrow, unfinished (as I hope it ever will be), a fright conceived and borne in iniquity by Herrera, who was called to the Escorial before his plans could be accomplished. It is covered with a hair-like grass and looks old and weather-beaten. I cannot conceive a drearier-looking pile, pseudo-classical in style, so and so many feet long and broad, and on the whole heroically homely. Why did Herrera wish us to expiate *his* sins by looking at it? Not even the sheeny satin of Castilian air can glorify it into anything beyond a crude abomination, conceived and borne in ugliness, a blemish on the pure clime in which it finds itself. All the sins of the cathedral, however, receive plenary indulgence when your idle feet bring you accidentally before the front of San Pablo, and the cornice and *patio* of San Gregorio adjacent. The same miraculously delicate carving which we see on the front of the University of Salamanca, blossoms here into a thousand thread-like Puck-on-Pegasus moldings: stars, shields, arabesques, canopies, pinnacles as exquisitely chiseled as a silversmith's masterpiece, succeed each other in tiers, till the whole is like a cashmere shawl in subtilty and fineness. It is more an efflorescence than a piece of handiwork: a quaint and airy melody wrought in stone, giving strange delectation to passing pilgrims, who hear it with a finer ear than the outward one. A dreamlet, passing through Puck's brain as he lay asleep in an asphodel, has been caught by some great magician and flashed upon us in this charming work. The cornice of San Gregorio is beautiful, formed of all sorts of animals intertwined and apparently engaged in a wild dance along the battlements. Within are a very elegant gallery and *patio*, with twisted pillars, Moorish *ajimez* windows, and a fine staircase and roof which admit meditative feet to an antique and antic world, where poetry and religion joined hands in loving rivalry and called into being this half rhythmical structure.

Valladolid, too, once had a famous university, and many royal palaces; libraries, theatres, and promenades are not wanting even to-day; and some of the squares and streets have here and there bits of canonized antiquity well worth visiting. The Plaza Mayor was a great jousting place, where jousts and tournaments alternated with gay entertainments, in which Lutherans were roasted. Its arcades, shops, and tiered balconies, with the rivulet-like streets debouching into the square, have witnessed many a scene of Castilian pageantry. I could not but think of the sad, silent face of Columbus amid all the throng of costumes and hidalgos brilliant with silk and satin — the sad, beautiful face which with all its force had something of saintliness in it, like Tasso's. In a few moments the plaza was transformed into the tableau which he saw, and not a stone of it was changed, — gliding señoras, Castilian lazzaroni, dark Spanish figures and faces, needed but the marvelous trick of moonlight to present a scene as poetic and pageant-like as any Veronese has painted for sleepy Venice. These arcaded streets then became in reverie an illuminated hall, with a thousand pillars; lights burned everywhere; and the sound of guitars rose plaintively to the moon. One could hear the pathetic romances of life and death rehearsed; sublime dreams of half-witted navigators peopled the shadows with their plenteous phantoms; and the lords and ladies of Velazquez stepped from their canvases and engaged in stately promenade through the eery square. With such illusions the history of Spain becomes a beautiful romance; noble discoverers and captains, painters and poets, princes and monks, form a rich procession before the mind's eye and leave not the heart untouched. The quiet beauty of a Spanish night and an old Spanish square have done it all; we become reconciled to the savagery of Alva, the sternness of the Gran Capitan, the bigotry of Ximénes, and the laxity of the Bourbons; but the sole illustrious figure is Columbus, the hero of this moonlit resurrection, sad and silent, full of dreams, full of events, by instinct greater than all the doctors of the church, by deeds childlike, trusting, transcendent.

VALLADOLID.

My heart was happy when I turned from Burgos to Valladolid;
My heart that day was light and gay — it bounded like a kid.
I met a palmer on the way, — my horse he bade me rein:
'I left Valladolid to-day, — I bring thee news of pain; —
The lady-love whom thou dost seek in gladness and in cheer,
Closed is her eye, and cold her cheek; I saw her on her bier.

'The priests went singing of the mass, — my voice their song did aid;
A hundred knights with them did pass to the burial of the maid;
And damsels fair went weeping there, and many a one did say,
'Poor cavalier! he is not here, — 't is well he 's far away.'
I fell when thus I heard him speak — upon the dust I lay;
I thought my heart would surely break, — I wept for half a day.

When evening came I rose again, the palmer held my
  steed ;
And swiftly rode I o'er the plain to dark Valladolid.
I came unto the sepulchre where they my love had laid, —
I bowed me down beside the bier, and there my moan I
  made :
'Oh take me, take me to thy bed, I fain would sleep with
  thee !
My love is dead, my hope is fled, — there is no joy for me.'

I heard a sweet voice from the tomb, — I heard her voice
  so clear :
'Rise up, rise up, my knightly love ! thy weeping well I
  hear ;
Rise up and leave this darksome place, — it is no place for
  thee.
God yet will send thee helpful grace in love and chivalry ;
Though in the grave my bed I have, — for thee my heart is
  sore :
'T will ease my heart if thou depart, — thy peace may God
  restore !'

LOCKHART.

XXI.

As Brahma walked over the earth the gold revealed itself to him saying, 'Here am I, Lord, do with me what thou wilt!' — LOWELL.

HAVE you ever turned over an ancient volume (say) printed by Wynken de Worde, or even earlier, a monkish manuscript where the vellum has bloomed into an edging of illuminated fruits and flowers; where there are mighty pictures covering a whole page; where there are quaint margins and curious vignettes but half-emerged from an old black-letter imagination; where there is a trick and tune of ancient felicities which no latter-day printer has ever learned or ever interwoven with the bald Roman script? The queen of Navarre's missal-book, or one of the lovely 'hour-books' with the arms of the Plantagenets, would give you glimpses into these irrecoverable times.

Just so it is with Burgos. After the pilgrimage over the Spanish sierras in search of a 'summer in Spain,' there is positive refreshment in reaching this last station of the Cross. Not only is Burgos but a few hours from yesterday's 'Gaulois;' not only is there a glimpse here and there of French cleanliness; not only are there avenues of pollard poplars, chestnuts, and walnuts particularly suggestive of the tri-color and the '*tras montes;*' but Burgos is in itself poetically satisfactory. There is a purity, a repose, a quaintness, an ancientness about the former capital of Castile which, added to its rare air, its tortuous river, its umbrageous environs, and its venerable associations, combine into one of the most perfect mediæval compositions left us by the great artist Time.

Many hours of weariness were spent at the Salamanca Junction waiting for the great northern mail train from Madrid, which maintains a feeble communication between that city and Paris. It was early September; the air seemed as rare and tense as if we were on a mountain-top; the great thin plains lifted their flanks to the yellow moon with a gleam like that of snow; a wind sharp as the edges of Toledo blades tempered with nitric acid stung one's cheeks in the impatient promenade up and down the station; the shut glass doors of the waiting-rooms were glazed with white breath from within, where a medley of individuals had gathered and spread themselves over the floors and benches, expectant like ourselves of the Ethelred-the-Unready train. Laughter, ribaldry, dram-drinking, joke-telling, songs, dialogues, politics, babies, — what a night! It seemed there was to be a bull-fight at Avila, I think; hence this caravansary of camping women, puling infants, dancing peasants, and village politicians. You felt sure they would have dozed there till doomsday, perhaps, for just one peep into the enchanted arena; and the thin air might have grown thinner, the wind might have sundered soul and spirit, and the Castilian nose and toes might have become as blue as the bluest blood in the peninsula. This hot, alcoholic blood of Spain does not seem to mind cold or inconvenience; it has its own unnatural warmth; and you see its sullen fires in what Calderon prettily calls '*las voces de los ojos*,' — the voices of the eyes. It was enough to put one in a 'marvelous dump and sadness,' as an old English writer has it, to wander among these sleeping bull-fighters, and feel the incisive air hour after hour making inroads into one's constitution. Finally, '*la journée est dure, mais elle — finira!*' — the train came, and we got in with a feeling of snugness, and made ourselves a nest among the comfortable cushions. Nobody, unless he is like Coleridge's cherub — nothing but wings and head — should think of traveling in any other way than first-class in Spain. Spaniards have a superstitious dread of foreigners, so you are often left delightfully to yourself, in what is decidedly the roomiest of European carriages; the second-class, being all thrown together in one large compartment holding forty-eight persons, is a sort of Smithfield market — 'seventy-five acres of meat' in miniature; while the third-class is too unclean to mention. No matter where you are, you are offered something to eat. If it be in the third-class, you become the martyr of hospitality, for wonderful are the objects presented for your reluctant acceptance. If it be the second-class, it is a shade more decent and dainty: huge baskets are brought out; wine and water are offered; Bologna sausages, like a small obelisk of Luxor, are dissected and handed round, and if the company be congenial, cheerfulness reigns supreme. In the first-class old Spanish etiquette prevails; offers are made, but declined courteously, and with due ceremony.

> 'Que necios cumplimientos,
> Que frases repetidas!'

A Spaniard seldom insists — possibly from the scantiness of the supply — and among them, at least, one can never imagine a Great Fire breaking out in Pudding Lane and ending in Pie Corner!

Between Medina (the Junction) and Burgos, however, we were fortunately spared the traveling picnic; everybody was asleep. 'Then they bound him to the stake and set fire to that most constant martyr:' so one feels in the Spanish cars. There is nothing to do but to endure.

Eventually they come to something; and, though it is seldom your station or your stopping-place, still there is a sort of abstract pleasure in seeing other people gratified; in hearing omnibuses rattling off with belated passengers; and in watching the surprise of the station-people that one should have arrived at all.

Late, late, we got to Burgos, the city of the Cid, of legendary Spain, of the Goths, Castilians, and Pedro the Cruel, of the people who describe themselves gayly as descendants of Noah's grandchildren, who manufacture cheese, paper, and cloth, who are the most unprogressive people in Spain, and who delight in ancient recollections. The deep breadth and beauty of the night, the cloudless darkness, stillness, and serenity, the silent old Gotho-Castilian city, plunged in sleep, the sense of immensely wide, spacious streets traversed but unseen, the long flicker of innumerable lamps filling the ashen darkness, and bringing out architectural forms with strange and exaggerated vastness; the very crackle of the frosty air, the very lateness and lonesomeness of the place and hour; — all made a weird and solemn impression on the imagination:

> 'Looking upward at the heavenes beams
> With nightës stars thick powder'd everywhere.'

A step from the train to the ancient omnibus had flung open the valves and admitted us to the moldy presence of Yesterday! You felt that there was a river meandering through this darkness, that there were bridges, monuments, gates; that the darkness was populous with figures as any background of Rembrandt; but all had vanished into the large tranquil night; whatever was harsh was now softened and harmonious; whatever was squalid and impure had melted away under the purple plenitude of the darkened heavens. A sharp turn and a swift drive brought us to the door of the inn; sleepy female waiters escorted us to our rooms; everything looked as old as the inn from which the Canterbury Pilgrims started on their journey; an ancient and musty smell, more befitting the crypt of an old Norman cathedral, greeted us as we ascended flight after flight of stairs up to the top of the hostelry; and the very mirror seemed to give back a face of the fifteenth century.

My first impulse was to open the windows, which had been sealed and cemented obviously from the time of the Cid: a dainty balcony!

How beautiful and still it was, looking down into the deep street or over at the trellised windows, or up and on till a cluster of exquisite spires fretted the sky to the east, and hung faint and spectre-like among the stars, — Burgos Cathedral! I have never seen a lovelier group of pinnacles. And they pricked the darkness and yearned heavenward with an almost human intensity; the faint, uncertain starlight played hide-and-seek among them; they took on an unnatural largeness and grandeur, and the gigantic church, lightened and lengthened by the illusions of the hour, seemed to stand a-tiptoe over the town, and to be a thing of glory and buoyance such as no other cathedral ever could be.

Again and again under the jasmine yellow of the Spanish sun I returned to gaze on the picture of these pinnacles: the ancient doorways of the cathedral, the Gate of Pardon, the pointed arches, the trefoils and rose-windows, the clustered pillarets, statues, and compartments of the façade, the open-work balustrades, the monograms of Christ and the Virgin here and there, the transparent delicacy and warmth of color of the two towers, three hundred feet high, the lovely concentric arches of the Gate of the Apostles fantastically peopled with statuettes and effigies; the Gate of Pilgrimage, looking like a piece of Tiffany's silverwork transferred to stone, with its beautiful detail in a thousand minute moldings, crowned by a cornice and scutcheon of the good bishop who paid for it; and the Archbishop's Gate, crowded with cherubs and seraphs playing musical instruments, and ending in the glorious blaze of a rose-window, wherein the dying fires of fifteenth century sunsets have been relighted and made to shed again their poetry and their effulgence over this great cathedral. It is difficult to say in what light such a wonder of Gothic art is best seen. The beauty of the clear Ontoria stone of which it is built catches the noon glamour wonderfully and fills with an exceeding richness as the shadows creep over the meridian. But it is the very poetry of dying light to see the sun fading among the pinnacles, throwing one into vivid distinctness, and another into inky shadow, throwing all its pallors and purities full on the embattled corona of the great lantern tower, or, while the west is one mighty fan-tracery, playing its battery of irradiation in among the steepled thicket of the congregated roof. I confess, too, to a feeling of deep poetry in the starlit pinnacles as they clustered close to the stars and filled the sky with their delicate lances.

Externally, Burgos Cathedral is the most striking in Spain, and inside it is hard to surpass. While many an English church has exceeded it in mere proportions, — it is three hundred feet long by two hundred and thirteen feet wide, — its rich and lofty interior is unexcelled anywhere in the world. It seems to have been the work more of the statuary than of the architect: it is a Shakspere among cathedrals in its infinite variety of carvings, in the elegance and quaintness of the riotous imagination that has presided over its decoration, in the sculptured whim and carven paradox in which it abounds, in the cadenced harmony of its proportions, and in the serene rigor of its virginally white spaces. It is so pure, so still, so severe, so white inside; there is a lustrous pavement of white Carrara marble, given by the Queen of Spain; the light is white, the three naves are white, the twenty octagonal pillars which separate these naves attain an airy elegance, lightness, and whiteness as they dash their pillared snow against the roof; there is a presence of white roses in these pure disembodied spaces, filled with the perfumes of many centuries; one feels as if the shed rose-leaves of all the Lamarques in the world were about, Roman fashion, to rain down upon one in a startled mist. The spectator, as he stands in the centre of the cathedral and looks up, feels as if spirits were descending, and bringing with them the star-shaped dome which rests over the intersections of the naves, — so delicate, so ethereally light and fair it is. Down from it, too, there seems to pour a torrent of seraphs, apostles, prophets, fruits, flowers, shells, busts, waving banners, scutcheons, and marble allegories, in the shape of four enormous tower-like piers literally smothered in these chiseled details, supporting the dome. There is an ambience, a tenderness, a spaciousness, a sweetness in this pure-stoned cathedral such as

I do not remember to have seen anywhere else in Europe. It is nearly two hundred feet from roof to floor; there is a singular luxuriance of tracery and carving; the great pillars rise out of a tumult of chisel-work, and mount with noble wings to the roof; all is stainless and great. Ducats without number were spent on the elaborate high altar, with its tombs, screens, and *rilievos*. All the Dark Ages, one thinks, wreathe over the one hundred and three walnut stalls of the choir, with their pilasters, medallions, and canopies, a choir which is one of the most exquisite books of illustrations ever made of that minor but inimitable talent which delights to make a story of a chairback, carve a legend on a footstool, or write a poem with a chisel round the frame of a miserere. While all is large, grandiose, lofty around, here all is small, delicious, prankish, as if the dainty spirits of the corridor in Faust had turned illustrators, and had stung the dead walnut into sprite-like life. Art-journals could, no doubt, be filled with the grotesqueries of these stalls and their tiers; there is nothing so good, even in Reineke Fuchs, as some of the satirical scenes in the choirs and misereres of these old Spanish cathedrals; one sees that they were the fairy-tale, the Arabian Nights, the Mother Goose's Melodies of that age of pleasant imaginations and child-like faith; they humanize the old monks to us, and make us like to imagine them sitting amid these marvelous scenes, or mayhap kneeling on a miserere containing a carving of St. Atendio riding the devil!

As the organs are not even two hundred years old, it is hardly worth while mentioning them. Thousands of ducats were spent on the reredos the filigree doors, the altar-pieces, and the columns of this choir. The armorial boots and shoes of a famous cardinal may, quaintly enough, be seen here figured on an open-work *reja* which he presented to the cathedral. Under the ample wings of this cathedral fifteen chapels are gathered, besides its own glorious spaces of whiteness and calm: some speckled and piebald, with all imaginable horrors of late Spanish taste; others, beautiful and rich with all that one might expect from Spanish romance. A peep into Santa Tecla's chapel, magnificent as it is, is more like a peep into an oratory of Castile soap, — streaks, stripes, garish color, a whole rhetoric and rainbow of shades and distinctions, meet the eye, and fever it with the glare. A step farther brings you to the chapel of Santa Ana, which is uninteresting except to a garter king-at-arms or a Sir Bernard Burke, containing, as it does, a sculptured genealogical tree of Christ. In it, however, there is nothing like the refreshing genealogies of Job given in the Talmud, some of which claim that he was contemporary with Moses, some that he married Abraham's daughter, and some that he never married or existed at all.

Next in the cathedral journey comes a staircase of thirty-eight steps, leading down — owing to the unevenness of the cathedral site — from the Puerta Alta to the church; and close by a dainty bit of still life in the outstretched sweetness and purity of a group of children entrapped, as it were, in the arch over a sepulchral altar, marble immortalities, ascribed to the epic poet of tombs, Torrigiano. The pearl of the cathderal is, however, undoubtedly, the chapel of the Constable, Fernando de Velasco. From the tombs of jasper to the flooded jewelry of the fourteen painted windows, from the four-sided columns and balustraded pillars to the great door by which you enter from the cathedral, from the cornices and laurel-crowned children to the infinity of minutiæ lavished on the arched semicircle and intricate niche-work above, from the stone scutcheons to the embroidered gloves and cushions, armor, and lap-dog, near which repose the effigies of the Constable and his 'very illustrious señora,' — all is one flow of poetry. A man who could call all this into being deserved to be five times viceroy of the realms, Lord High Constable, and whatever else the most Catholic kings could make him, — last of all, to show that he was a poet-laureate in virtue of this delightful creation of the darker centuries. Children here support the cornices, as if they were born to it; each statuette stands beneath the airiest marble canopy; the whole thing swarms with pinnacles, clusters, figures, parables in stone, and has so wonderfully escaped the gray and ancient disaster of time that it looks as if its yesterday had hardly passed.

The chapel of Santiago — the saint whom Fra Luis de Leon so charmingly commemorates in his Spanish ballad — is large enough to be the parish church, which purpose it serves to such of the good Burgolese as from time to time wend their way thither. The martial patron of Spain — Santa Theresa is the *padrona* — is even seen astride a horse, riding in huge array over the high altar; while the alabaster and jasper tombs, greatly scandalized at this performance, look on in silent contempt. The triumphant figure of the same cavalier is seen a-horseback over the jasper-pedestaled railing, gayly disporting him amid the surrounding sanctities. Such an embodiment of life and health is welcome anywhere, and much more so amid the symbolic dust and frozen allegories of a mortuary chapel. Then the new sacristy, with its garments and ecclesiastical fashions, and the chapel of San Enrique, come next on the list. In the chapel of San Juan de Saha-

gan is a tomb of St. Lesmes, who is quaintly
enough called 'Son of Burgos, Advocate of Kidney Complaint,' — not because, forsooth, he advocated that complaint, but because he had a
miraculous gift of cure for it. It seems his own
saintly carcase was tormented by the '*dolor de
riñones;*' and with such exemplary patience and
fortitude (Heaven bless him) did he bear the
dolor, that it was awarded to him as a special
honor to alleviate other people's. I am sure this
is a far better reason for canonization than many
a thousand of the other Catholic saints can urge.
Of course there is the usual list of nodding virgins, venerated images, flounced and furbelowed
beatitudes, and writhing martyrs; no Spanish
church can get along without them. The reliquary of Burgos Cathedral is a small museum of
desiccated saints. There is an image of Christ
with real hair, beard, eyelashes, and thorns, that
sweats on Fridays, and bleeds now and then for
a change, — truly the 'crucified phantom,' which
it is called by a French writer. Horror and disgust are the sole emotions, in contemplating such
things; yet every Spanish church has more than
one niche devoted to them. A dose of jalap
could hardly be more effective in purging one's
imagination.

A vigorous push on what seems like a wall
ajar admits you to the cloisters, where it is hard

to tell what attracts you most, — the massive solidity of the whole structure, the pure ogival arches, the long vistas of arched and ambient gloom, the walls inlaid with abbots and canons, who rest around them in splendid tombs, the Moorish windows, the moldering mezzo-relievos, or the foliage, lancet-work, and trefoils that break the continuity of lines, and lighten the ponderous masses of the stone. Like an Oxford quadrangle, the cloisters enclasp a space dedicated to verdure and sunshine. Sunshine and verdure are the only things that never fade; here the light lingers as in a deep well, and here its goldenness and summer joy have been stored from the time when old Geoffrey was tuning his lyre to the Duchess Blaunche, and John of Gaunt was getting him a new wife by marrying the poet's sister-in-law. Altogether charming is such a place; suggestive, too, for beneath in the crypt no end of scholars and warriors await the millennium, when they shall gather up their tangled limbs and personalities, and haste them to meet the Master. The whole place is a silent Benedicite and Blessed-are-ye : the lightest shoe treads historic dust and leaves a print in it.

And to retire from this built-in niche of paradise and mingle again with the tawdry world outside ; to forget these pinnacles, starlit or sunlit, as the case may be, and go one's way back into a Spanish inn; to turn from mitred abbots to mincing chambermaids, and from this rich air of many centuries to the reek of a five o'clock dinner, — this is a part of Spain in summer!

Almost had I forgot the blessed Cid, on whom Burgos prides herself far more than on the cathedral! Here he was born, and here he is buried, irreverently enough, to be sure, for his naked ashes are displayed in a glass case in quite as matter-of-fact a style as the jar of an apothecary labeled 'Camomile.' I am sure the doughty warrior has killed as many people since his death by their attempt to wade through his interminable 'rhymed chronicle' and 'romance,' as ever he did Moors and infidels in his valiant life-time. Whether one takes it in Herder's German or in scraps of Lockhart, Frere, and Longfellow, the ballad of Childe Rodrigo is a trial of patience. And one's recollections of him immediately mount on stilts in the alexandrines of Corneille. The prettiest thing ever said of the Cid was what he said of himself on his death-bed at the daybreak of the twelfth century, in 1099: 'No paid mourners shall follow me; the tears of my wife will suffice!' Such a terse, true sentence as this gives far deeper insight into the man's character than all the 'romanceros' ever written.

They show an old trunk, too, which once contained the sand which the Cid deposited with a

Jew as surety for the red gold he had borrowed when he was once in distress — the 'dean of all the trunks in the world,' says Gautier, — the ancestor of all the lordly descendants that annually visit the spas of the continent for their health. Burgos clings to the old box as if it were a bit of the true cross, and not all the temptations of St. Anthony could sever the tie which binds the old burg and the old box tenderly together.

The other churches of Burgos, — Santa Agueda, San Esteban, and San Gil, — though immensely old, have little of interest save the hallowing touch of legend on their silvery heads. As you walk up the busy *alameda* you come on a gate, the Arco de Santa Maria, one of the most effective architectural masses to be seen. It is just such a grand gate as one imagines opening and letting out the lords and ladies of Ivanhoe, or Count Robert of Paris; it is turreted and battlemented till it is delightful to see, and stands over the spot whence Don Pedro hurled the poet Garcilaso de la Vega from a tower now no longer in existence. It is a perfect picture, and one of those charming things that makes you long to be an artist, that you may transfer its antique pomp of bastion and pride of battlemented wall straightway to your sketch-book. About the old *Castle* there is a tender perfume that blows to us from English history, for here

Edward I. married that Eleanor of Castile whose death caused so many crosses to be erected wherever her body rested, on its long journey to London, giving rise to the poetic but unphilological etymology, *Charing Cross* (Chère Reine Cross, — rather from *Charan*, to turn, because the street made a bend there).[1] The Cid was born and married within its walls; but nearly all its memories and beauties were blown up in the air when Wellington and Soult contended for it early in this century, and a great explosion took place, shivering to a thousand atoms the beautiful and irrecoverable painted windows of the cathedral. And what more than a piece of painted glass was the old Duke himself? Fragments of fourteenth, fifteenth, and sixteenth century domestic life may be seen intact in certain venerable houses of those dates still standing, with now a noble courtyard and series of pillars, now an old palace, and now a group of armorial bearings belonging to some of the haughtiest blood in Spain. A charming feature about Burgos is its dilapidated market-places, colonnaded all around, and fraught with a vivacity that never seems to die out; the long avenues of twinkling poplars; the deep streets, with their uneven pavement; the intensity of the Spanish type there indigenous; the old pumps, portals, and shops; the hundreds of

---

[1] Hare, *Walks in London.*

gilded and trellised *miradores* running up three or four stories, and presenting the aspect of show-windows, continued on the outside all the way to the top of the house.

Imagine all this weird yet winsome detail gathered about the feet of a mighty church; imagine the church itself resting like a mother among her children, and casting over the place a spell of grace and peace; trace the morning and the evening shadows over all this life; stop to listen a moment to the proverbs dropping from these Spanish lips; think of the narrowest, intensest, most poetic, most unintellectual existence ever dreamt of by a village Plato:—then look in your oldest Spanish dictionary, and you will find, in answer to the quest: BURGOS.

The Burgos guides point the pilgrim to the environs of the old city as worth seeing: so the reader will follow me or not, as he thinks fit, while I briefly describe them.

'The convent of Las Huelgas,' says a recent writer, 'is situated on the high-road to Valladolid, and was founded by Alfonso VIII. and his queen, Leonora, daughter of Henry II., of England, in 1180, on the site of some pleasure-grounds (*huelgas*, from *Holgar*, to rest = sans souci). It has been often augmented and repaired in subsequent periods, and is therefore not homogeneous in either style or shape. Of the former palace, or villa, nothing more, it is said, remains than the small cloister with fantastical capitals, and Byzantine semicircular arch. The church was consecrated in 1279, and was the work of King St. Ferdinand. It is of a good pure Gothic, severe, and well characterized. The interior of the church is not very interesting, the altars *churrigueresque* and gaudy, with a Christ dressed with a most profane crinoline, an offering of the present lady abbess. The abbesses of Huelgas used formerly to be most powerful, and inferior to no one in dignity besides the queen; they were mitred '*Señoras de horca y cuchillo*' (*i. e.* with right of life and death), lorded over fifty-one villages and boroughs, named their alcaldes, curates, chaplains, and possessed the style of '*Por la gracia de Dios*' and '*nullius diocesis.*' It is one of the few remaining convents which have preserved, though considerably diminished, extensive landed property, amounting to some fifteen thousand *fanegas*, several villages, and many thousand head of merino sheep. The order is Cistercian; and to gain admission the nuns must, besides the ordinary exigencies of the rule, bring a dowry, and belong to the nobility. The confinement is most strict, and the nuns can only be visited by ladies. On Sundays, during high mass, they may be nevertheless seen sitting in their magnificently carved stalls, singing and praying, and clad in a most becoming dress. As the building was also intended for the burial-house of the kings of Castile, there are several tombs worthy of a rapid glance. In this church the marriage took place of the Infante de la Cerda with Blanche, daughter of St. Louis of France, at which the kings of Castile, Aragon, Navarre, the Moorish king of Granada, Prince Edward of England (son of Henry III.), the Empress of Constantinople, the French Dauphin, and twenty or thirty other crowned heads and princes were present. Amongst the nuns of rank that have lived and died here, were Berenguela, daughter of St. Ferdinand; Maria of Aragon, aunt of Charles V., etc. In the chapel of Santiago is preserved an image of this warrior saint, in which some springs move the arms. Here aspirants to knighthood used to '*velar las armas*' (keep the vigil), and when they were knighted, a sword was fastened to the right hand of the image which, by moving a spring, fell gently on the recipient's shoulder, and thus their dignity was saved; for otherwise, it was an offence to receive the accolade (dub of knighthood) from a man.'

The Carthusian Convent and church of La Cartuja, near which the railroad passes, must also be seen for the fine tombs, the elegance of the architecture, the altar gilt with the gold brought by Columbus in his second voyage from

America, and the splendid *retablo* behind the altar. The place breathes of Isabella and her dead brother, to whom she raised one of these striking commemorative tombs: tombs which are a sort of animal, vegetable, and mineral kingdom in the small, whereon the tropic wealth of erudite imaginations has exhausted itself, and the stricken stone almost cries out, like Pygmalion's statue. There is a sunny and strange pathos about the place: Silence, the Carthusian god, reigns supreme, in company with its brother Desolation; there is no telling how many of the old brethren a turn of the spade might bring to light in the burial-ground; a sorrowing sisterhood of cypresses throws its heart-shaped shade athwart the motionless air; the air has a lament in it as it wanders among the flying buttresses and florid Gothic of the aged church, and all around invisible fingers have written: Thou shalt die.

Just where France and Spain meet, in one corner of the Cantabrian Sea, is San Sebastian. It is a compact little town, new as the newest, built on a peninsula, with high mountains all around, a wide passage opening to the sea, a great roll and undulation of sunny hills to the southward, a train at its back door, and forty omnibuses, manned by sturdy Basques, in waiting for your worship when you arrive. It is a little place that has sprung up almost Thebes-like to the Amphion-lyre of good fish, good bathing, striking scenery, and most gracious accessibility to the rest of Europe. It is now one of the two places that rank as 'cities' in the Basque Provinces. To drop in at such a place, after a long railway roll among the moth-eaten cities of Spain; to enjoy its quaint, fresh life; to see the Spanish grandees and notabilities that have escaped from the dust of Madrid, and have come to inhale its salt air; to hear the soft and melodious Basque spoken by men in blue *boinas*, and women in hoods of Aragon and Navarre; to feast on the beautiful apple-orchards literally crimson and gold with autumn apples; and to go to bed in clean sheets, in a new hotel that has a perfectly new and unsophisticated proprietor, — all the trials of summer pilgrims in Spain are forgotten in such a place. It then becomes grateful, from such a coigne of vantage, to look back over the journey accomplished, the conscience quieted, and the store of recollections garnered. It must be like the bees when the winter comes: from how many bitter flowers the honey flows! One has crossed the very valley of the shadow, and has half become one of the eternal lotus-eaters: the mind, like the grave accent, turns backward, and catches only the light of the lovelier days; there is a joy of things accomplished and things remembered; and over the wide hills and the yellow valleys there rests a transfiguration. It is not difficult, then, to forgive Spain all she has done to us, — to pass over the slow trains, the sluggish life, the empty compliments, the narrow prejudices, the ignorance, saint-worship, and indecency, the pitiful dislike to foreigners, the lack of newspapers, inns, and clean linen, the vice, squalor, and impenitence. One can even overlook the priests that dot the land like asterisks and obeluses, — designed to refer the spectator to other ages. There is so much that is bright and eloquent in Spain, but fortitude must be exercised in seeing it.

>'Han dejado
>Sepulcros para memorias!'

Exclaims Lope of the ages of Spanish influence and affluence. The period when, according to an old *romancero*, Spaniards were 'like steel among men, like wax among women,' has passed away. Fra Luis de Leon's 'rich wound of the eternal side' flows no longer for them. Rolling in through these fair and bounteous gates of southwestern France, or over the wonderful verdure of the Barcelona coast, the traveler would have little idea of what was in store for him. There is a sudden plenteousness of vegetation which makes him marvel, and brings him to think of those olden days of luxuriance and wealth when gold

and spices flowed in from all the Indies, and
Philip could lavish millions on his ugly ash-heap.
But the slow coiling and twining of the train
through the Pyrenees, the slow march of the diligence from Perpignan, soon bring him down into
immeasurable flats, jaundiced vegetation, rivers
like gum Arabic, and the huge pallor of a colorless and extinguished landscape. Due penance
is done for the weariness caused by the greenery
of France; weeks and weeks may pass without
a single flash of green along a river, a single
glint of gold in fruity orchards.

San Sebastian, Biarritz, Santander, Hendaya,
Irun, San Juan de Luz, are exceptions to the
general wanness of the country. As soon as one
reaches the country of pale blue granites, Basque
villages, hay-fields and wheat-fields; as soon as
the poppies and the corn-flowers begin to brighten
the grain; as soon as the subtle chill of the sea
thrusts its lance through the heavy air and pricks
the Seven Sleepers of Spain into wakefulness and
vigilance; so soon does an astonishing change
come over the face of the earth: there are rushing mill-wheels, smoking factories, active industries, population, life, intelligence. The Basques
deserve better than to be known only from having given the under-petticoat to the Spanish
women. They have always been renowned for
sprightliness, poetic temperament, rugged inde-

pendence, and purity; their strange legends and dances, the wild poetry of their wandering singers and improvisatores, their simple faith, constancy, and fortitude, the oddities of the *fueros*, or local customs that control the confederation of Basque hamlets and fishing towns, the peculiarities of their un-European and as yet unclassified language, have for generations attracted attention and invited research. Wentworth Webster, Prince Bonaparte, Sayce, and several French and Spanish scholars, have lately thrown light on this curious people and their *Euskara* dialect, as they call it. The country-folk are seen trooping into San Sebastian, or gathered in Teniers-like groups in the market-places: wise, kind, sober people of economic instincts, social habits, and ancient prejudices. They pride themselves greatly on having given birth to Ignatius Loyola, whose sumptuous college, convent, and church, called the 'wonder of Guipuzcoa,' are shown in the neighborhood of Azcoitia. One of the holy man's fingers adorns the reliquary of this establishment: there are silver altars, marbles, terraces, staircases; a mighty dome caps the church; opulent estates and revenues yield goodly provision to the establishment; and the whole foundation lies in a beautiful plain where there are sulphur springs, — into which it should be dipped twice a day for purification. Guipuzcoa, as the natives call the province, abounds in little mountain baths, vegas, valleys, streams that shoot down the glady slopes and mingle their waters with the Bay of Biscay. The Basques could not escape the 'pesky' Wellington; so the light of 1813 is still traceable here and there over their battle-scarred Province. A feeble chapter of 'celebrated men' usually accompanies the San Sebastian guide-books; but it is hardly worth while to discover to the world such names as Elcano, Churruca, Oquendo, Legazpi, Urdaneta, Zumalacarregui, and Idiaquez, many of which have a strange resemblance to Aztec names. Nor, perhaps, would the other twenty thousand inhabitants of San Sebastian thank us for selecting half a dozen of the illustrious and leaving the unillustrious throng uncommemorated. San Sebastian is too bright and charming a place to enter into guide-book details of its name, antiquity, fortresses, coat-of-arms, notable deeds, climate, population, and sea-baths. Its 'actuality,' as the Spanish say, or present condition, compares favorably with that of the most celebrated resorts. The length and breadth of churches, the height or lowness of barometers, has little to do with its present prosperity. Its ancient walls and fortifications have unfortunately disappeared in the general march of improvement; the 'new horizons' so much coveted in France and Germany — acquired by leveling to the earth the most precious relics of the buttressed and battlemented Past — have been acquired here; 'the heat of new ideas, peace and fraternity,' has dissolved the crystallizations of ancient fancy and convenience; and San Sebastian now looks to the sea over wide streets, elmed and lindened boulevards, and nail-new mansard roofs quite to its satisfaction. Oh, that Monsieur Mansard had perished before he gave his name to this fatal roof! San Sebastian is an example of what the Spaniards call 'a near and smiling future,' — though what causes the smile of the future is rather hard to see. The local guide-book lately published heaps a litany of curses on war, hate, desire of vengeance, and thirst of blood; all which, according to this authority, convert humanity (with a delightful complexity of metaphor) into thirsty hyenas, ruin, and tears! And the litany of curses is followed by a litany of benedictions on the peace that maketh men brethren, on the tranquillity that develops moral and material interests, on the nations as they travel down the illimitable path of progress (whatever that is), and on the mission of civilization that fulfilleth and perfecteth the designs of Providence! After the good people have thus cleared their throats and consciences, they betake themselves to devout meditation, to church, and to the

Middle Ages; they go to sleep for a century, while all the brilliant fumes of their painted imaginations go up a chimney built three hundred years ago! Such is a picture of aspirations and realities in Spain.

Volvamos empero á nuestro tema.

Why the San Sebastianos should chuckle over their razed fortifications it is difficult to see; but they say that the present state of things as compared with the past presents a most pleasing and consolatory spectacle. One agrees to the beauty, but Rachel refuses to be comforted. A flowery alameda planted with trees has replaced the old wall; a market-place has sprung from the very mouths of the cannon; the furious sea has been kept from the long menaced city; broad and spacious streets, excellently paved and lighted, replace bristling fort and fosse; and shops streaming with the glories of Paris open their lighted apartments to the promenader. The ancient military importance of the place is gone, but *que importa?* The city breathes free from its walls; and while its former maritime importance is gone too, it has risen to be a decided moral force in the Spanish empire. More than twenty thousand foreigners visited the place as long ago as the summer of 1870. The fine sea-shore of this part of the country, — Spain has over eight hundred miles of Atlantic and seventeen hundred miles of Mediterranean sea-coast, — the numerous water-cures and mineral springs, the medicinal repute of the sulphur and saline baths, conspire to develop the place prodigiously and fill it with a summer sparkle of fashionable life. Spanish people tell you of magnificent edifices, varied spectacles, new centres of recreation, large spring colonies, annual augmentation of passionate pilgrims, — in short, sing the usual Spanish ballad over what is by no means the usual Spanish watering-place. In fourteen or fifteen years an entirely new population has taken possession of the old town; and the new wine is almost too much for the old bottles. Without going into the alphabetical list of its streets, the mysteries of its civil administration, or the careers of its local celebrities, there is much of interest to see; there are fine walks and drives, as picturesque as anything in Savoy or the French Pyrenees; there are environs which may be described as delicious; precious *paseos*, hills rich in panoramas and vistas, military music on many a fine evening, superb moonlight a-shine through the livelong August nights, fives-courts, country houses, and clubs. The abundance of comforts makes one rub one's eyes : is it Spain? High sounding literary and musical societies are not wanting; a casino; a bull-ring; a mercantile and industrial 'cercle,' after the fashion of France; a circus-theatre and various play-houses; movable bath-houses without number along the seashore; and lastly, the *Pearl of the Ocean*, an elegant bathing establishment luxuriously furnished in every direction and with everything. Minute directions are given as to the period, characteristics, duration, and hygiene of the baths; and if you are curious, formidable papers bristling with statistics, physical and chemical properties of sea-water, chemical analyses, tables of carbonic acid, the latest specific gravity according to the last results of Gay-Lussac, — not to speak of electro-magnetic properties and phosphorescence, — are at your service. The savor and the odor, the degree of saline saturation and the rate of evaporation, how to dress and what to do, if you happen to be a rheumatic old gentleman or a nervous old lady, whether you are delicate or debilitated, — all is made straight for you by these statistical John the Baptists, and you have nothing to do but to pay. A chapter on hydrography tells you all about what the San Sebastianos did to get wells of sweet water, and how it is distributed, followed by columns of figures going solemnly into the linear measure of water-pipes, and the liquid measure of *azumbres* of water in twenty-four hours. An isle with a light-house on it lies at the entrance of the shell-shaped bay — called La Concha — of San Sebastian; whereupon the Spanish chronicler takes occasion to go

into the genealogy and etymology of light-houses;
pointing to the Pharos of Alexandria, which was
one of the wonders of the world, the light-house
of the promontory of Sigæum, in the Troad, and
the ancient light-house of Boulogne, by which the
Romans lighted themselves to Britain. A fine
castle defends the port, and is surrounded by a
whole dragon-brood of ramparts, mines, chambers, and military prisons. The railroad hours
are most convenient; travel is cheap; stage
coaches are abundant; and everybody has plenty
of time. A really surprising number of newspapers and periodicals see the light in San Sebastian; whether the light of day or the light of fire,
an inspection of their contents will speedily de-
termine. With true Spanish gallantry, there is
one called 'The Friend of the Ladies,' devoted
— not to men — but to modes. Banks, insurance
companies, philanthropic associations, asylums,
schools, civil edifices, churches, might all be vol-
uminously described, if they had the least interest to the untraveled. Every other house is a hotel, or a boarding-house, or a *casa de huespedes*.
Every other *a* has the English breadth or the
French lightness. Every other cravat you see
came from the Bon Marché. Women-haters and
man-hunters pass you at every few steps; eremites
of Chartreuse and *habitués* of Mabille saunter in
the wide-thrown light of the gas lamps, and listen

to the music issuing from a gorgeous pavilion in the *alameda*. The beginning and the end of the social alphabet seem to be on terms of friendly equality. The French talk Spanish and the Spanish talk French, in amiable condescension. No matter what country you come from, some obliging waiter will inform you that he has been there. Everywhere you meet acquaintances, — people that you have dived with down into the bowels of the Escorial, or toiled with up the heights of the Alhambra; old ladies with *Murray* clasped to their hearts, and *Baedeker* written all over their faces; army officers, who startle you by peremptorily demanding to see the corpses of Ferdinand and Isabella, five hundred miles from where they are buried; foreign consuls, who have married Andalusian chamber-maids, and cultivate art; English cockneys, talking out of their throats, and dispensing sovereigns; old maiden artists, who travel third-class, go all over Algeria and Morocco alone, sketch Mohammedan mosques, and get remittances from home (oblivious of *h*'s) in ten-pound notes; all of these scenes and faces dart out of one's *memorabilia* pocket-book, and claim a notice with acute accents. San Sebastian is the place to see them! Spence's Anecdotes — nay, Walpole's Letters — might be written afresh in these Cantabrian latitudes; the 'laced petticoats of my lady Castlemaine,' that 'did' old

Pepys 'so much good,' might do another Pepys good under the shadow of the Pyrenees; and one is sure that old Fuller, under the elms of San Sebastian, could indefinitely increase the 'Worthies' whom he so blithesomely describes.

'O cúan dulce y suavisima memoria!'

cries a Spanish poet in words applicable as well to the memory of San Sebastian. The other day the cannon's mouth flamed with the red roses and wreathing smoke-flowers of war, and all the hills around it roared under the Spanish guns; but all this has failed to wreck the glory, or stay the summer that lingers over the place. Nature has here shown a chance combination of rare grace. Castelar and the poets love the place; it has a pleasantness all its own; San Sebastian and its suburbs might be wrought up into a brilliant chapter. I know people who delight in it, and who would go back to it as gladly as the storks go to Egypt, or the swallows follow the South.

> So may God let thee, Reader, gather fruit
> From this thy reading.
> DANTE.

www.ingramcontent.com/pod-product-compliance
Lightning Source LLC
Chambersburg PA
CBHW022144300426
44115CB00006B/340